175 HOT & SPICY
VEGETARIAN

175 HOT & SPICY VEGETARIAN

Fire up your cooking with sizzling meat-free dishes, shown in 195 tempting photographs

EDITED BY BEVERLEY JOLLANDS

southwater

This edition is published by Southwater, an imprint of Anness Publishing Ltd, Hermes House, 88–89 Blackfriars Road, London SE1 8HA; tel. 020 7401 2077; fax 020 7633 9499

www.southwaterbooks.com; www.annesspublishing.com

© Anness Publishing Ltd 2010

If you like the images in this book and would like to investigate using them for publishing, promotions or advertising, please visit our website www.practicalpictures.com for more information.

UK distributor: Book Trade Services; tel. 0116 2759086; fax 0116 2759090; uksales@booktradeservices.com; exportsales@booktradeservices.com
North American agent/distributor: National Book Network; tel. 301 459 3366; fax 301 429 5746; www.nbnbooks.com
Australian agent/distributor: Pan Macmillan Australia; tel. 1300 135 113; fax 1300 135 103; customer.service@macmillan.com.au
New Zealand agent/distributor: David Bateman Ltd; tel. (09) 415 7664; fax (09) 415 8892

Publisher: Joanna Lorenz
Editors: Joanne Rippin and Anne Hildyard
Proofreading Manager: Lindsay Zamponi
Production Controller: Christine Ni

A CIP catalogue record for this book is available from the British Library.

ETHICAL TRADING POLICY

At Anness Publishing we believe that business should be conducted in an ethical and ecologically sustainable way, with respect for the environment and a proper regard to the replacement of the natural resources we employ. As a publisher, we use a lot of wood pulp to make high-quality paper for printing, and that wood commonly comes from spruce trees. We are therefore currently growing more than 750,000 trees in three Scottish forest plantations: Berrymoss (130 hectares/320 acres), West Touxhill (125 hectares/305 acres) and Deveron Forest (75 hectares/185 acres). The forests we manage contain more than 3.5 times the number of trees employed each year in making paper for the books we manufacture.

Because of this ongoing ecological investment programme, you, as our customer, can have the pleasure and reassurance of knowing that a tree is being cultivated on your behalf to naturally replace the materials used to make the book you are holding.

Our forestry programme is run in accordance with the UK Woodland Assurance Scheme (UKWAS) and will be certified by the internationally recognized Forest Stewardship Council (FSC). The FSC is a non-government organization dedicated to promoting responsible management of the world's forests. Certification ensures forests are managed in an environmentally sustainable and socially responsible way. For further information about this scheme, go to www.annesspublishing.com/trees

PUBLISHER'S NOTE

Although the advice and information in this book are believed to be accurate and true at the time of going to press, neither the authors nor the publisher can accept any legal responsibility or liability for any errors or omissions that may be made nor for any inaccuracies nor for any loss, harm or injury that comes about from following instructions or advice in this book.

Front cover shows Tofu in a Tangy Chilli Sauce p35

Previously published as part of a larger volume, *500 Hot & Spicy Recipes*

CONTENTS

Introduction

More and more people enjoy vegetarian dishes or feel they should include more vegetables in their diet, but are not sure how to jazz up plain vegetables, tofu and beans. This book offers a wonderful collection of over 175 spiced vegetarian recipes that are full of flavour, colour and taste, as well as being good for you.

Vegetarians eat no meat, poultry, game, fish, shellfish, animal products and animal fats, but many vegetarians do eat free-range eggs from healthy birds.

For modern vegetarians, there are numerous exciting, colourful vegetables available, and innovative recipes from many countries to inspire you to make the best use of good-quality ingredients. Gone are the days when vegetables or beans were just an adjunct to the meat course; now they can be the star of the show.

Spices make the perfect partner for vegetables, lentils, beans and tofu. Adding blends of spices creates different tastes: warm and aromatic, hot and spicy, or just subtle enough to hint at the flavour.

Judicious use of spices can enhance any food or give a kick to the blandest ingredient, and you can turn up the heat by adding extra chillies to fire up the taste buds.

Throughout history, spices have been prized and regarded as precious, perhaps because they were only obtained after long and dangerous journeys. Now, however, exotic and aromatic spices from around the world are readily available from supermarkets, Asian shops and delicatessens everywhere, and they are inexpensive enough to use them in everyday cooking.

It is the particular mix of spices and seasonings that gives each cuisine its distinctive flavour. For instance, in South American and Mexican cooking fresh and dried chillies are top of the list to pep up recipes for rice, tortillas, beans and vegetables, with the addition of cumin and cinnamon, while in North Africa, an explosive paste, harissa, which is made from red chillies, is served on the side to add extra fire and flavour. More subtle spicing is prevalent in Spain, where saffron, cumin, cloves, cayenne and paprika appear in many dishes, while in central Europe, spices such as caraway, dill, cardamom, cinnamon and fennel are used in both sweet and savoury dishes. In northern Europe, the warm spices nutmeg, cinnamon and cloves are popularly added to biscuits, puddings, cakes and pastries.

Around the Middle East and the Mediterranean, it is the warm spices, such as cinnamon, cumin, coriander and saffron that create the distinctive mixture that is added to classic tagines, fresh colourful salads and barbecues, and in Turkey, enticing tastes are created with red chillies, allspice, cumin, cinnamon and caraway used to spice up meze, soups and vegetarian dishes.

The renowned spice basket of the world, India, boasts a huge range of dried spices including ginger, cumin, coriander, cinnamon, turmeric, mustard seeds, fennel seeds and caraway seeds. Cooks in India prepare their curry powders daily, often grinding as many as 20 spices together, and each region in India has developed its own style of cooking and spice blend to create subtly different aromatic flavours for mild and fiery curries, rice dishes and savoury breads.

Other Asian countries such as China and Japan favour spices such as sesame seeds and star anise, and use generous quantities of fresh ginger and garlic in stir-fries and in steamed, simmered and deep-fried dishes.

In this easy-to-use book, you will discover how to prepare a fantastic range of spicy recipes from all these countries, using blends of spice pastes or powders. You will be able to create appealing vegetarian soups, appetizers and light meals, main meals, side dishes and accompaniments, and desserts and bakes. Each recipe is clearly explained in step-by-step instructions and has a superb colour photograph to inspire you and ensure a great result. Nutritional notes for every recipe allow you to plan a healthy menu.

Containing a feast of authentic and tempting recipes for creative cooks who want to spice up their vegetarian menus, the dishes in this book are imaginative, and easy to prepare and cook. With over 175 recipes to choose from, you are sure to find many delicious dishes that you can add to your repertoire of meals for any occasion.

Hot Red Lentil Soup

Red lentils and vegetables are cooked and puréed, then sharpened with lots of lemon juice. In hot weather, the soup is also good served cold, with the addition of more lemon. This soup is also known as Esau's soup and is sometimes served as part of a sabbath meal in Jewish households.

Serves 4
45ml/3 tbsp olive oil
1 onion, chopped
2 celery sticks, chopped
1–2 carrots, sliced
8 garlic cloves, chopped
1 potato, peeled and diced
250g/9oz/generous 1 cup
    red lentils
1 litre/1¾ pints/4 cups
    vegetable stock
2 bay leaves
1–2 lemons, halved
2.5ml/½ tsp ground cumin, or
    to taste
cayenne pepper or Tabasco sauce,
    to taste
salt and ground black pepper
lemon slices and chopped
    fresh flat leaf parsley leaves,
    to serve

1 Heat the oil in a large pan. Add the onion and cook for about 5 minutes, or until softened. Stir in the celery, carrots, half the garlic and all the potato. Cook for a few minutes until beginning to soften.

2 Add the lentils and stock to the pan and bring to the boil. Reduce the heat, cover and simmer for about 30 minutes, until the potato and lentils are tender.

3 Add the bay leaves, remaining garlic and half the lemons to the pan and cook the soup for a further 10 minutes. Remove the bay leaves. Squeeze the juice from the remaining lemons, then stir into the soup, to taste.

4 Pour the soup into a food processor or blender and process until smooth. (You may need to do this in batches.) Tip the soup back into the pan, stir in the cumin, cayenne pepper or Tabasco sauce, and season with salt and pepper.

5 Ladle the soup into bowls and top each portion with lemon slices and a sprinkling of chopped fresh flat leaf parsley.

Lentil Soup with Cumin and Fenugreek

Lentil soups are popular in many countries around the world. This Turkish soup is light and subtly spiced, and is served as an appetizer or a snack. With the addition of some crusty bread and cheese, it can be served as a meal on its own.

Serves 4–6
30–45ml/2–3 tbsp olive or
    sunflower oil
1 large onion, finely chopped
2 garlic cloves, finely chopped
1 fresh red chilli, seeded and
    finely chopped
5–10ml/1–2 tsp cumin seeds
5–10ml/1–2 tsp coriander seeds
1 carrot, finely chopped
scant 5ml/1 tsp ground fenugreek
5ml/1 tsp sugar
15ml/1 tbsp tomato
    purée (paste)
250g/9oz/generous 1 cup split
    red lentils
1.75 litres/3 pints/7½ cups
    vegetable stock
salt and ground black pepper

To serve
1 small red onion, finely chopped
1 large bunch of fresh flat leaf
    parsley, finely chopped
4–6 lemon wedges

1 Heat the oil in a heavy pan and stir in the onion, garlic, chilli, cumin and coriander seeds. When the onion begins to colour, toss in the carrot and cook for 2–3 minutes. Add the fenugreek, sugar and tomato purée and stir in the lentils.

2 Pour in the stock, stir well and bring to the boil. Lower the heat, partially cover the pan and simmer for 30–40 minutes, until the lentils have broken up.

3 If the soup is too thick, thin it down with a little water. Season with salt and pepper to taste.

4 Serve the soup straight from the pan or, if you prefer a smooth texture, whizz it in a blender, then reheat if necessary.

5 Ladle the soup into bowls and sprinkle liberally with the chopped onion and parsley. Serve with a wedge of lemon to squeeze over the soup.

Hot Red Lentil Soup Energy 235kcal/991kJ; Protein 13g; Carbohydrate 28.4g, of which sugars 3.7g; Fat 8.9g, of which saturates 2.2g; Cholesterol 0mg; Calcium 66mg; Fibre 2.9g; Sodium 40mg.
Lentil Soup with Cumin Energy 203kcal/856kJ; Protein 11.1g; Carbohydrate 31.8g, of which sugars 7.3g; Fat 4.4g, of which saturates 0.6g; Cholesterol 0mg; Calcium 45mg; Fibre 3.5g; Sodium 26mg.

Spiced Bean Soup with Cumin and Turmeric

This delicious soup, of black-eyed beans is flavoured with tangy lemon and speckled with chopped fresh coriander. It is a Sephardi Jewish recipe, and shows the influence of western Mediterranean cuisines – those of North Africa and the Iberian Peninsula – in its use of tomatoes, garlic and spices.

Serves 4

175g/6oz/1 cup black-eyed beans (peas)
15ml/1 tbsp olive oil
2 onions, chopped
4 garlic cloves, chopped
1 medium-hot or 2–3 mild fresh chillies, chopped
5ml/1 tsp ground cumin
5ml/1 tsp ground turmeric
250g/9oz fresh or canned tomatoes, diced
600ml/1 pint/2¹/₂ cups vegetable stock
1 small bunch fresh coriander (cilantro), stalks removed, leaves roughly chopped
juice of ¹/₂ lemon
pitta bread, to serve

1 Bring the beans and cold water to the boil, then cook for 5 minutes. Remove from the heat, cover and stand for 2 hours.

2 Heat the olive oil, add the onions, garlic and chilli and cook for 5 minutes, stirring, until the onion is soft but not browned.

3 Stir in the cumin, turmeric, tomatoes, stock, half the chopped coriander and the beans and simmer for 20–30 minutes.

4 Stir in the lemon juice and remaining coriander and serve at once accompanied by pitta bread.

> **Cook's Tip**
> Black-eyed beans are small and cream-coloured with a nutty, earthy flavour. To save preparation time, make this soup using canned beans, draining and rinsing them well before adding them to the pan.

Spiced North African Soup

Known as *harira*, this traditional Moroccan soup is often served in the evening as a starter, but it also makes a hearty and satisfying lunch.

Serves 6

1 large onion, chopped
1.2 litres/2 pints/5 cups vegetable stock
5ml/1 tsp ground cinnamon
5ml/1 tsp turmeric
15ml/1 tbsp grated fresh root ginger
pinch cayenne pepper
2 carrots, diced
2 celery sticks, diced
400g/14oz can chopped tomatoes
450g/1lb floury potatoes, diced
5 strands saffron
400g/14oz can chickpeas, drained
30ml/2 tbsp chopped fresh coriander (cilantro)
15ml/1 tbsp lemon juice
salt and ground black pepper
fried wedges of lemon, to serve

1 Place the onion in a large pot with 300ml/¹/₂ pint/1¹/₄ cups of the vegetable stock. Simmer gently for about 10 minutes.

2 Meanwhile, mix together the cinnamon, turmeric, ginger, cayenne pepper and 30ml/2 tbsp of stock to form a paste. Stir into the onion mixture with the carrots, celery and the remaining stock.

3 Bring the mixture to a boil, reduce the heat, then cover and gently simmer for 5 minutes.

4 Add the tomatoes and potatoes and simmer gently, covered, for 20 minutes. Add the saffron, chickpeas, coriander and lemon juice. Season to taste and when piping hot serve with fried wedges of lemon.

> **Cook's Tip**
> This recipe is a vegetarian version of the soup, but in Morocco it is often made with cubed lean lamb, and enriched with eggs beaten into the hot soup just before serving, turning it into a substantial meal. It is traditionally served with hard-boiled eggs sprinkled with cumin, dried fruits and sweetmeats.

Spiced Bean Soup Energy 161kcal/682kJ; Protein 9.9g; Carbohydrate 23g, of which sugars 3g; Fat 3.5g, of which saturates 0.6g; Cholesterol 0mg; Calcium 47mg; Fibre 5.6g; Sodium 507mg.
Spiced North African Soup Energy 134kcal/556kJ; Protein 2.1g; Carbohydrate 14g, of which sugars 9.3g; Fat 8.1g, of which saturates 2.8g; Cholesterol 8mg; Calcium 65mg; Fibre 4.9g; Sodium 44mg.

Cinnamon-scented Chickpea and Lentil Soup

This soup is believed to have originated from a semolina gruel that the Berbers prepared to warm themselves during the cold winters in the Atlas Mountains. It is served to break the fast during the Muslim month of Ramadan.

Serves 8
30–45ml/2–3 tbsp olive oil
2 onions, halved and sliced
2.5ml/½ tsp ground ginger
2.5ml/½ tsp ground turmeric
5ml/1 tsp ground cinnamon
pinch of saffron threads
2 × 400g/14oz cans chopped
   tomatoes
5–10ml/1–2 tsp sugar
175g/6oz/¾ cup brown or green
   lentils, picked over and rinsed
about 1.75 litres/3 pints/7½ cups
   vegetable stock, or water
200g/7oz/1 generous cup dried
   chickpeas, soaked overnight,
   drained and boiled in plenty of
   water until tender
200g/7oz/1 generous cup dried
   broad (fava) beans, soaked
   overnight, drained and boiled
   until tender
small bunch of fresh coriander
   (cilantro), chopped
small bunch of flat leaf parsley,
   chopped
salt and ground black pepper

1 Heat the olive oil in a stockpot or large pan. Add the onions and cook gently, stirring, for about 15 minutes, or until they are soft but not browned.

2 Add the ground ginger, turmeric, cinnamon and saffron to the cooked onions in the pan, followed by the chopped tomatoes and a little sugar. Stir in the rinsed lentils and pour in the stock or water.

3 Bring to the boil, then reduce the heat, cover and simmer for about 25 minutes, or until the lentils are tender.

4 Stir in the cooked chickpeas and beans, bring back to the boil, cover and simmer for a further 10–15 minutes.

5 Stir in the fresh herbs and season to taste. Serve piping hot with warm crusty bread or rolls.

Curried Parsnip Soup with Sesame Naan Croûtons

The mild sweetness of parsnips is given an exciting lift with a blend of spices in this simple soup.

Serves 4
30ml/2 tbsp olive oil
1 onion, chopped
1 garlic clove, crushed
1 small green chilli, seeded and
   finely chopped
15ml/1 tbsp grated fresh
   root ginger
5 large parsnips, diced
5ml/1 tsp cumin seeds
5ml/1 tsp ground coriander
2.5ml/½ tsp ground turmeric
30ml/2 tbsp mango chutney
1.2 litres/2 pints/5 cups water
juice of 1 lime
salt and ground black pepper
chopped fresh coriander (cilantro),
   to garnish (optional)
60ml/4 tbsp natural (plain) yogurt
   and mango chutney, to serve

**For the sesame naan
croûtons**
45ml/3 tbsp olive oil
1 large naan, cut into
   small dice
15ml/1 tbsp sesame seeds

1 Heat the oil in a large pan and add the onion, garlic, chilli and ginger. Cook for 4–5 minutes, until the onion has softened. Add the parsnips and cook for 2–3 minutes. Sprinkle in the cumin seeds, coriander and turmeric, and cook for 1 minute, stirring.

2 Add the chutney and the water. Season well and bring to the boil. Reduce the heat and simmer for 15 minutes, until the parsnips are soft. Cool the soup slightly, then process it in a food processor or blender until smooth, and return it to the pan. Stir in the lime juice.

3 To make the croûtons, heat the oil in a large frying pan and cook the diced naan for 3–4 minutes, stirring, until golden all over. Remove from the heat and drain off any excess oil. Add the sesame seeds to the croûtons and return to the heat for 30 seconds, until the seeds are pale golden.

4 Ladle the soup into bowls. Spoon a little yogurt into each bowl, then top with mango chutney and some of the croûtons. Garnish with chopped fresh coriander, if you like.

Cinnamon Chickpea Soup Energy 288kcal/1222kJ; Protein 14g; Carbohydrate 50.4g, of which sugars 7g; Fat 4.8g, of which saturates 0.9g; Cholesterol 1mg; Calcium 137mg; Fibre 5.8g; Sodium 36mg.
Curried Parsnip Soup Energy 118kcal/497kJ; Protein 3.2g; Carbohydrate 19.8g, of which sugars 10.9g; Fat 3.5g, of which saturates 0.6g; Cholesterol 0mg; Calcium 84mg; Fibre 6g; Sodium 66mg.

Velvety Pumpkin Soup with Rice and Cinnamon

Modern Moroccan streets and markets are full of colourful seasonal produce that inspire you to buy, go home and start cooking. The pumpkin season is particularly delightful, with the huge orange vegetables piled up on stalls and wooden carts. The sellers patiently peel and slice the pumpkins ready for making this delicious winter soup.

Serves 4
1kg/2¼lb pumpkin
750ml/1¼ pints/3 cups
    vegetable stock
750ml/1¼ pints/3 cups milk
10–15ml/2–3 tsp sugar
75g/3oz/½ cup cooked
    white rice
salt and ground black pepper
5ml/1 tsp ground cinnamon,
    to serve

1 Remove any seeds or fibre from the pumpkin, cut off the peel and chop the flesh. Put the prepared pumpkin in a pan and add the stock, milk, sugar and seasoning. Bring to the boil, then reduce the heat and simmer for about 20 minutes, or until the pumpkin is tender.

2 Drain the pumpkin, reserving the liquid, and purée it in a food processor, then return it to the pan.

3 Bring the soup back to the boil again, throw in the rice and simmer for a few minutes, until the grains are heated through. Check the seasoning, pour into bowls and dust with cinnamon. Serve piping hot, with chunks of bread.

Variations
• *Pumpkin makes a delicious soup, but you could also use butternut squash in this recipe.*
• *For a nutty flavour and a chewier texture, substitute cooked brown rice for the white rice.*
• *Sprinkle a handful of toasted pumpkin seeds over the top of each bowl before serving the soup.*

Garlic and Butternut Squash Soup with Chilli Salsa

This is a wonderful, richly flavoured soup, given bite by the spicy tomato salsa.

Serves 6
2 garlic bulbs, outer papery
    skin removed
a few fresh thyme sprigs
75ml/5 tbsp olive oil
1 large butternut squash, halved
2 onions, chopped
5ml/1 tsp ground coriander
1.2 litres/2 pints/5 cups
    vegetable stock

30–45ml/2–3 tbsp fresh oregano
    or marjoram, stems removed,
    leaves chopped
salt and ground black pepper

For the salsa
4 large ripe tomatoes, halved
    and seeded
1 red (bell) pepper
1 large fresh red chilli, seeded
30ml/2 tbsp extra virgin
    olive oil
15ml/1 tbsp balsamic vinegar
pinch of caster (superfine) sugar

1 Preheat the oven to 220°C/425°F/Gas 7. Wrap the garlic bulbs in foil with the thyme and 7.5ml/1½ tsp of the oil. Put the parcel on a baking sheet with the squash and the tomatoes, pepper and fresh chilli for the salsa. Brush the squash with 10ml/2 tsp of the remaining oil. Roast for 25 minutes, then remove the tomatoes, pepper and chilli. Reduce the oven temperature to 190°C/375°F/Gas 5 and roast the squash and garlic for a further 20–25 minutes, or until tender.

2 Heat the remaining oil in a large non-stick pan and cook the onions and ground coriander gently for about 10 minutes.

3 Meanwhile, skin the pepper and chilli, then process them with the tomatoes and the oil for the salsa. Stir in the vinegar and seasoning to taste, adding a pinch of sugar if necessary.

4 Squeeze the roasted garlic out of its skin into the onions and add the squash, scooped out of its skin. Add the stock, season with salt and pepper, and simmer for 10 minutes. Stir in half the chopped fresh herbs then process or strain the soup. Reheat and taste for seasoning. Serve in warmed bowls topped with a spoonful of salsa and sprinkled with the remaining herbs.

Pumpkin Soup Energy 148kcal/627kJ; Protein 8.8g; Carbohydrate 20.7g, of which sugars 13.5g; Fat 4g, of which saturates 2.4g; Cholesterol 11mg; Calcium 308mg; Fibre 2.8g; Sodium 81mg.
Garlic and Butternut Soup Energy 238kcal/986kJ; Protein 2.9g; Carbohydrate 11.9g, of which sugars 10.3g; Fat 20.2g, of which saturates 3.1g; Cholesterol 0mg; Calcium 79mg; Fibre 4.1g; Sodium 11mg.

Ginger and Star Anise Miso Broth

The Japanese eat miso broth, a simple but highly nutritious soup, almost every day – it is standard breakfast fare and is also eaten with rice or noodles later in the day.

Serves 4
1 bunch of spring onions (scallions) or 5 baby leeks
15g/½oz fresh coriander (cilantro)

3 thin slices fresh root ginger
2 star anise
1 small dried red chilli
1.2 litres/2 pints/5 cups vegetable stock
225g/8oz pak choi (bok choy) or other Asian greens, thickly sliced
200g/7oz firm tofu, cut into 2.5cm/1in cubes
60ml/4 tbsp red miso
30–45ml/2–3 tbsp shoyu
1 fresh red chilli, seeded and shredded

1 Cut the green tops off the spring onions or baby leeks and slice the rest of the spring onions or leeks finely. Place the green tops in a large saucepan with the coriander stalks, fresh root ginger, star anise, dried chilli and vegetable stock.

2 Heat the mixture gently until boiling, then lower the heat and simmer for 10 minutes. Strain, return to the pan and reheat until simmering. Add the green portion of the sliced spring onions or leeks to the soup with the pak choi or greens and tofu. Cook for 2 minutes.

3 Mix 45ml/3 tbsp of the miso with a little of the hot soup in a bowl, then stir it into the soup. Taste the soup and add more miso with soy sauce to taste.

4 Chop the coriander leaves and stir most of them into the soup with the white part of the spring onions or leeks. Cook for 1 minute, then ladle the soup into warmed bowls. Sprinkle with the remaining coriander and the red chilli. Serve at once.

> **Cook's Tips**
> *Shoyu is a Japanese soy sauce, which is available in most Asian and Chinese stores.*

Curried Butternut Squash Soup with Horseradish Cream

The combination of cream, curry powder and horseradish makes a wonderful topping for this beautiful golden soup. The gentle sweetness of the squash and apple are enlivened with curry spices.

Serves 6
1 butternut squash
1 cooking apple
25g/1oz/2 tbsp butter

1 onion, finely chopped
5–10ml/1–2 tsp curry powder
900ml/1½ pints/3¾ cups vegetable stock
5ml/1 tsp chopped fresh sage
150ml/¼ pint/⅔ cup apple juice
salt and ground black pepper
curry powder, to garnish

For the horseradish cream
60ml/4 tbsp double (heavy) cream
10ml/2 tsp horseradish sauce
2.5ml/½ tsp curry powder

1 Peel the squash, remove the seeds and chop the flesh. Peel, core and chop the apple.

2 Heat the butter in a large pan. Add the onion and cook, stirring occasionally, for 5 minutes until soft. Stir in the curry powder. Cook to bring out the flavour, stirring constantly, for 2 minutes.

3 Add the stock, squash, apple and sage. Bring to the boil, lower the heat, cover and simmer for 20 minutes until the squash and apple are soft.

4 Meanwhile, make the horseradish cream. Whip the cream in a bowl until stiff, then stir in the horseradish sauce and curry powder. Cover and chill until required.

5 Purée the soup in a blender or food processor. Return to the clean pan and add the apple juice, with salt and pepper to taste. Reheat gently, without allowing the soup to boil.

6 Serve the soup in individual bowls, topping each portion with a spoonful of horseradish cream and a dusting of curry powder. Garnish with a few lime shreds, if you like.

Butternut Squash Soup Energy 120kcal/502kJ; Protein 11.4g; Carbohydrate 5.1g, of which sugars 3.8g; Fat 6.2g, of which saturates 3.5g; Cholesterol 124mg; Calcium 87mg; Fibre 1.7g; Sodium 125mg.
Ginger and Star Anise Miso Energy 64kcal/267kJ; Protein 6.9g; Carbohydrate 2.7g, of which sugars 2.3g; Fat 3g, of which saturates 0.4g; Cholesterol 0mg; Calcium 394mg; Fibre 1.6g; Sodium 617mg.

Castilian Garlic and Paprika Soup

This rich, dark garlic soup, from central Spain, divides people into two groups: you either love it or hate it. The pitiless sun beats down on La Mancha, one of the poorest regions of Spain, and the local soup has harsh, strong tastes to match the climate. Poaching a whole egg in each bowl just before serving transforms the soup into a complete meal.

Serves 4

30ml/2 tbsp olive oil
4 large garlic cloves, peeled
4 slices stale country bread
20ml/4 tsp paprika
1 litre/1¾ pints/4 cups
  vegetable stock
1.5ml/¼ tsp ground cumin
4 free-range (farm-fresh) eggs
salt and ground black pepper
chopped fresh parsley, to garnish

1 Preheat the oven to 230°C/450°F/Gas 8. Heat the olive oil in a large pan. Add the whole peeled garlic cloves and cook until they are golden, then remove and set aside. Fry the slices of bread in the oil until golden, then set these aside.

2 Add 15ml/1 tbsp of the paprika to the pan, and fry for a few seconds. Stir in the vegetable stock, cumin and remaining paprika, then add the reserved garlic, crushing the cloves with the back of a wooden spoon. Season to taste, then cook for about 5 minutes.

3 Break up the slices of fried bread into bitesize pieces and stir them into the soup. Ladle the soup into four ovenproof bowls.

4 Carefully break an egg into each bowl of soup and place in the oven for about 3 minutes, until the eggs are set. Sprinkle the soup with chopped fresh parsley and serve immediately.

> **Variation**
> *If you prefer, you can simply whisk the eggs into the soup while it is very hot, before ladling it into bowls. The heat of the soup will cook them lightly.*

Spanish Onion Soup with Saffron and Almonds

The Spanish combination of onions, sherry and saffron gives this pale yellow soup a beguiling flavour that is perfect for the opening course of a meal.

Serves 4

40g/1½oz/3 tbsp butter
2 large yellow onions, thinly sliced
1 small garlic clove,
  finely chopped
pinch of saffron threads

50g/2oz blanched almonds,
  toasted and finely ground
750ml/1¼ pints/3 cups
  vegetable stock
45ml/3 tbsp fino sherry
2.5ml/½ tsp paprika
salt and ground black pepper

For the garnish
30ml/2 tbsp flaked or slivered
  almonds, toasted
chopped fresh parsley

1 Melt the butter in a heavy pan over a low heat. Add the onions and garlic, stirring to ensure that they are thoroughly coated in the melted butter, then cover the pan and cook very gently, stirring frequently, for about 20 minutes, or until the onions are soft and golden yellow.

2 Add the saffron threads to the pan and cook, uncovered, for 3–4 minutes, then add the finely ground almonds and cook, stirring the ingredients constantly, for a further 2–3 minutes.

3 Pour in the chicken or vegetable stock and sherry into the pan and stir in 5ml/1 tsp salt and the paprika. Season with plenty of black pepper. Bring to the boil, then lower the heat and simmer gently for about 10 minutes.

4 Pour the soup into a food processor and process until smooth, then return it to the rinsed pan. Reheat slowly, without allowing the soup to boil, stirring occasionally. Taste for seasoning, adding more salt and pepper if required.

5 Ladle the soup into heated bowls, garnish with the toasted flaked or slivered almonds and a little chopped fresh parsley and serve immediately.

Garlic and Paprika Soup Energy 299kcal/1249kJ; Protein 11.6g; Carbohydrate 24.6g, of which sugars 2.8g; Fat 18g, of which saturates 3.1g; Cholesterol 190mg; Calcium 170mg; Fibre 3g, Sodium 323mg.
Spanish Onion Soup Energy 233kcal/966kJ; Protein 7.2g; Carbohydrate 16.2g, of which sugars 12.3g; Fat 16g, of which saturates 5.2g; Cholesterol 27mg; Calcium 51mg; Fibre 3.3g; Sodium 398mg.

Garlic and Tomato Soup with Couscous

Israeli couscous is a toasted, round pasta, which is much larger than regular couscous. It makes a wonderful addition to this warm and comforting soup, which is easy to make and uses largely store-cupboard ingredients. For a really garlicky flavour, an extra clove of chopped raw garlic is added just before serving.

Serves 4–6

30ml/2 tbsp olive oil
1 onion, chopped
1–2 carrots, diced
400g/14oz can chopped tomatoes
6 garlic cloves, roughly chopped, plus 1 extra garlic clove to serve
1.5 litres/2½ pints/6¼ cups vegetable stock
200–250g/7–9oz/1–1½ cups Israeli couscous
2–3 mint sprigs, chopped, or several pinches of dried mint
1.5ml/¼ tsp ground cumin
¼ bunch fresh coriander (cilantro), or about 5 sprigs, chopped
cayenne pepper, to taste
salt and ground black pepper

1 Heat the oil in a large pan, add the onion and carrots and cook gently for about 10 minutes until softened.

2 Add the tomatoes to the onion and carrot mixture. Stir in half the roughly chopped garlic, the stock, couscous, mint, ground cumin, coriander, and cayenne pepper, and season with salt and pepper to taste.

3 Bring the soup to the boil, add the remaining chopped garlic, then reduce the heat slightly and simmer gently for 7–10 minutes, stirring occassionally, or until the couscous is just tender. Chop the extra clove of garlic finely and stir it into the soup. Serve piping hot, ladled into individual serving bowls.

> **Variation**
> If you can't get Israeli couscous, also known as pearl couscous, substitute small soup pasta shapes, such as stellete or risi.

Ras el Hanout Moroccan Tomato Soup

Ras el hanout, a subtle Moroccan mixture of dozens of different spices, gives it a lovely, warming kick. Garlic lovers may like to add a crushed garlic clove and a little salt to the yogurt that is swirled into the soup before serving. This is the daily soup in many Moroccan households.

Serves 4

45–60ml/3–4 tbsp olive oil
3–4 cloves
2 onions, chopped
1 butternut squash, peeled, seeded and cut into chunks
4 celery stalks, chopped
2 carrots, peeled and chopped
8 large, ripe tomatoes, skinned and roughly chopped
5–10ml/1–2 tsp sugar
15ml/1 tbsp tomato purée (paste)
5–10ml/1–2 tsp ras el hanout
2.5ml/½ tsp ground turmeric
large bunch of fresh coriander (cilantro), chopped (reserve a few sprigs for garnish)
1.75 litres/3 pints/7½ cups vegetable stock
a handful dried egg noodles or capellini, broken into pieces
salt and ground black pepper
60–75ml/4–5 tbsp creamy natural (plain) yogurt, to serve

1 In a deep, heavy pan, heat the oil and add the cloves, onions, squash, celery and carrots. Fry until they begin to colour, then stir in the tomatoes and sugar. Cook the tomatoes until the water reduces and they begin to pulp.

2 Stir in the tomato purée, ras el hanout, turmeric and chopped coriander. Pour in the stock and bring the liquid to the boil. Reduce the heat and simmer for 30–40 minutes until the vegetables are very tender and the liquid has reduced a little.

3 Leave the liquid to cool slightly before processing in a food processor or blender, then return to the pan and add the pasta. Alternatively, simply add the pasta to the unblended soup and cook for a further 8–10 minutes, or until the pasta is soft.

4 Season the soup to taste and ladle it into bowls. Spoon a swirl of yogurt into each one, garnish with the extra coriander and serve with freshly baked bread.

Spiced Mango Soup with Chillies and Yogurt

This delicious, light soup is an unusual combination of fruit and spices. It makes a refreshing, fruity start to a spicy meal.

Serves 4
2 ripe mangoes
15ml/1 tbsp gram flour
120ml/4fl oz/½ cup natural (plain) yogurt
900ml/1½ pints/3¾ cups cold water
2.5ml/½ tsp grated fresh root ginger
2 fresh red chillies, seeded and finely chopped
30ml/2 tbsp olive oil
2.5ml/½ tsp mustard seeds
2.5ml/½ tsp cumin seeds
8 curry leaves
salt and ground black pepper
fresh mint leaves, shredded and natural (plain) yogurt, to garnish

1 Peel the mangoes, remove the stones and cut the flesh roughly into chunks. Put into a food processor or blender and purée until smooth.

2 Pour into a pan and stir in the gram flour, yogurt, water, ginger and chillies. Bring the mixture slowly to the boil, stirring occasionally. Simmer for 4–5 minutes until thickened slightly, then remove from the heat and set aside.

3 Heat the oil in a frying pan. Add the mustard seeds and cook for a few seconds until they begin to pop, then add the cumin seeds.

4 Add the curry leaves and continue to cook for 5 minutes. Stir the spice mixture into the soup, return it to the heat and cook for 10 minutes.

5 Press the soup through a sieve (strainer), if you wish to remove the spices, then season to taste. Leave the soup to cool completely, then chill for at least 1 hour.

6 Ladle the soup into bowls, and top each bowl with a spoonful of yogurt. Garnish the soup with mint and serve.

Avocado Soup with Cumin and Paprika

Andalusia is home to both avocados and gazpacho, so it is not surprising that this soup, which is also known as green gazpacho, was invented there. In southern Spain, this deliciously mild, creamy soup is the perfect chilled summer appetizer.

Serves 4
3 ripe avocados
1 bunch spring onions (scallions), white parts only, trimmed and roughly chopped
2 garlic cloves, chopped
juice of 1 lemon
1.5ml/¼ tsp ground cumin
1.5ml/¼ tsp paprika
450ml/¾ pint/scant 2 cups vegetable stock
300ml/½ pint/1¼ cups iced water
salt and ground black pepper
roughly chopped fresh flat leaf parsley, to garnish

1 Starting half a day ahead, put the flesh of one avocado in a food processor or blender. Add the spring onions, garlic and lemon juice and purée until smooth. Add the second avocado and purée, then the third, with the spices and seasoning. Purée until smooth.

2 Gradually add the vegetable stock. Pour the soup into a metal bowl and chill.

3 To serve, stir in the iced water, then season to taste with plenty of salt and black pepper. Garnish with chopped parsley and serve immediately.

Cook's Tips
- *Hass avocados, with bumpy skin that turns purplish black when ripe, generally have the best flavour. They should be perfectly ripe for this recipe.*
- *Avocado flesh blackens when exposed to air, but the lemon juice in this recipe preserves the colour of the soup.*

Spiced Mango Soup Energy 83kcal/354kJ; Protein 3g; Carbohydrate 14.4g, of which sugars 12.7g; Fat 2g, of which saturates 0.5g; Cholesterol 0mg; Calcium 72mg; Fibre 2g; Sodium 28mg.
Avocado Soup with Cumin Energy 148kcal/613kJ; Protein 1.9g; Carbohydrate 2.2g, of which sugars 1.1g; Fat 14.6g, of which saturates 3.1g; Cholesterol 0mg; Calcium 18mg; Fibre 2.9g; Sodium 6mg.

Spinach and Nutmeg Spring Rolls

In Morocco, these little savoury pastries may be filled with cheese and herbs, or, as in this recipe, spinach with freshly grated nutmeg added. The pastries are easy to make, and they are always shaped into cigars or triangles. The filling can be prepared ahead of time but the pastry should not be unwrapped until you are ready to make the pastries, otherwise it will dry out.

Makes 32
8 sheets of filo pastry
sunflower oil, for deep-frying

For the spinach filling
50g/2oz/¼ cup butter
1 onion, finely chopped
275g/10oz fresh spinach, cooked, drained and chopped
small bunch of fresh coriander (cilantro), finely chopped
pinch of freshly grated nutmeg
salt and ground black pepper

1 To make the spinach filling, melt the butter in a small heavy pan. Add the chopped onion and cook over a low heat for 15 minutes, stirring occasionally, until softened but not browned. Stir in the spinach and coriander. Season with nutmeg, salt and pepper, then set aside to cool.

2 Lay a sheet of *ouarka* or filo pastry on a work surface, keeping the other sheets covered with a damp cloth or in a plastic bag. Cut the sheet widthways into four strips.

3 Spoon a little of the filling mixture on to the first strip, at the end nearest to you. Fold the corners of the pastry over the mixture to seal it, then roll up the pastry and filling away from you into a tight cigar. As you reach the end of the strip, brush the edges with a little water and continue to roll up the cigar to seal in the filling. Repeat, placing the finished rolls under a damp cloth.

4 Heat the sunflower oil for deep-frying to 180°C/350°F, or until a cube of day-old bread browns in 30 seconds. Add the rolls to the oil in batches and fry over a medium heat until golden brown. Drain on kitchen paper. Serve the rolls while they are still warm.

Sweet Potato Cakes

These sweet potato balls from Cambodia are delicious dipped in chilli sauce. Simple to make, they are ideal for serving as nibbles with drinks.

Serves 4
450g/1lb sweet potatoes or taro root, boiled or baked, and peeled
30ml/2 tbsp sugar
15ml/1 tbsp Indian curry powder
25g/1oz fresh root ginger, peeled and grated
150g/5oz/1¼ cups glutinous rice flour or plain (all-purpose) flour
salt
sesame seeds or poppy seeds
vegetable oil, for deep-frying
chilli sauce, to serve
vegetarian nuoc cham, to serve

1 In a bowl, mash the cooked sweet potatoes or taro root. Beat in the sugar, curry powder, and ginger. Add the rice flour or plain flour (the latter should be sifted before adding) and salt, and work into a stiff dough – adding more flour if necessary.

2 Pull off lumps of the dough and mould them into small balls using your hands – you should be able to make roughly 24 balls. Roll the balls on a bed of sesame seeds or poppy seeds until they are completely coated.

3 Heat enough oil for deep-frying in a wok. Fry the sweet potato balls in batches, until golden. Drain on kitchen paper. Serve the balls with wooden skewers to make it easier to dip them into the *nuoc cham*.

Cook's Tips
• *Taro root is a staple in South-east Asia. It is used in similar ways to the potato, but has a pronounced nutty taste. The peel can irritate the skin, so it is wise to wear gloves when handling the raw vegetable.*
• *Nuoc cham is a piquant Vietnamese dipping sauce made with chillies, garlic, vinegar and nuoc mam. The vegetarian version is made with seaweed.*

Spinach Spring Rolls Energy 41kcal/171kJ; Protein 0.6g; Carbohydrate 2.8g, of which sugars 0.3g; Fat 3.1g, of which saturates 1g; Cholesterol 3mg; Calcium 23mg; Fibre 0.4g; Sodium 22mg.
Sweet Potato Cakes Energy 354kcal/1495kJ; Protein 5g; Carbohydrate 61g, of which sugars 14.8g; Fat 11.8g, of which saturates 1.5g; Cholesterol 0mg; Calcium 84mg; Fibre 3.9g; Sodium 50mg.

Curry-spiced Pakoras

These delicious bites make a
wonderful snack drizzled
with the fragrant chutney.

Makes 25
15ml/1 tbsp sunflower oil
20ml/4 tsp cumin seeds
5ml/1 tsp black mustard seeds
1 small onion, finely chopped
10ml/2 tsp grated fresh
 root ginger
2 green chillies, seeded
 and chopped
600g/1lb 5oz potatoes, cooked
200g/7oz fresh peas
juice of 1 lemon
90ml/6 tbsp chopped fresh
 coriander (cilantro) leaves
115g/4oz/1 cup gram flour

25g/1oz/¼ cup self-raising (self-
 rising) flour
40g/1½oz/⅓ cup rice flour
large pinch of turmeric
10ml/2 tsp crushed
 coriander seeds
350ml/12fl oz/1½ cups water
vegetable oil, for frying
salt and ground black pepper

For the chutney
105ml/7 tbsp coconut cream
200ml/7fl oz/scant 1 cup natural
 (plain) yogurt
50g/2oz mint leaves, finely
 chopped
5ml/1 tsp golden caster
 (superfine) sugar
juice of 1 lime

1 Heat a wok over a medium heat and add the sunflower oil.
When hot, fry the cumin and mustard seeds for 1–2 minutes.
Add the onion, ginger and chillies to the wok and cook for
3–4 minutes. Add the cooked potatoes and peas and stir-fry
for a further 5–6 minutes. Season, then stir in the lemon
juice and coriander leaves. Leave the mixture to cool slightly,
then divide into 25 portions. Shape each portion into a ball
and chill.

2 To make the chutney, place all the ingredients in a blender
and process until smooth. Season, then chill. To make the batter,
put the gram flour, self-raising flour and rice flour in a bowl.
Season and add the turmeric and coriander seeds. Gradually
whisk in the water to make a smooth batter.

3 Fill a wok one-third full of oil and heat to 180°C/350°F.
Working in batches, dip the chilled balls in the batter, then drop
into the oil and deep-fry for 1–2 minutes, or until golden. Drain
on kitchen paper, and serve immediately with the chutney.

Spiced Tofu with Soy Dressing

The silky consistency of
firm tofu absorbs the dark
smoky taste of the soy
dressing in this rich and
flavourful dish from Korea.
Tofu has a nutty quality that
blends agreeably with the
salty sweetness of soy sauce
and the hints of garlic and
spring onion in the dressing.
Serve it as an appetizer,
alone as a light meal, or as
an accompaniment to a
South-east Asian meal.

Serves 2
2 blocks firm tofu
salt

For the dressing
10ml/2 tsp finely sliced spring
 onion (scallion)
5ml/1 tsp finely chopped garlic
60ml/4 tbsp dark soy sauce
10ml/2 tsp chilli powder
5ml/1 tsp sugar
10ml/2 tsp sesame seeds

1 To make the dressing, mix the spring onion and garlic in a
bowl with the soy sauce, chilli powder, sugar and sesame seeds.
Leave the dressing to stand for a few minutes, allowing the
flavours to mingle.

2 Meanwhile, bring a large pan of water to the boil, and add a
pinch of salt. Place the whole blocks of tofu in the water, being
careful not to let them break apart.

3 Blanch the tofu for about 3 minutes. Remove from the
pan very carefully and place on kitchen paper to remove
any excess water.

4 Transfer the blocks of tofu to a serving dish, and cover with
the dressing. Leave for 10 minutes to absorb the dressing then
serve, slicing the tofu as desired.

Cook's Tip
*Koreans traditionally eat this dish without slicing the tofu,
preferring instead to either eat it directly with a spoon or pick it
apart with chopsticks. It may be easier, however, to slice it in
advance if you are serving it as an accompanying dish.*

Spiced Pakoras Energy 126kcal/525kJ; Protein 4.1g; Carbohydrate 8.3g, of which sugars 2.6g; Fat 8.8g, of which saturates 5.2g; Cholesterol 0mg; Calcium 35mg; Fibre 1.3g; Sodium 16mg.
Spiced Tofu Energy 160kcal/669kJ; Protein 16.1g; Carbohydrate 6.7g, of which sugars 5.6g; Fat 7.8g, of which saturates 0.9g; Cholesterol 0mg; Calcium 954mg; Fibre 0.1g; Sodium 2144mg.

Red Lentil and Tomato Dhal

This is Indian comfort food at its best – there's nothing like a bowl of dhal spiced with mustard seeds, cumin and coriander to clear away the blues.

Serves 4

30ml/2 tbsp sunflower oil
1 green chilli, halved
2 red onions, halved and
    thinly sliced
10ml/2 tsp finely grated garlic
10ml/2 tsp finely grated fresh
    root ginger
10ml/2 tsp black mustard seeds
15ml/1 tbsp cumin seeds

10ml/2 tsp crushed
    coriander seeds
10 curry leaves
250g/9oz/generous 1 cup red
    lentils, rinsed and drained
2.5ml/½ tsp turmeric
2 plum tomatoes, roughly
    chopped
salt
coriander (cilantro) leaves
    and crispy fried onion, to
    garnish (optional)
natural (plain) yogurt, poppadums
    and griddled flatbread or
    naans, to serve

1 Heat a wok over a medium heat and add the sunflower oil. When hot add the green chilli and onions, lower the heat and cook gently for 10–12 minutes, until the onions are softened. Increase the heat slightly and add the garlic, ginger, mustard seeds, cumin seeds, coriander seeds and curry leaves and stir-fry for 2–3 minutes.

2 Add the lentils to the wok with 700ml/1 pint 2fl oz/scant 3 cups water, the turmeric and tomatoes and season with plenty of salt. Bring the mixture to the boil, cover, reduce the heat and cook very gently for 25–30 minutes, stirring occasionally.

3 Check the seasoning, then garnish with coriander leaves and crispy fried onion, if liked, and serve with yogurt, poppadums and flatbread or naans.

Variation
Use yellow split peas in place of the lentils. Like red lentils, they do not need to be soaked before cooking.

Green Chilli Stuffed Tofu

These squares of fried tofu have a crispy coating, surrounding a creamy texture with a crunchy filling. They are stuffed with a blend of chilli and chestnut, which gives a piquant contrast with the delicate flavour of the tofu. This Korean-style dish makes an easy accompaniment for a main course, or a great appetizer.

Serves 2

2 blocks firm tofu
30ml/2 tbsp soy sauce
5ml/1 tsp sesame oil
2 eggs
7.5ml/1½ tsp cornflour
    (cornstarch)
vegetable oil, for shallow-frying

For the filling

2 green chillies, finely chopped
2 chestnuts, finely chopped
6 garlic cloves, crushed
10ml/2 tsp sesame seeds

1 Cut the tofu into 2cm/¾in slices, then cut each slice in half. Place the slices on kitchen paper to absorb any excess water.

2 Mix together the soy sauce and sesame oil. Transfer the tofu slices to a plate and coat them with the mixture. Leave to marinate for 20 minutes. Meanwhile, put all the filling ingredients into a bowl and combine. Set aside.

3 Beat the eggs in a shallow dish. Add the cornflour and whisk until well combined. Take the slices of tofu and dip them into the beaten egg mixture, coating them evenly on all sides.

4 Place a frying pan over medium heat and add the vegetable oil. Add the tofu slices to the pan and sauté, turning over once, until golden brown.

5 Once cooked, make a slit down the middle of each slice with a sharp knife, without cutting all the way through. Gently stuff a large pinch of the filling into each slice, and serve.

Variation
Serve the tofu with a light soy dip instead of the spicy filling.

Lentil and Tomato Dhal Energy 295kcal/1242kJ; Protein 16.1g; Carbohydrate 43.7g, of which sugars 8.5g; Fat 7.6g, of which saturates 1g; Cholesterol 0mg; Calcium 71mg; Fibre 4.7g; Sodium 30mg.
Chilli Stuffed Tofu Energy 291kcal/1213kJ; Protein 23g; Carbohydrate 7.8g, of which sugars 1.3g; Fat 19.1g, of which saturates 3.4g; Cholesterol 209mg; Calcium 1014mg; Fibre 0.8g; Sodium 88mg.

Corn on the Cob with Chillies

You can barbecue, grill or oven-bake corn on the cob in this way. Keeping the husks on the corn protects the kernels and encloses the butter, so the flavours are contained. Fresh corn cobs with the husks intact are perfect, but banana leaves or a double layer of foil will also work as a protective layer.

Serves 6

3 dried chipotle chillies
250g/9oz/generous 1 cup
    butter, softened
7.5ml/1½ tsp lemon juice
45ml/3 tbsp chopped fresh flat
    leaf parsley
6 corn on the cob, with
    husks intact
salt and ground black pepper

1 Heat a heavy frying pan. Add the dried chillies and roast them by stirring them continuously for 1 minute without letting them scorch. Put them in a bowl with almost boiling water to cover. Use a saucer to keep them submerged, and leave them to rehydrate for up to 1 hour.

2 Drain, remove the seeds and chop the chillies finely. Place the butter in a bowl and add the chillies, lemon juice and parsley. Season to taste and mix well.

3 Peel back the husks from each cob without tearing them. Remove the silk. Smear about 30ml/2 tbsp of the chilli butter over each cob. Pull the husks back over the cobs, ensuring that the butter is well hidden. Put the rest of the butter in a pot, smooth the top and chill to use later. Place the cobs in a bowl of cold water and leave in a cool place for 1–3 hours; longer if that suits your work plan better.

4 Prepare the barbecue. Remove the corn cobs from the water and wrap in pairs in foil. Once the flames have died down, position a lightly oiled grill rack over the coals to heat. When the coals are medium-hot, or have a moderate coating of ash, grill the corn for 15–20 minutes. Remove the foil and cook the corn cobs for about 5 minutes more, turning them often to char the husks a little. Serve hot, with the rest of the butter.

Quesadillas with Green Chillies

Barbecuing gives these vegetables a wonderful smoky flavour, enhanced by the bite of green chillies.

Serves 4

8 long baby aubergines
    (eggplants), total weight about
    175g/6oz, halved lengthways
2 red onions, cut into wedges,
    leaving the roots intact
2 red (bell) peppers, quartered
1 yellow and 1 orange (bell)
    pepper, quartered

30ml/2 tbsp olive oil
400g/14oz block mozzarella
    cheese
2 fresh green chillies, seeded and
    sliced into rounds
15ml/1 tbsp Mexican
    tomato sauce
8 corn or wheat flour tortillas
handful of fresh basil leaves
salt and ground black pepper

1 Toss the aubergines, onions and peppers in the oil on a large baking tray. Place the peppers, skin side down, on the griddle or directly on the grill rack of a medium hot barbecue and cook until seared and browned underneath. If the food starts to char, remove the rack until the coals cool down.

2 Put the peppers in a bowl, cover with clear film (plastic wrap) and set aside. Grill the onions and aubergines until they have softened slightly and are branded with brown grill marks, then set them aside. Rub the skins off the peppers with your fingers, cut each piece in half and add to the other vegetables.

3 Cut the mozzarella into 20 slices. Place them, together with the roasted vegetables, in a large bowl and add the sliced chillies and the tomato sauce. Stir well to mix, and season with salt and pepper.

4 Place a griddle over the heat. When it is hot, lay a tortilla on the griddle and pile a quarter of the vegetable mixture into the centre. Sprinkle over some basil leaves. When the tortilla has browned underneath, put another tortilla on top, cooked-side down. Turn the quesadilla over and continue to cook until the underside has browned. Keep warm while you cook the remaining quesadillas.

Corn with Chillies Energy 435kcal/1805kJ; Protein 3.4g; Carbohydrate 27.1g, of which sugars 10g; Fat 35.6g, of which saturates 21.9g; Cholesterol 89mg; Calcium 28mg; Fibre 1.8g; Sodium 525mg.
Quesadillas with Chilli Energy 233kcal/971kJ; Protein 11.8g; Carbohydrate 17.1g, of which sugars 8.5g; Fat 13.6g, of which saturates 7.4g; Cholesterol 29mg; Calcium 214mg; Fibre 2.7g; Sodium 268mg.

Artichoke Hearts with Ginger and Preserved Lemons

In this Moroccan dish, tender globe artichoke hearts are poached in a delicious sweet-sour sauce flavoured with honey, garlic, herbs and preserved lemon. The dish can be eaten warm or cold as a first course or as part of a buffet, but it also makes a perfect accompaniment for barbecued meat.

Serves 4
30–45ml/2–3 tbsp olive oil
2 garlic cloves, crushed
scant 5ml/1 tsp ground ginger
pinch of saffron threads
juice of ½ lemon
15–30ml/1–2 tbsp honey
peel of 1 preserved lemon,
    finely sliced
8 artichoke hearts, quartered
150ml/¼ pint/⅔ cup water
salt

1 Heat the olive oil in a small heavy pan and stir in the garlic. Before the garlic begins to colour, stir in the ginger, saffron, lemon juice, honey and preserved lemon.

2 Add the artichokes to the pan and toss them in the spices and honey. Pour in the water, add a little salt and heat until the liquid is simmering.

3 Cover the pan and simmer for 10–15 minutes until the artichokes are tender, turning them occasionally. If the liquid has not reduced, take the lid off the pan and boil for about 2 minutes until reduced to a coating consistency. Serve warm or at room temperature.

Cook's Tip
To prepare the artichoke hearts, remove the outer leaves and cut off the stems. Carefully separate the remaining leaves and use a teaspoon to scoop out the choke with all the hairy bits. Trim the hearts and immerse them in water mixed with a squeeze of lemon juice to prevent them from turning black. Frozen prepared hearts are available in some supermarkets and they can be used for this recipe.

Sweet Potato and Fresh Ginger Rösti Cakes

This dish is a speciality of Hanoi in Vietnam, where the street sellers are well known for their varied recipes, which are all delicious. Traditionally, the patties are served with herbs and lettuce leaves for wrapping.

Serves 4
50g/2oz/½ cup plain
    (all-purpose) flour
50g/2oz/½ cup rice flour
4ml/scant 1 tsp baking powder
10ml/2 tsp sugar
2.5cm/1in fresh root ginger,
    peeled and grated
2 spring onions (scallions),
    finely sliced
1 slim sweet potato, about
    225g/8oz, peeled and cut into
    fine matchsticks
vegetable oil, for deep-frying
salt and ground black pepper
chopped fresh coriander (cilantro),
    to garnish
lettuce leaves and soy sauce or
    other dipping sauce, to serve

1 Sift the plain and rice flour and baking powder into a bowl. Add the sugar and about 2.5ml/½ tsp each of salt and pepper. Gradually stir 250ml/8fl oz/1 cup water into the mixture, until thoroughly combined.

2 Add the grated ginger and sliced spring onions to the batter and leave to stand for 30 minutes for the flavours to develop. Add extra ginger if you like a strong flavour.

3 Add the sweet potato matchsticks to the batter and fold them in, making sure they are well coated. Heat enough oil for deep-frying in a wok.

4 Lower a heaped tablespoon of the mixture into the oil, pushing it off the spoon so that it floats in the oil. Fry for 2–3 minutes, turning it over so that it is evenly browned. Drain on kitchen paper. Continue with the rest of the batter.

5 Arrange the patties on lettuce leaves, garnish with coriander, and serve immediately with soy sauce or another dipping sauce of your choice.

Artichoke Hearts Energy 142kcal/586kJ; Protein 1.6g; Carbohydrate 4.1g, of which sugars 1.9g; Fat 11.3g, of which saturates 1.6g; Cholesterol 0mg; Calcium 40mg; Fibre 1.6g; Sodium 47mg.
Sweet Potato and Ginger Rösti Energy 276kcal/1159kJ; Protein 11g; Carbohydrate 35g, of which sugars 6g; Fat 11g, of which saturates 1g; Cholesterol 85mg; Calcium 83mg; Fibre 81g; Sodium 200mg.

Smoky Aubergine and Red Pepper Pâté

Cooking the aubergines whole, over an open flame, gives them a distinctive smoky flavour and aroma, as well as tender, creamy flesh. The subtle flavour of the roasted aubergine contrasts wonderfully with the sweet flavour of the red peppers.

Serves 4–6
2 aubergines (eggplants)
2 red (bell) peppers
3–5 garlic cloves, chopped, or
    more to taste
2.5ml/½ tsp ground cumin
juice of ½–1 lemon, to taste
2.5ml/½ tsp sherry or
    wine vinegar
45–60ml/3–4 tbsp extra virgin
    olive oil
1–2 shakes of cayenne pepper,
    Tabasco or other hot
    pepper sauce
coarse sea salt
chopped fresh coriander (cilantro),
    to garnish
pitta bread wedges or thinly sliced
    French bread or ciabatta bread,
    sesame seed crackers and
    cucumber slices, to serve

1 Place the aubergines and peppers directly over a medium-low gas flame or on the coals of a barbecue. Turn the vegetables frequently until deflated and the skins are charred.

2 Put the aubergines and peppers in a plastic bag or in a bowl and seal tightly. Leave to cool for 30–40 minutes.

3 Peel the vegetables, reserving the juices, and roughly chop the flesh. Put the flesh in a bowl and add the juices, garlic, cumin, lemon juice, vinegar, olive oil, hot pepper seasoning and salt. Mix well to combine. Turn the mixture into a serving bowl and garnish with coriander. Serve with bread, sesame seed crackers and cucumber slices.

> **Cook's Tip**
> *Enclosing the hot vegetables in a bag or bowl traps plenty of steam, which helps to loosen the skin from the flesh. It can then be rubbed or peeled off in long pieces.*

Spicy Zahlouk with Courgette and Cauliflower Salad

Zahlouk is a delicious, spicy aubergine and tomato salad from Morocco that can be served as an appetizer, with lots of bread to scoop it up, or use it as one of the dishes in a *meze* spread.

Serves 4
3 large aubergines (eggplants),
    peeled and cubed
3–4 large tomatoes, peeled and
    chopped to a pulp
5ml/1 tsp sugar
3–4 garlic cloves, crushed
60ml/4 tbsp olive oil
juice of 1 lemon
scant 5ml/1 tsp harissa
5ml/1 tsp cumin seeds, roasted
    and ground
small bunch of flat leaf
    parsley, chopped
salt

For the courgette and cauliflower salad
1 cauliflower broken into florets
3 small courgettes (zucchini)
60ml/4 tbsp olive oil
juice of 1 lemon
2–3 garlic cloves, crushed
small bunch of parsley,
    finely chopped
salt and ground black pepper
5ml/1 tsp paprika and flat bread,
    to serve

1 To make the zahlouk, boil the aubergines in plenty of salted water for about 15 minutes, until they are very soft. Drain and squeeze out the excess water, then chop and mash with a fork.

2 Put the pulped tomatoes in a pan, stir in the sugar, and cook over a gentle heat until they are reduced to a thick sauce. Stir in the mashed aubergines. Add the garlic, olive oil, lemon juice, harissa, cumin and parsley and stir until thoroughly mixed. Season to taste.

3 To make the cauliflower salad, steam the cauliflower until tender. Slice the courgettes and fry in half the olive oil. Drain on kitchen paper.

4 Mash the cauliflower lightly with the remaining olive oil, add the courgette slices, lemon juice and garlic, season to taste then sprinkle the top with paprika. Serve at room temperature with plenty of flat bread and the zahlouk.

Aubergine Pâté Energy 51kcal/213kJ; Protein 2.2g; Carbohydrate 8.9g, of which sugars 8.3g; Fat 1g, of which saturates 0.2g; Cholesterol 0mg; Calcium 22mg; Fibre 4.4g; Sodium 7mg.
Spicy Zahlouk Energy 302kcal/1251kJ; Protein 8.3g; Carbohydrate 12.6g, of which sugars 11.5g; Fat 24.7g, of which saturates 3.7g; Cholesterol 0mg; Calcium 139mg; Fibre 8.6g; Sodium 36mg.

Paprika-spiced Butternut and Aubergine Salad

This delightful salad, served warm, is all the reason you need to get the griddle out in the colder months. Not only do the colour combinations please the eye, but the flavours really work. Look out for slivered pistachios in Middle Eastern shops: they combine brilliantly with the orange butternut squash.

Serves 4

2 aubergines (eggplants)
1 butternut squash, about 1kg/2¼lb
120ml/4fl oz/½ cup extra virgin olive oil
5ml/1 tsp paprika
150g/5oz feta cheese
50g/2oz/⅓ cup pistachio nuts, roughly chopped
salt and ground black pepper

1 Slice the aubergines widthways into 5mm/¼in rounds. Spread them out on a tray and sprinkle with a little salt. Leave for 30 minutes.

2 Peel the squash and scoop out the seeds with a spoon, then slice it in the same way. Place the butternut squash slices in a bowl, season lightly with salt and pepper and toss with 30ml/2 tbsp of the oil.

3 Heat the griddle until a few drops of water sprinkled on to the surface evaporate instantly. Lower the heat a little and sear the butternut squash slices in batches. Cook for about 1½ minutes on each side, then put them on a tray. Continue until all the slices have been cooked, then dust them with a little of the paprika.

4 Pat the aubergine slices dry. Toss with the remaining oil and season lightly. Cook in the same way as the squash. When all the slices are cooked, mix the aubergine and squash together in a serving bowl.

5 While the salad is still warm, crumble the feta over the top, sprinkle with the chopped pistachio nuts and dust with the remaining paprika. Serve immediately.

Seven-spice Aubergines

Thai seven-spice powder is a commercial blend of spices, including coriander seeds, cumin, cinnamon, star anise, chilli pepper, cloves and lemon peel, as well as ginger and garlic. The mix gives these aubergines a lovely warm flavour. After coating the aubergines in a light, spicy batter and deep-frying them, they become crisp and golden. If you are unable to find this spice mix, you can use Chinese five-spice powder instead.

Serves 4

500g/1¼lb aubergines (eggplants)
2 egg whites
90ml/6 tbsp cornflour (cornstarch)
5ml/1 tsp salt
15ml/1 tbsp Thai seven-spice powder
15ml/1 tbsp mild chilli powder
sunflower oil, for frying
fresh mint leaves, to garnish
steamed rice or noodles and hot chilli sauce, to serve

1 Slice the aubergines into thin discs and pat them dry with kitchen paper.

2 Whisk the egg whites in a bowl until light and foamy, but not dry. Combine the cornflour, salt, seven-spice powder and chilli powder and spread the mixture evenly on to a large plate.

3 Fill a wok one-third full of sunflower oil and heat to 180°C/350°F (or until a cube of bread, dropped into the oil, browns in 30 seconds).

4 Working in batches, dip the aubergine slices in the egg white and then into the spiced flour mixture to coat. Deep-fry for 3–4 minutes, or until crisp and golden.

5 Remove the aubergine slices from the oil with a wire skimmer or slotted spoon and drain well on kitchen paper. Keep warm while you cook the remaining slices.

6 Serve the aubergines immediately, garnished with mint leaves and accompanied with steamed rice or noodles, and hot chilli sauce for dipping.

Butternut Salad Energy 385kcal/1593kJ; Protein 10.7g; Carbohydrate 9.2g, of which sugars 7g; Fat 34.2g, of which saturates 9.1g; Cholesterol 26mg; Calcium 231mg; Fibre 4.8g; Sodium 608mg.
Seven-spice Aubergines Energy 203kcal/850kJ; Protein 2.7g; Carbohydrate 23.5g, of which sugars 2.5g; Fat 11.7g, of which saturates 1.4g; Cholesterol 0mg; Calcium 17mg; Fibre 2.5g; Sodium 45mg.

Asian-spiced Courgette Tempura

This is a twist on the classic Japanese tempura, using besan, or chickpea flour, in the batter. Also known as gram flour, golden besan is more commonly used in Indian cooking and gives a wonderfully crisp texture while the courgette inside becomes meltingly tender.

Serves 4

600g/1lb 5oz courgettes
  (zucchini)

90g/3½oz/¾ cup gram flour
5ml/1 tsp baking powder
2.5ml/½ tsp turmeric
10ml/2 tsp ground coriander
5ml/1 tsp ground cumin
5ml/1 tsp chilli powder
250ml/8fl oz/1 cup beer
sunflower oil, for frying
salt
steamed basmati rice, natural
  (plain) yogurt and pickles,
  to serve

1 Cut the courgettes into thick, finger-sized batons and set aside. Sift the gram flour, baking powder, turmeric, ground coriander, cumin and chilli powder into a large bowl.

2 Season the mixture with salt and gradually add the beer, mixing to make a thick batter – do not overmix.

3 Fill a large wok one-third full with sunflower oil and heat to 180°C/350°F (or until a cube of bread, dropped into the oil, browns in 15 seconds).

4 Working in batches, dip the courgette batons in the spiced batter and then deep-fry for 1–2 minutes, or until crisp and golden. Lift out of the wok using a slotted spoon and drain on kitchen paper.

5 Serve the courgettes immediately with steamed basmati rice, yogurt, pickles and chutney.

> **Cook's Tip**
> *You can cook all kinds of vegetables in this way. Try using onion rings, aubergine (eggplant) slices, or even whole mild chillies.*

Grilled Aubergine with Harissa and Ginger

Hot, spicy, sweet and fruity are classic flavours of North African cooking and all are abundant in this Moroccan dish. For a spread of tantalizing tastes, serve with artichoke heart and orange salad and the garlicky dip, bissara. Baby aubergines are very effective for this dish as you can slice them in half lengthways and hold them by their stalks.

Serves 4

2 aubergines (eggplants), peeled
  and thickly sliced
olive oil, for frying
2–3 garlic cloves, crushed
5cm/2in piece of fresh root ginger,
  peeled and grated
5ml/1 tsp ground cumin
5ml/1 tsp harissa
75ml/5 tbsp clear honey
juice of 1 lemon
salt
fresh bread, to serve

1 Preheat the grill (broiler) or a griddle. Dip each slice of aubergine in olive oil and cook in a pan under the grill or in a griddle pan. Turn the slices so that they are lightly browned on both sides.

2 In a wide frying pan, fry the garlic in a little olive oil for a few seconds, then stir in the ginger, cumin, harissa, honey and lemon juice. Add enough water to cover the base of the pan and to thin the mixture, then lay the aubergine slices in the pan. Cook the aubergines gently for about 10 minutes, or until they have absorbed all the sauce.

3 Add a little extra water, if necessary, season to taste with salt, and serve at room temperature, with chunks of fresh bread to mop up the juices.

> **Variations**
> *Courgettes (zucchini) can also be cooked in this way. If you want to make a feature out of this sumptuous dish, serve it with other grilled (broiled) vegetables and fruit, such as (bell) peppers, chillies, tomatoes, oranges, pineapple and mangoes.*

Courgette Tempura Energy 241kcal/999kJ; Protein 7.3g; Carbohydrate 15.3g, of which sugars 4.6g; Fat 15.6g, of which saturates 1.9g; Cholesterol 0mg; Calcium 83mg; Fibre 3.8g; Sodium 15mg.
Aubergine with Harissa Energy 151kcal/631kJ; Protein 1.4g; Carbohydrate 17.6g, of which sugars 17.3g; Fat 8.9g, of which saturates 1.3g; Cholesterol 0mg; Calcium 16mg; Fibre 3g; Sodium 5mg.

Spiced Herby Mushrooms

Button mushrooms caramelize beautifully in their own juice, but still retain their moistness and nutty flavour. Turkish cooks often serve them as a side dish, or as a hot or cold *meze* dish with chunks of bread to mop up the tasty cooking juices, but they are also good served on toasted crusty bread as a light lunch with a salad. You can use whatever herbs and spices you enjoy and have available to flavour this dish.

Serves 4
45ml/3 tbsp olive oil
15ml/1 tbsp butter
450g/1lb button (white)
  mushrooms, wiped clean
3–4 garlic cloves, peeled and
  finely chopped
10ml/2 tsp allspice
  berries, crushed
10ml/2 tsp coriander seeds
5ml/1 tsp dried mint
1 small bunch each of fresh
  sage and flat leaf parsley,
  chopped
salt and ground black pepper
lemon wedges, to serve

1 Heat the oil and butter in a wide, heavy pan, then stir in the mushrooms with the garlic, crushed allspice berries and the coriander seeds. Cover and cook for about 10 minutes, shaking the pan from time to time, until the mushrooms start to caramelize and their liquid evaporates.

2 Remove the lid and toss in the mint with some of the sage and parsley. Cook for a further 5 minutes, until most of the liquid has evaporated, then season with salt and pepper.

3 Tip the mushrooms into a serving dish and sprinkle the rest of the sage and parsley over the top. Serve hot or at room temperature, with lemon wedges for squeezing.

> **Cook's Tip**
> *Choose small mushrooms for this dish and keep them whole, trimming the ends of the stalks if necessary. Avoid washing them before cooking as they will absorb a lot of water. Instead, use a soft brush to remove any grit and wipe the caps with a clean damp cloth.*

Turkish Spiced Apples

Vegetables and fruits stuffed with an aromatic pilaff are a great favourite in Turkey. This recipe is for apples, but you can use the same filling for other fruit or vegetables.

Serves 4
4 cooking apples, or any firm, sour
  apple of your choice
30ml/2 tbsp olive oil
juice of ½ lemon
10ml/2 tsp sugar
salt and ground black pepper
1 tomato, 1 lemon and fresh mint
  or basil leaves, to serve

For the filling
30ml/2 tbsp olive oil
a little butter
1 onion, finely chopped
2 garlic cloves
30ml/2 tbsp pine nuts
30ml/2 tbsp currants, soaked in
  warm water and drained
5–10ml/1–2 tsp ground
  cinnamon
5–10ml/1–2 tsp ground allspice
5ml/1 tsp sugar
175g/6oz/scant 1 cup short grain
  rice, rinsed and drained
1 bunch each of fresh flat leaf
  parsley and dill, finely chopped

1 To make the filling, heat the oil and butter in a heavy pan, stir in the onion and garlic and cook until they soften. Add the pine nuts and currants and cook until the nuts turn golden.

2 Stir in the spices, sugar and rice, and mix well. Pour in enough water to cover the rice – roughly 1–2cm/½–¾in above the grains – and bring to the boil. Season with salt and pepper and stir, then lower the heat and simmer for about 10–12 minutes, until almost all the water has been absorbed. Toss in the herbs and turn off the heat. Cover and leave to steam for 5 minutes.

3 Preheat the oven to 200°C/400°F/Gas 6. Using a sharp knife, cut the stalk ends off the apples and keep to use as lids. Core each apple, removing some flesh to create a cavity. Take spoonfuls of the rice and pack it into the apples. Replace the lids and stand the apples, tightly packed, in a small baking dish.

4 Mix together 100ml/3½fl oz/scant ½ cup water with the oil, lemon juice and sugar. Pour this mixture around the apples, then bake for 30–40 minutes, until the apples are tender and the cooking juices are slightly caramelized. Serve with a tomato and lemon garnish and a sprinkling of mint or basil leaves.

Cumin-spiced Hummus

This classic Middle Eastern appetizer is made from cooked chickpeas, ground to a paste and flavoured with garlic, lemon juice, tahini, olive oil and cumin. It is delicious served with wedges of toasted pitta bread or crudités. It is traditionally made with dried chickpeas, soaked overnight then simmered in water until tender, but using canned chickpeas gives a satisfactory result and makes it very quick and easy to prepare.

Serves 4–6
400g/14oz can chickpeas, drained
60ml/4 tbsp tahini
2–3 garlic cloves, chopped
juice of ½–1 lemon
cayenne pepper
small pinch to 1.5ml/¼ tsp ground cumin, or more to taste
salt and ground black pepper

1 Put the chickpeas into a bowl and mash them coarsely using a potato masher or a fork. If you prefer a smoother purée, process the chickpeas in a food processor or blender until you have the texture you require.

2 Mix the tahini into the chickpea purée, then stir in the garlic, lemon juice, cayenne, cumin and salt and pepper to taste, adding the ingredients to the processor or blender if you are using one. If the mixture seems too stiff, add a little water. Serve at room temperature.

Cook's Tip
Cans of chickpeas usually contain water to which sugar and salt has been added. Drain the chickpeas and rinse them thoroughly under the tap before mashing them.

Variation
Process two roasted red (bell) peppers with the chickpeas, then continue as above. Serve sprinkled with lightly toasted pine nuts and paprika mixed with olive oil.

Feta and Roast Pepper Dip

This is a familiar *meze* in northern Greece, where it is eaten as a dip with pittas, as an accompaniment to other dishes, or with toast to serve with a glass of ouzo. The strong, salty feta cheese with the smoky peppers and hot chillies makes a powerful combination to enliven the taste buds. In Greek it is known as *htipiti*, which literally means 'that which is beaten'.

Serves 4
1 yellow or green (bell) pepper
1–2 fresh green chillies
200g/7oz feta cheese
60ml/4 tbsp extra virgin olive oil
juice of 1 lemon
45–60ml/3–4 tbsp milk
ground black pepper
a little finely chopped fresh flat leaf parsley, to garnish
slices of toasted Greek bread or pittas, to serve

1 Thread the pepper and the chillies on metal skewers and turn them over a flame or under the grill (broiler), until the skins are charred all over.

2 Put the pepper and chillies in a plastic bag or in a covered bowl and set them aside until cool enough to handle.

3 Peel off as much of the pepper and chilli skins as possible and brush off the blackened bits with kitchen paper. Slit the pepper and chillies lengthways and discard the seeds and stems.

4 Put the pepper and chilli flesh into a food processor. Add all the other ingredients except the parsley and blend to a fairly smooth paste. Add a little more milk if the mixture seems too stiff. Spread on slices of toast, sprinkle a hint of parsley on top and serve.

Variation
Add 75g/3oz sun-dried tomatoes bottled in oil, drained, to the mixture in the food processor.

Cumin-spiced Hummus Energy 140kcal/586kJ; Protein 6.9g; Carbohydrate 11.2g, of which sugars 0.4g; Fat 7.8g, of which saturates 1.1g; Cholesterol 0mg; Calcium 97mg; Fibre 3.6g; Sodium 149mg.
Feta and Pepper Dip Energy 244kcal/1010kJ; Protein 8.8g; Carbohydrate 4.4g, of which sugars 4.3g; Fat 21.4g, of which saturates 8.5g; Cholesterol 35mg; Calcium 205mg; Fibre 0.7g; Sodium 731mg.

Libyan Spicy Pumpkin Dip

This spicy dip is a beautiful warm orange colour and its flavour, spiced with paprika and ginger, is equally warming. It is great to serve at a Thanksgiving feast. It can be stored for at least a week in the refrigerator. Serve chunks of bread or raw vegetables to dip into it.

Serves 6–8
45–60ml/3–4 tbsp olive oil
1 onion, finely chopped
5–8 garlic cloves, roughly chopped
675g/1½lb pumpkin, peeled and diced
5–10ml/1–2 tsp ground cumin
5ml/1 tsp paprika
1.5–2.5ml/¼–½ tsp ground ginger
1.5–2.5ml/¼–½ tsp curry powder
75g/3oz chopped canned tomatoes or diced fresh tomatoes
15–30ml/1–2 tbsp tomato purée (paste)
½–1 red jalapeño or serrano chilli, chopped, or cayenne pepper, to taste
pinch of sugar, if necessary
juice of ½ lemon, or to taste
salt
30ml/2 tbsp chopped fresh coriander (cilantro) leaves, to garnish

1 Heat the oil in a frying pan, add the onion and half the garlic and fry until softened. Add the pieces of pumpkin, then cover the pan and cook for about 10 minutes, or until the pumpkin is half tender.

2 Add the spices to the pan and cook for 1–2 minutes. Stir in the tomatoes, tomato purée, chilli, sugar and salt and cook over a medium-high heat until the liquid has evaporated.

3 When the pumpkin is tender, mash to a coarse purée. Add the remaining garlic and taste for seasoning, then stir in the lemon juice to taste. Serve at room temperature, sprinkled with the chopped fresh coriander.

> **Variation**
> Use butternut squash, or any other winter squash, in place of the pumpkin.

Garlic-infused Spicy Bean Dip

Broad (fava) beans are among the oldest vegetables in cultivation, and are a staple ingredient in the cuisines of North Africa, where they are native and are eaten both fresh and dried. This garlicky dip comes from Morocco. Sprinkled with paprika or dried thyme, it makes a tasty appetizer, and is best served with flat bread.

Serves 4
350g/12oz/1¾ cups dried broad (fava) beans, soaked overnight
4 garlic cloves
10ml/2 tsp cumin seeds
60–75ml/4–5 tbsp olive oil
salt
paprika or dried thyme to garnish

1 Drain the beans, remove their wrinkly skins and place them in a large pan with the garlic and cumin seeds. Add enough water to cover the beans and bring to the boil. Boil for 10 minutes, then reduce the heat, cover the pan and simmer gently for about 1 hour, or until the beans are tender.

2 Drain the beans and, while they are still warm, pound or process them with the olive oil until the mixture forms a smooth dip. Season to taste with salt and serve warm or at room temperature, sprinkled with paprika.

Beetroot and Yogurt Relish

Spiked with garlic, this is a smooth, creamy relish that is suitable to eat as part of a selection of meze dishes. It is delicious served with warm pitta bread or slices of fresh baguette.

Serves 4
4 raw beetroot (beets)
500g/1¼ lb/2¼ cups natural (plain) yogurt
2 garlic cloves, crushed
salt and ground black pepper
fresh mint leaves to garnish

1 Boil the beetroot until tender. Drain and refresh. then peel off the skins and grate on to a plate. Pat off excess water. In a bowl, beat the yogurt with garlic, salt and pepper, add the beetroot and mix well. Garnish with mint leaves.

Spicy Pumpkin Dip Energy 54kcal/224kJ; Protein 0.9g; Carbohydrate 2.9g, of which sugars 2.3g; Fat 4.4g, of which saturates 0.7g; Cholesterol 0mg; Calcium 37mg; Fibre 1.3g; Sodium 3mg.
Spicy Bean Dip Energy 155kcal/650kJ; Protein 7.4g; Carbohydrate 18.4g, of which sugars 3.9g; Fat 6.3g, of which saturates 0.9g; Cholesterol 0mg; Calcium 96mg; Fibre 6.9g; Sodium 394mg.
Beetroot Relish Energy 95kcal/403kJ; Protein 7.8g; Carbohydrate 14.4g, of which sugars 13g; Fat 1.4g, of which saturates 0.6g; Cholesterol 2mg; Calcium 249mg; Fibre 1.3g; Sodium 137mg.

Chickpea Purée with Paprika

This recipe for baked hummus is an eastern Anatolian speciality. Add yogurt to make it light, and serve it hot as an appetizer or light lunch with a tomato and herb salad.

Serves 4
225g/8oz/1¼ cups dried chickpeas, soaked overnight
about 50ml/2fl oz/¼ cup olive oil
juice of 2 lemons
3–4 garlic cloves, crushed
10ml/2 tsp cumin seeds, crushed
30–45ml/2–3 tbsp light tahini
45–60ml/3–4 tbsp thick natural (plain) yogurt
30–45ml/2–3 tbsp pine nuts
40g/1½oz/3 tbsp butter or ghee
5–10ml/1–2 tsp paprika
salt and ground black pepper

1 Drain the chickpeas, tip them into a pan and fill the pan with plenty of cold water. Bring to the boil and boil for 1 minute, then lower the heat and partially cover the pan. Simmer the chickpeas for about 1 hour, until they are soft and easy to mash. Drain, rinse under running water and remove any loose skins.

2 Preheat the oven to 200°C/400°F/Gas 6. Using a large mortar and pestle, pound the chickpeas with the oil, lemon juice, garlic and cumin. Or process the ingredients in a food processor or blender.

3 Beat in the tahini (at this point the mixture will be very stiff), then beat in the yogurt until the purée is light and smooth. Season to taste. Transfer the purée to an ovenproof dish – preferably an earthenware one – and smooth the top with the back of a spoon.

4 Dry-roast the pine nuts in a small heavy pan over a medium heat until golden brown. Lower the heat, add the butter and let it melt, then stir in the paprika.

5 Pour the mixture of pine nuts and spiced butter over the hummus and bake it for about 25 minutes, until it has risen slightly and the butter has been absorbed. Serve the purée straight from the oven.

Artichoke and Cumin Dip

This dip is so easy to make and is unbelievably tasty. Serve it with olives, hummus and wedges of pitta bread to make a summery snack selection. Grilled artichokes bottled in oil have a fabulous flavour and can be used instead of canned artichokes. You can also vary the flavourings – try adding chilli powder in place of the cumin and add a handful of torn basil leaves to the artichokes before blending the dip.

Serves 4
2 x 400g/14oz cans artichoke hearts, drained
2 garlic cloves, peeled
2.5ml/½ tsp ground cumin
olive oil
salt and ground black pepper
pitta bread, warmed and thickly sliced, to serve

1 Put the artichoke hearts in a food processor or blender, and add the garlic and ground cumin. Pour in a generous drizzle of olive oil.

2 Process to a smooth purée and season with plenty of salt and ground black pepper to taste.

3 Spoon the purée into a serving bowl. Drizzle a little extra olive oil in a swirl over the top and serve with slices of warm pitta bread to scoop up the purée.

Tahini Dip

This is a delightful and very simple dip from Anatolia, often served as an appetizer with toasted pitta bread and a glass of raki.

Serves 2
45ml/3 tbsp tahini
juice of 1 lemon
15–30ml/1–2 tsp dried mint
lemon wedges, to serve

1 Beat the tahini and lemon juice together in a bowl. Add the mint and beat again until thick and creamy. Spoon the dip into a small dish and serve at room temperature with lemon wedges for squeezing.

Artichoke Dip Energy 76kcal/315kJ; Protein 2g; Carbohydrate 3.8g, of which sugars 2g; Fat 6g, of which saturates 0.8g; Cholesterol 0mg; Calcium 84mg; Fibre 2.7g; Sodium 121mg.
Tahini Dip Energy 160kcal/664kJ; Protein 4.3g; Carbohydrate 6.4g, of which sugars 6.2g; Fat 13.3g, of which saturates 1.9g; Cholesterol 0mg; Calcium 155mg; Fibre 1.8g; Sodium 6mg.
Chickpea Purée Energy 433kcal/1803kJ; Protein 15g; Carbohydrate 29.5g, of which sugars 3g; Fat 29.2g, of which saturates 7.7g; Cholesterol 21mg; Calcium 160mg; Fibre 6.8g; Sodium 91mg.

Chilli-spiced Turkish Salad

This Turkish *meze* dish is simply a mixture of chopped fresh vegetables. Along with a few simple dishes such as cubes of honey-sweet melon and feta, or plump, juicy olives spiked with red pepper and oregano, it is *meze* at its simplest and best. Popular in kebab houses in Turkey, this dish makes a tasty snack or appetizer, and is good served with chunks of warm, crusty bread or toasted pitta.

Serves 4
2 large tomatoes, skinned, seeded and finely chopped
2 Turkish green peppers or 1 green (bell) pepper, finely chopped
1 onion, finely chopped
1 green chilli, seeded and finely chopped
1 small bunch of fresh flat leaf parsley, finely chopped
a few fresh mint leaves, finely chopped
15–30ml/1–2 tbsp olive oil
salt and ground black pepper

1 Put all the finely chopped ingredients in a bowl and mix well together.

2 Toss the mixture with the olive oil to bind the ingredients, and season to taste with salt and pepper.

3 Leave the dish to sit for a short time for the flavours to blend. Serve at room temperature, in individual bowls or one large dish.

Variations
• *The salad can be turned into a paste. When you bind the chopped vegetables with the olive oil, add 15–30ml/1–2 tbsp tomato purée (paste) with a little extra chilli and 5–10ml/1–2 tsp sugar. The mixture will become a tangy paste to spread on fresh, crusty bread or toasted pitta, and it can also be used as a sauce for grilled (broiled), roasted or barbecued meats.*
• *Add other salad vegetables to the mixture, such as chopped cucumber and spring onions (scallions).*

Carrot and Caraway Purée with Yogurt

Long, thin carrots that are orange, yellow, red and purple are a colourful feature in the vegetable markets throughout Turkey. Used mainly in salads, lentil dishes and stews, they are also married with garlic-flavoured yogurt for *meze* – sliced and deep-fried drizzled with yogurt, grated and folded in, or steamed and puréed, then served with the yogurt in the middle, as in this recipe. Try serving the carrot purée while it is still warm, with chunks of crusty bread or warm pitta to scoop it up. The caraway seeds give it an interesting, anise-like flavour, which is sharpened with lemon juice.

Serves 4
6 large carrots, thickly sliced
5ml/1 tsp caraway seeds
30–45ml/2–3 tbsp olive oil
juice of 1 lemon
225g/8oz/1 cup thick and creamy natural (plain) yogurt
1–2 garlic cloves, crushed
salt and ground black pepper
a few fresh mint leaves, to garnish

1 Steam the carrots for about 25 minutes, until they are very soft. While they are still warm, mash them to a smooth purée, or process them in a food processor or blender.

2 Beat the caraway seeds into the carrot purée, followed by the oil and lemon juice. Season with salt and pepper.

3 Beat the yogurt and garlic together in a separate bowl, and season with salt and pepper. Spoon the warm carrot purée around the edge of a serving dish, or pile into a mound and make a well in the middle. Spoon the yogurt into the middle, and garnish with mint.

Cook's Tip
It is always best to steam, rather than boil, vegetables, so they retain their taste, texture and goodness. This purée would not taste nearly as good if the carrots were boiled and watery.

Baba Ganoush with Lebanese Flatbread

Baba Ganoush is a delectable aubergine dip from the Middle East. Tahini – sesame seed paste – and ground cumin are the main flavourings, giving a subtle hint of spice.

Serves 6
2 small aubergines (eggplants)
1 garlic clove, crushed
60ml/4 tbsp tahini
25g/1oz/¼ cup ground almonds

juice of ½ lemon
½ tsp ground cumin
30ml/2 tbsp fresh mint leaves
30ml/2 tbsp olive oil
salt

For the Lebanese flatbread
4 pitta breads
45ml/3 tbsp toasted
    sesame seeds
45ml/3 tbsp fresh thyme leaves
45ml/3 tbsp poppy seeds
150ml/¼ pint/⅔ cup olive oil

1 Start by making the Lebanese flatbread. Split the pitta breads horizontally through the middle and carefully open them out flat, cut-side up. Mix the sesame seeds, chopped thyme and poppy seeds in a mortar. Crush them lightly with a pestle to release their flavour.

2 Stir the olive oil into the spice mixture. Spread the mixture lightly over the cut sides of the pitta bread. Grill (broil) until golden brown and crisp. When cool enough to handle, break into rough pieces and set aside.

3 Grill the aubergines, turning them frequently, until the skin is blackened and blistered. Remove the peel, chop the flesh roughly and leave to drain in a colander.

4 Squeeze out as much liquid from the aubergine as possible. Place the flesh in a blender or food processor. Add the garlic, tahini, ground almonds, lemon juice and cumin, with salt to taste and process to a smooth paste. Roughly chop half the mint and stir into the dip.

5 Spoon into a bowl, sprinkle the remaining leaves on top and drizzle with olive oil. Serve with the Lebanese flatbread.

Turkish Eggs on Spiced Yogurt

This dish of poached eggs on a bed of garlic-flavoured yogurt is surprisingly delicious. In Turkey it is served as a hot *meze* dish or snack, but it works equally well as a supper dish with a green salad. Hen's eggs or duck's eggs can be used, whichever you prefer or have at hand, and you can either poach or fry them. Spiked with paprika, and served with toasted flat bread or chunks of a warm, crispy loaf, this is a simple dish to prepare, but it is very satisfying.

Serves 2
500g/1¼lb/2¼ cups thick
    natural (plain) yogurt
2 garlic cloves, crushed
30–45ml/2–3 tbsp white
    wine vinegar
4 large eggs
15–30ml/1–2 tbsp butter
5ml/1 tsp paprika
a few dried sage leaves, crumbled
salt and ground black pepper

1 Beat the yogurt with the garlic and seasoning. Spoon into a serving dish or on to individual plates, spreading it flat to create a thick bed for the eggs.

2 Fill a pan with water, add the vinegar to seal the egg whites, and bring to a rolling boil. Stir the water with a spoon to create a whirlpool and crack in the first egg. As the egg spins and the white sets around the yolk, stir the water for the next one. Poach the eggs for 2–3 minutes so the yolks are still soft.

3 Lift the eggs out of the water with a slotted spoon and place them on the yogurt bed.

4 Quickly melt the butter in a small pan. Stir in the red pepper or paprika and sage leaves, then spoon the mixture over the eggs. Eat immediately.

Cook's Tip
Leave the yogurt at room temperature to form a contrast with the hot eggs, or heat it by placing the dish in a cool oven, or by sitting it in a covered pan of hot water.

Baba Ganoush Energy 451kcal/1878kJ; Protein 9.3g; Carbohydrate 29.5g, of which sugars 3.1g; Fat 33.8g, of which saturates 4.7g; Cholesterol 0mg; Calcium 204mg; Fibre 4.2g; Sodium 225mg.
Turkish Eggs Energy 345kcal/1438kJ; Protein 25.4g; Carbohydrate 19.1g, of which sugars 19.1g; Fat 19.8g, of which saturates 8.3g; Cholesterol 400mg; Calcium 534mg; Fibre 0.1g; Sodium 393mg.

Spring Onions with Chilli Sauce

A piquant sauce is an excellent accompaniment to deep-fried spring onions in their crisp batter.

Serves 6
18–24 plump spring onions (scallions), trimmed
sea salt and ground black pepper
lemon wedges, to serve

For the batter
225g/8oz/2 cups self-raising (self-rising) flour
150ml/¼ pint/⅔ cup lager
175–200ml/6–7fl oz/¾ water
groundnut (peanut) oil, for deep-frying

1 large egg white
2.5ml/½ tsp cream of tartar

For the sauce
2–3 large mild dried red chillies, such as Spanish ñoras or Mexican anchos or guajillos
1 large red (bell) pepper, halved
2 large tomatoes, halved and seeded
4–6 large garlic cloves, unpeeled
75–90ml/5–6 tbsp olive oil
4 slices French bread, about 2cm/¾in thick
25g/1oz/¼ cup hazelnuts, blanched and dry roasted
15ml/1 tbsp sherry vinegar
chopped fresh parsley, to garnish

1 Soak the dried chillies in hot water for about 30 minutes. Preheat the oven to 220°C/425°F/Gas 7. Place the pepper halves, tomatoes and garlic on a baking sheet and drizzle with 15ml/1 tbsp olive oil. Roast, uncovered, for about 30–40 minutes, until the pepper is blistered and blackened. Cool slightly, then peel the pepper, tomatoes and garlic.

2 Fry the bread in the olive oil until light brown on both sides, Drain the chillies, discard the seeds, then place in a food processor. Add the pepper, tomatoes, garlic, hazelnuts and bread with the oil from the pan. Add the vinegar and process to a paste. Thin the sauce with more oil, if necessary. Set aside.

3 To make the batter, sift the flour into a bowl, season, then gradually whisk in the lager, then water. Whisk the egg white with the cream of tartar until stiff, then fold it into the batter. Heat the oil for deep-frying to 180°C/350°F. Dip the spring onions in the batter and fry in batches for 4–5 minutes. Drain thoroughly on kitchen paper and sprinkle with a little sea salt. Serve hot with the sauce and lemon wedges.

Thai-spiced Potato Samosas

Most samosas are deep-fried, but these are baked, making them a healthier option. They are also perfect for parties as no deep-frying is involved.

Makes 25
1 large potato, about 250g/9oz, diced
15ml/1 tbsp groundnut (peanut) oil

2 shallots, finely chopped
1 garlic clove, finely chopped
60ml/4 tbsp coconut milk
5ml/1 tsp Thai red or green curry paste
75g/3oz/¾ cup peas
juice of ½ lime
25 samosa wrappers or 10 x 5cm/4 x 2in strips of filo pastry
salt and ground black pepper
oil, for brushing

1 Preheat the oven to 220°C/425°F/Gas 7. Bring a small pan of water to the boil, add the diced potato, cover and cook for 10–15 minutes, until tender. Drain and set aside.

2 Meanwhile, heat the groundnut oil in a large frying pan and cook the shallots and garlic over a medium heat, stirring occasionally, for 4–5 minutes, until softened and golden.

3 Add the drained potato, coconut milk, red or green curry paste, peas and lime juice to the frying pan. Mash coarsely with a wooden spoon. Season to taste with salt and pepper and cook over a low heat for 2–3 minutes, then remove the pan from the heat and set aside until the mixture has cooled a little.

4 Lay a samosa wrapper or filo strip flat on the work surface. Brush with a little oil, then place a generous teaspoonful of the mixture in the middle of one end. Turn one corner diagonally over the filling to meet the long edge.

5 Continue folding over the filling, keeping the triangular shape as you work down the strip. Brush with a little more oil if necessary and place on a baking sheet. Prepare all the other samosas in the same way.

6 Bake for 15 minutes, or until the pastry is golden and crisp. Leave to cool slightly before serving.

Spring Onions with Chilli Energy 428kcal/1791kJ; Protein 7.9g; Carbohydrate 47.9g, of which sugars 4.9g; Fat 24.1g, of which saturates 3g; Cholesterol 0mg; Calcium 103mg; Fibre 3.2g; Sodium 181mg.
Thai Samosas Energy 42kcal/178kJ; Protein 1.2g; Carbohydrate 8.5g, of which sugars 0.6g; Fat 0.6g, of which saturates 0.1g; Cholesterol 0mg; Calcium 14mg; Fibre 0.5g; Sodium 4mg.

Spiced Onion Pakora

These delicious Indian onion fritters are made with chickpea flour, otherwise known as gram flour or besan. Serve with chutney or a yogurt dip.

Serves 4–5
675g/1 1/2lb onions, halved and
   thinly sliced
5ml/1 tsp salt
5ml/1 tsp ground coriander
5ml/1 tsp ground cumin
2.5ml/1/2 tsp ground turmeric
1–2 green chillies, seeded and
   finely chopped
45ml/3 tbsp chopped fresh
   coriander (cilantro)
90g/3 1/2oz/3/4 cup gram flour
2.5ml/1/2 tsp baking powder
vegetable oil, for deep-frying

To serve
lemon wedges (optional)
fresh coriander (cilantro) sprigs
yogurt and cucumber dip

1 Place the onions in a colander, add the salt and toss. Place on a plate and leave to stand for 45 minutes, tossing once or twice. Rinse the onions, then squeeze out any excess moisture.

2 Place the onions in a bowl. Add the ground coriander, cumin, turmeric, chillies and fresh coriander. Mix well.

3 Add the gram flour and baking powder, then use your hands to mix the ingredients thoroughly. Shape the mixture by hand into 12–15 pakoras, about the size of golf balls.

4 Heat the oil for deep-frying to 180–190°C/350–375°F or until a cube of day-old bread browns in 30–45 seconds. Fry the pakoras, 4–5 at a time, until they are deep golden brown all over. Drain each batch on kitchen paper and keep warm until all the pakoras are cooked. Serve with lemon wedges, coriander sprigs and a yogurt dip.

> **Cook's Tip**
> *For a cucumber dip, stir half a diced cucumber and 1 seeded and chopped fresh green chilli into 250ml/8fl oz/1 cup natural (plain) yogurt. Season with salt and cumin.*

Braised Spiced Onion Salad

If you can find the small, flat Italian *cipolla* or *borettane* onions, they are excellent in this recipe – otherwise you can use pickling onions, small red onions or shallots.

Serves 6
105ml/7 tbsp olive oil
675g/1 1/2lb small onions, peeled
150ml/1/4 pint/2/3 cup dry white
   wine
2 bay leaves
2 garlic cloves, bruised
1–2 small dried red chillies
15ml/1 tbsp coriander seeds,
   toasted and lightly crushed
2.5ml/1/2 tsp sugar
a few fresh thyme sprigs
30ml/2 tbsp currants
10ml/2 tsp chopped
   fresh oregano
5ml/1 tsp grated lemon rind
15ml/1 tbsp chopped fresh flat
   leaf parsley
30–45ml/2–3 tbsp pine
   nuts, toasted
salt and ground black pepper

1 Place 30ml/2 tbsp olive oil in a wide pan. Add the onions and cook gently over a medium heat for about 5 minutes, or until they begin to colour. Remove the onions from the pan and set aside.

2 Add the remaining oil, the wine, bay leaves, garlic, chillies, coriander, sugar and thyme to the pan. Bring the mixture to the boil and cook briskly for 5 minutes, then return the onions to the pan.

3 Stir in the currants, then reduce the heat and cook gently for 15–20 minutes, or until the onions are completely tender but not falling apart. Use a draining spoon to transfer the onions to a serving dish.

4 Boil the liquid remaining in the pan over a high heat until it has reduced considerably. Taste it and adjust the seasoning, if necessary, then pour the reduced liquid over the onions. Sprinkle the oregano over the onions, set aside to cool and then chill them.

5 Just before serving, stir the onions to coat them in the sauce and sprinkle over the grated lemon rind, chopped parsley and toasted pine nuts.

Spiced Onion Pakora Energy 207kcal/861kJ; Protein 5.4g; Carbohydrate 19.8g, of which sugars 8.2g; Fat 12.3g, of which saturates 1.4g; Cholesterol 0mg; Calcium 84mg; Fibre 4.3g; Sodium 14mg.
Spiced Onion Salad Energy 224kcal/926kJ; Protein 2.1g; Carbohydrate 17.3g, of which sugars 13.4g; Fat 16.9g, of which saturates 2.4g; Cholesterol 0mg; Calcium 60mg; Fibre 2.4g; Sodium 6mg.

Fruit and Nut Couscous

In Morocco this dish of steamed couscous with dried fruit and nuts, topped with sugar and cinnamon, is served on special celebrations. It is often presented as a course on its own, just before the dessert, but it is delicious served with spicy vegetable tagines.

Serves 6

500g/1¼lb medium couscous
600ml/1 pint/2½ cups
    warm water
5ml/1 tsp salt

pinch of saffron threads
45ml/3 tbsp sunflower oil
30ml/2 tbsp olive oil
a little butter
115g/4oz/½ cup dried apricots,
    cut into slivers
75g/3oz/½ cup dried
    dates, chopped
75g/3oz/generous ½ cup
    seedless raisins
115g/4oz/1 cup blanched
    almonds, cut into slivers
75g/3oz/¾ cup pistachio nuts
10ml/2 tsp ground cinnamon
45ml/3 tbsp sugar

1 Preheat the oven to 180°C/350°F/Gas 4. Put the couscous in a bowl. Mix the water, salt and saffron and pour the mixture over the couscous, stirring. Leave to stand for 10 minutes, or until the grains have plumped up and become tender. Add the sunflower oil and, using your fingers, rub it evenly through the couscous grains.

2 In a heavy pan, heat the olive oil and butter and stir in the apricots, dates, raisins, most of the almonds (reserving some to garnish the dish) and the pistachio nuts. Cook over a gentle heat until the raisins plump up, then tip the nuts and fruit into the couscous and toss together.

3 Tip the couscous into an ovenproof dish and cover with foil. Place in the oven for about 20 minutes, until heated through. Meanwhile, toast the reserved slivered almonds.

4 Pile the hot couscous in a mound on a large warmed serving dish and sprinkle with the cinnamon and sugar – these are traditionally added in vertical stripes down the mound of couscous. Sprinkle the toasted almonds over the top of the dish and serve immediately.

Sweet Potato Tagine

The vegetables in this succulent, syrupy tagine are chosen for their sweetness and should be slightly caramelized. They are at their best when served with grilled meats, couscous or with lots of warm, crusty bread, accompanied by a leafy, herb-filled salad.

Serves 4–6

45ml/3 tbsp olive oil
a little butter
25–30 pearl or button onions,
    blanched and peeled

900g/2lb sweet potatoes, peeled
    and cut into bitesize chunks
2–3 carrots, cut into
    bitesize chunks
150g/5oz/generous ½ cup
    ready-to-eat pitted prunes
5ml/1 tsp ground cinnamon
2.5ml/½ tsp ground ginger
10ml/2 tsp clear honey
450ml/¾ pint/scant 2 cups
    vegetable stock
small bunch of fresh coriander
    (cilantro), finely chopped
small bunch of mint,
    finely chopped
salt and ground black pepper

1 Preheat the oven to 200°C/400°F/Gas 6. Heat the olive oil in a flameproof casserole with the butter and stir in the peeled onions. Cook the onions over medium heat for about 5 minutes until they are tender, then remove half the onions from the pan and set aside.

2 Add the sweet potatoes and carrots to the pan and cook until the vegetables are lightly browned. Stir in the prunes with the cinnamon, ginger and honey, then pour in the stock. Bring to the boil, season well, cover the casserole and transfer to the oven for about 45 minutes.

3 Stir in the reserved onions and bake for a further 10 minutes. Gently stir in the fresh coriander and mint, and serve the tagine immediately.

> **Cook's Tip**
> *Sweet potatoes have dark red or orange skin and orange flesh with a flavour reminiscent of chestnuts. Buy fresh, firm specimens that do not "give" when pressed.*

Fruit and Nut Couscous Energy 576kcal/2403kJ; Protein 12.5g; Carbohydrate 73g, of which sugars 29.4g; Fat 27.8g, of which saturates 3.1g; Cholesterol 0mg; Calcium 102mg; Fibre 4.2g; Sodium 74mg.
Sweet Potato Tagine Energy 388kcal/1638kJ; Protein 5.4g; Carbohydrate 74.8g, of which sugars 37.5g; Fat 9.6g, of which saturates 1.5g; Cholesterol 0mg; Calcium 129mg; Fibre 11g; Sodium 120mg.

Stuffed Vine Leaves with Cumin

The important ingredients in these stuffed vine leaves are the spices and fresh herbs, which give the brown rice filling its zest.

Serves 6–8
250g/9oz/1¼ cups brown rice
30–45ml/2–3 tbsp natural
(plain) yogurt
3 garlic cloves, chopped
1 egg, lightly beaten
5–10ml/1–2 tsp ground cumin
2.5ml/½ tsp ground cinnamon
several handfuls of raisins
3–4 spring onions (scallions),
thinly sliced

½ bunch fresh mint, plus extra
to garnish
about 25 preserved vine leaves,
rinsed and drained
salt, if necessary

For cooking
8–10 unpeeled garlic cloves
juice of ½–1 lemon
90ml/6 tbsp olive oil

To serve
1 lemon, cut into wedges or
half slices
15–25 Greek black olives
150ml/¼ pint/⅔ cup natural
(plain) yogurt

1 Put the rice in a pan with 300ml/½ pint/1¼ cups water. Bring to the boil, reduce the heat, cover and simmer for 30 minutes, or until just tender. Drain well and leave to cool slightly.

2 Put the cooked rice in a bowl, add the yogurt, garlic, egg, cumin and cinnamon, raisins, spring onions and mint and mix.

3 Lay the vine leaves on a board, shiny side down. Place 15–30ml/1–2 tbsp of the mixture near the stalk of each leaf. Fold each one up, starting at the bottom, turning in the sides then rolling up towards the top to enclose the filling.

4 Carefully layer the rolls in a steamer and stud with the whole garlic cloves. Fill the base of the steamer with water and drizzle the lemon juice and olive oil evenly over the rolls.

5 Cover the steamer tightly and cook over a medium-high heat for about 40 minutes, adding more water if necessary. Remove from the heat and set aside to cool slightly. Arrange the vine leaves on a serving dish and serve warm. Garnish and serve with lemon, olives and a bowl of yogurt, for dipping.

Casablancan Couscous with Harissa

This dish is based on the classic Moroccan couscous recipe for a stew containing seven vegetables, which is believed to bring good luck. Serve with a dollop of thick and creamy yogurt and a spoonful of fiery harissa.

Serves 6
3 red onions, peeled and
quartered
2–3 courgettes (zucchini), halved
lengthways and cut across into
2–3 pieces each
2–3 red, green or yellow (bell)
peppers, quartered
2 aubergines (eggplants), cut into
6–8 long segments
2–3 leeks, trimmed and cut into
long strips

2–3 sweet potatoes, peeled and
cut into long strips
4–6 tomatoes, quartered
6 garlic cloves, crushed
25g/1oz fresh root ginger, sliced
a few large fresh rosemary sprigs
about 150ml/¼ pint/⅔ cup
olive oil
10ml/2 tsp sugar or clear honey
salt and ground black pepper
natural (plain) yogurt, harissa and
bread, to serve

For the couscous
500g/1¼lb/3 cups medium
couscous
5ml/1 tsp salt
600ml/1 pint/2½ cups
warm water
45ml/3 tbsp sunflower oil
about 25g/1oz/2 tbsp butter

1 Preheat the oven to 200°C/400°F/Gas 6. Arrange all the vegetables in a roasting pan with the garlic, ginger and rosemary. Pour olive oil over the vegetables, sprinkle with the sugar or honey, salt and pepper, and roast for about 1½ hours.

2 Meanwhile stir the salt into the water, then pour it over the couscous. Leave to stand for 10 minutes to plump up then, using your fingers, rub the sunflower oil into the grains to air them and break up any lumps. Tip the couscous into an ovenproof dish, arrange the butter over the top, cover with foil and heat in the oven for about 20 minutes.

3 Fork the melted butter into the grains of couscous and fluff it up, then pile it on a large dish and shape into a mound with a little pit at the top. Spoon some vegetables into the pit and arrange the rest around the dish. Pour the oil from the pan over the couscous. Serve with yogurt, harissa and bread.

Vine Leaves with Cumin Energy 220kcal/924kJ; Protein 3.5g; Carbohydrate 31.1g, of which sugars 6g; Fat 9.9g, of which saturates 1.6g; Cholesterol 24mg; Calcium 27mg; Fibre 1.2g; Sodium 18mg.
Couscous with Harissa Energy 561kcal/2340kJ; Protein 10.4g; Carbohydrate 78.8g, of which sugars 18.7g; Fat 24.6g, of which saturates 3.5g; Cholesterol 0mg; Calcium 101mg; Fibre 7.2g; Sodium 51mg.

Spiced Vegetable Casserole

Here's a meal cooked in a single pot that's suitable for feeding large numbers of people. It's lightly spiced and includes plenty of garlic, and is popular with everyone.

Serves 4

60ml/4 tbsp olive oil
1 large onion, chopped
2 small–medium aubergines (eggplants), cut into small cubes
4 courgettes (zucchini), cut into small chunks
1 green (bell) pepper, chopped
1 red or yellow (bell) pepper, chopped
115g/4oz/1 cup fresh or frozen peas

115g/4oz French beans
450g/1lb new or salad potatoes, cubed
2.5ml/½ tsp cinnamon
2.5ml/½ tsp ground cumin
5ml/1 tsp paprika
4–5 large ripe tomatoes, skinned
400g/14oz can chopped tomatoes
30ml/2 tbsp chopped fresh parsley
3–4 garlic cloves, crushed
350ml/12fl oz/1½ cups vegetable stock
salt and ground black pepper
black olives, to garnish
fresh parsley, to garnish

1 Preheat the oven to 190°C/375°F/Gas 5. Heat 45ml/3 tbsp of the oil in a heavy pan, add the onion and fry until golden. Add the aubergines and sauté for about 3 minutes, then add the courgettes, green and red or yellow peppers, peas, beans and potatoes, together with the spices and seasoning.

2 Continue to cook for 3 minutes, stirring all the time. Transfer to a shallow ovenproof dish.

3 Halve, seed and chop the fresh tomatoes and mix with the canned tomatoes, chopped parsley, garlic and the remaining olive oil in a bowl.

4 Pour the stock over the aubergine mixture and then spoon over the prepared tomato mixture.

5 Cover and bake the dish for 30–45 minutes until the vegetables are tender. Serve hot, garnished with black olives and parsley.

Spiced Pumpkin Gnocchi

Pumpkin adds a sweet richness to these gnocchi, which are superb on their own or served with meat.

Serves 4

450g/1lb pumpkin, peeled, seeded and chopped
450g/1lb potatoes, boiled
2 egg yolks
200g/7oz/1¾ cups plain (all-purpose) flour, plus more if necessary
pinch of ground allspice
1.5ml/¼ tsp cinnamon
pinch of freshly grated nutmeg
finely grated rind of ½ orange
salt and ground pepper

For the sauce

30ml/2 tbsp olive oil
1 shallot, finely chopped
175g/6oz/2½ cups fresh chanterelles, sliced, or 15g/½oz/½ cup dried, soaked in warm water for 20 minutes, then drained
10ml/2 tsp almond butter
150ml/¼ pint/⅔ cup crème fraîche
a little milk or water
75ml/5 tbsp chopped fresh parsley
50g/2oz/½ cup Parmesan cheese, freshly grated

1 Wrap the pumpkin in foil and bake at 180°C/350°F/Gas 4 for 30 minutes. Pass the pumpkin and cooked potatoes through a food mill into a bowl. Add the egg yolks, flour, spices, orange rind and seasoning and mix well to make a soft dough. If the mixture is too loose add a little flour to stiffen it.

2 To make the sauce, heat the oil in a pan and fry the shallot until soft. Add the chanterelles and cook briefly, then add the almond butter. Stir to melt and stir in the crème fraîche. Simmer briefly, add the parsley and season to taste. Keep hot.

3 Flour a work surface. Spoon the gnocchi dough into a piping bag fitted with a 1cm/½in plain nozzle. Pipe on to the flour to make a 15cm/6in sausage. Roll in flour and cut crossways into 2.5cm/1in pieces. Repeat. Mark each piece lightly with a fork and drop into a pan of fast boiling salted water.

4 The gnocchi are done when they rise to the surface, after 3–4 minutes. Lift them out, drain and turn into bowls. Spoon the sauce over, sprinkle with Parmesan, and serve at once.

Spiced Vegetable Casserole Energy 573kcal/2416kJ; Protein 32.5g; Carbohydrate 81.5g, of which sugars 19.5g; Fat 15.3g, of which saturates 2.5g; Cholesterol 0mg; Calcium 250mg; Fibre 25.7g; Sodium 60mg.
Spiced Pumpkin Gnocchi Energy 553kcal/2317kJ; Protein 15.6g; Carbohydrate 61.7g, of which sugars 5.9g; Fat 28.8g, of which saturates 14.7g; Cholesterol 156mg; Calcium 299mg; Fibre 4.5g; Sodium 166mg.

Picnic Pie with Ginger

This is a homely vegetarian version of the more elaborate and traditional Moroccan meat pie. It would be a delightful meal on a summer day, and make a tasty addition to a picnic.

Serves 6
30ml/2 tbsp olive oil
115g/4oz/½ cup butter
8 spring onions (scallions), trimmed and chopped
2 garlic cloves, chopped
25g/1oz fresh root ginger, peeled and chopped
225g/8oz/2 cups cashew nuts, roughly chopped
5–10ml/1–2 tsp ground cinnamon, plus extra to garnish
5ml/1 tsp paprika
2.5ml/½ tsp ground coriander, plus extra for dusting
6 eggs, beaten
bunch of flat leaf parsley, finely chopped
large bunch of fresh coriander (cilantro), finely chopped
8 sheets of fresh or frozen filo pastry
salt and ground black pepper

1 Preheat the oven to 200°C/400°F/Gas 6. Heat the olive oil with a little of the butter in a heavy pan and stir in the spring onions, garlic and ginger. Add the cashew nuts and cook for a few minutes, then stir in the cinnamon, paprika and ground coriander. Season well, then add the eggs. Cook, stirring, until the eggs begin to scramble but remain moist. Remove from the heat, add the parsley and fresh coriander, and leave to cool.

2 Melt the remaining butter. Separate the sheets of filo and keep them under a slightly damp cloth. Brush an ovenproof dish with a little of the melted butter and cover with a sheet of pastry, allowing the sides to flop over the rim. Brush the pastry with a little more melted butter and place another sheet on top. Repeat with another two sheets to make four layers. Spread the nut mixture over the pastry and fold the pastry edges over the filling.

3 Cover with the remaining sheets of pastry, brushing each one with melted butter and tucking the edges under the pie, as though making a bed. Brush the pie with the remaining melted butter and bake for 25 minutes, or until the pastry is crisp and golden. Dust the pie with a little cinnamon before serving.

Tofu in a Tangy Chilli Sauce

This is a light, tasty Vietnamese dish. Because tofu is high in protein, it is perfect for a vegetarian diet.

Serves 4
vegetable or groundnut (peanut) oil, for deep-frying
450g/1lb firm tofu, rinsed and cut into bitesize cubes
4 shallots, finely sliced
1 Thai chilli, seeded and chopped
25g/1oz fresh root ginger, peeled and finely chopped
4 garlic cloves, finely chopped
6 large ripe tomatoes, skinned, seeded and finely chopped
30ml/2 tbsp soy sauce
10ml/2 tsp sugar
mint leaves and strips of red chilli, to garnish
ground black pepper

1 Heat enough oil for deep-frying in a wok or heavy pan. Fry the cubes of tofu, in batches, until crisp and golden. Remove each batch as it is done with a slotted spoon and drain on kitchen paper.

2 When the tofu is cooked, pour off most of the oil, reserving 30ml/2 tbsp in the wok. Add the shallots, chilli, ginger and garlic and stir-fry until they are fragrant. Stir in the tomatoes, soy sauce and sugar.

3 Reduce the heat and simmer for 10–15 minutes until the liquid ingredients form a sauce. Stir in 105ml/7 tbsp water and bring to the boil.

4 Season the sauce with a little pepper to taste and return the tofu to the pan. Mix well and simmer gently for 2–3 minutes to heat through. Garnish with mint leaves and chilli strips and serve immediately.

Cook's Tip
This recipe is delicious as a side dish but can also be eaten as a main dish with noodles or rice.

Picnic Pie Energy 528kcal/2190kJ; Protein 15.9g; Carbohydrate 17.6g, of which sugars 3.1g; Fat 44.5g, of which saturates 15.9g; Cholesterol 231mg; Calcium 93mg; Fibre 2.4g; Sodium 300mg.
Tofu in Chilli Sauce Energy 423kcal/1749kJ; Protein 17.9g; Carbohydrate 7.8g, of which sugars 4.5g; Fat 35.8g, of which saturates 5.3g; Cholesterol 0mg; Calcium 607mg; Fibre 2.8g; Sodium 296mg.

Potato Rösti and Tofu

Although this dish features various different components, it is not difficult to make. Allow enough time to marinate the tofu for at least an hour before you start to cook it, to allow it to absorb the flavours of the ginger, garlic and tamari.

Serves 4

425g/15oz/3¾ cups tofu, cut into 1cm/½in cubes
4 large potatoes, about 900g/2lb total weight, peeled
sunflower oil, for frying
salt and ground black pepper
30ml/2 tbsp sesame seeds, toasted

For the marinade

30ml/2 tbsp tamari or dark soy sauce
15ml/1 tbsp clear honey
2 garlic cloves, crushed
4cm/1½in piece fresh root ginger, grated
5ml/1 tsp toasted sesame oil

For the sauce

15ml/1 tbsp olive oil
8 tomatoes, halved, seeded and chopped

1 Mix all the marinade ingredients in a bowl and add the tofu. Leave to marinate in the refrigerator for at least 1 hour, turning the tofu occasionally to allow the flavours to infuse.

2 To make the rösti, par-boil the potatoes for 10–15 minutes until almost tender. Leave to cool, then grate coarsely. Season well. Preheat the oven to 200°C/400°F/Gas 6. Drain the tofu, reserving the marinade, and spread out on a baking tray. Bake for 20 minutes, turning occasionally, until golden and crisp.

3 Meanwhile, to make the sauce, heat the oil in a pan, add the marinade and tomatoes and bring to the boil. Reduce the heat and simmer, covered, for 10 minutes. Pass through a sieve (strainer) to make smooth and keep warm.

4 Form the potato mixture into four cakes. Heat a frying pan with enough oil to cover the base. Place the cakes in the frying pan, flattening them slightly with a spatula. Cook until golden and crisp then flip over to cook the other side. To serve, place on four serving plates. Sprinkle the tofu on top, spoon over the tomato sauce and sprinkle with sesame seeds.

Spicy Stuffed Peppers

This is an unusual Thai version of this familiar dish, in that the stuffed peppers are steamed rather than baked, but the result is beautifully light and tender. The filling incorporates typical Thai ingredients such as red curry paste and mushroom ketchup, spiked with the zesty flavour of kaffir lime leaves. Choose firm, small mushrooms with a good flavour, which will be enhanced by the mushroom ketchup, for the stuffing.

Serves 4

3 garlic cloves, finely chopped
2 coriander (cilantro) roots, finely chopped
400g/14oz/3 cups mushrooms, quartered
5ml/1 tsp Thai red curry paste
1 egg, lightly beaten
15ml/1 tbsp Thai mushroom ketchup
15ml/1 tbsp light soy sauce
2.5ml/½ tsp sugar
3 kaffir lime leaves, finely chopped
4 yellow (bell) peppers, halved lengthways

1 In a mortar or spice grinder pound or blend the garlic with the coriander roots. Scrape into a bowl.

2 Put the mushrooms in a food processor and pulse briefly until they are finely chopped. Add to the garlic mixture, then stir in the curry paste, beaten egg, ketchup, soy sauce, sugar and kaffir lime leaves.

3 Place the pepper halves, cut-side up, in a single layer in a steamer basket. Spoon the mixture loosely into the pepper halves. Do not pack the mixture down tightly or the filling will dry out too much.

4 Bring the water in the steamer to the boil, then lower the heat to a simmer. Steam the peppers for 15 minutes, or until the flesh is tender. Serve hot.

> **Variation**
> Use red or orange (bell) peppers if you prefer, or a combination of the two.

Potato Rösti and Tofu Energy 433kcal/1811kJ; Protein 15g; Carbohydrate 42.3g, of which sugars 8.6g; Fat 23.7g, of which saturates 3.3g; Cholesterol 0mg; Calcium 618mg; Fibre 4.6g; Sodium 46mg.
Spicy Stuffed Peppers Energy 267kcal/1116kJ; Protein 13.9g; Carbohydrate 26.1g, of which sugars 15.3g; Fat 12.5g, of which saturates 4.7g; Cholesterol 37mg; Calcium 81mg; Fibre 4.4g; Sodium 84mg.

Red-cooked Tofu Stir-fry

"Red-cooked" is a term applied to Chinese dishes that are cooked with dark soy sauce. This tasty dish can be served as either a side dish or main meal.

Serves 2–4
225g/8oz firm tofu
45ml/3 tbsp dark soy sauce
30ml/2 tbsp Chinese rice wine or medium-dry sherry
10ml/2 tsp soft dark brown sugar
1 garlic clove, crushed
15ml/1 tbsp grated fresh root ginger
2.5ml/½ tsp Chinese five-spice powder
pinch of ground roasted Szechuan peppercorns
6 dried Chinese black mushrooms
5ml/1 tsp cornflour (cornstarch)
30ml/2 tbsp groundnut (peanut) oil
5–6 spring onions (scallions), sliced into 2.5cm/1in lengths
small basil leaves, to garnish
rice noodles, to serve

1 Drain the tofu, pat dry with kitchen paper and cut into 2.5cm/1in cubes. Place in a shallow dish. In a small bowl, mix together the soy sauce, rice wine or sherry, sugar, garlic, ginger, five-spice powder and ground roasted Szechuan peppercorns. Pour the marinade over the tofu, toss well and leave to marinate for about 30 minutes. Drain, reserving the marinade.

2 Meanwhile, just cover the dried black mushrooms in warm water and soak for 20–30 minutes until softened. Drain, reserving 90ml/6 tbsp of the soaking liquid. Squeeze the mushrooms, discard the tough stalks and slice the caps. In a small bowl, blend the cornflour with the reserved marinade and the mushroom liquid.

3 Heat a wok until hot, add the oil and swirl it around. Add the tofu and fry for 2–3 minutes until evenly golden. Remove from the wok and set aside. Add the mushrooms and white parts of the spring onions to the wok and stir-fry for 2 minutes. Pour in the marinade mixture and stir for 1 minute until thickened. Return the tofu to the wok with the green parts of the onions. Simmer for 1–2 minutes. Garnish with basil leaves and serve with noodles.

Tagine of Butter Beans

Serve this hearty butter bean dish with rice or couscous. It is, however, substantial enough to be served on its own, accompanied by a leafy salad and fresh, crusty bread.

Serves 4
115g/4oz/⅔ cup butter (lima) beans, soaked overnight
30–45ml/2–3 tbsp olive oil
1 onion, chopped
2–3 garlic cloves, crushed
25g/1oz fresh root ginger, peeled and chopped
pinch of saffron threads
16 cherry tomatoes
generous pinch of sugar
handful of fleshy black olives, pitted
5ml/1 tsp ground cinnamon
5ml/1 tsp paprika
small bunch of flat leaf parsley
salt and ground black pepper
rice or couscous, to serve

1 Rinse the beans in cold water in a sieve (strainer) and place them in a large pan with plenty of water. Bring to the boil and boil for about 10 minutes, then reduce the heat and simmer gently for 1–1½ hours until tender. Drain the beans and refresh under cold water.

2 Heat the olive oil in a heavy pan. Add the onion, garlic and ginger, and cook for about 10 minutes, or until softened but not browned. Stir in the saffron threads, followed by the cherry tomatoes and a sprinkling of sugar.

3 As the tomatoes begin to soften, stir in the butter beans. When the tomatoes have heated completely through, stir in the olives, ground cinnamon and paprika. Season to taste and sprinkle the parsley over. Serve immediately with rice or couscous, if using.

Variation
If you are in a hurry, use two 400g/14oz cans butter beans for this tagine. Rinse the beans well before adding.

Tofu Stir-fry Energy 118kcal/491kJ; Protein 9.3g; Carbohydrate 2.9g, of which sugars 1.1g; Fat 7.4g, of which saturates 0.9g; Cholesterol 0mg; Calcium 456mg; Fibre 1.2g; Sodium 455mg.
Tagine of Butter Beans Energy 146kcal/615kJ; Protein 7.4g; Carbohydrate 16.2g, of which sugars 3.8g; Fat 6.3g, of which saturates 0.9g; Cholesterol 0mg; Calcium 62mg; Fibre 6g; Sodium 16mg.

Spicy Chickpeas with Ginger

Chickpeas are filling, nourishing and cheap. Here they are served with a refreshing raita made with spring onions and mint. Serve as a snack or as part of a main meal.

Serves 4–6
225g/8oz dried chickpeas
30ml/2 tbsp vegetable oil
1 small onion, chopped
4cm/1½in piece fresh root ginger, finely chopped
2 garlic cloves, finely chopped
1.5ml/¼ tsp ground turmeric

450g/1lb tomatoes, peeled, seeded and chopped
30ml/2 tbsp chopped fresh coriander (cilantro)
10ml/2 tsp garam masala
salt and pepper
fresh coriander sprigs, to garnish

For the raita
150ml/¼ pint/⅔ cup natural (plain) yogurt
2 spring onions (scallions), finely chopped
5ml/1 tsp roasted cumin seeds
30ml/2 tbsp chopped fresh mint
pinch of cayenne pepper

1 Put the chickpeas in a large bowl and pour over enough cold water to cover. Leave to soak overnight. Next day, drain the chickpeas and put them into a large pan with fresh cold water to cover them. Bring to the boil and boil hard for 10 minutes, then lower the heat and simmer gently for 1½–2 hours until tender. Drain well.

2 Heat a wok until hot, add the oil and swirl it around. Add the onion and stir-fry for 2–3 minutes, then add the ginger, garlic and turmeric. Stir-fry for a few seconds more.

3 Add the tomatoes, chickpeas and seasoning. Bring to the boil, then simmer for 10–15 minutes, until the tomatoes have reduced to a thick sauce.

4 Meanwhile, make the raita. Mix together the yogurt, spring onions, roasted cumin seeds, mint and cayenne pepper to taste. Set aside.

5 Just before the end of cooking, stir the chopped coriander and garam masala into the chickpeas. Serve at once, garnished with coriander sprigs and accompanied by the raita.

Vegetable Korma

The blending of spices is an ancient art in India. In this curry the aim is to produce subtle flavours rather than assaulting the senses.

Serves 4
50g/2oz/¼ cup butter
2 onions, sliced
2 garlic cloves, crushed
2.5cm/1in piece fresh root ginger, grated
5ml/1 tsp ground cumin
15ml/1 tbsp ground coriander
6 cardamoms
5cm/2in cinnamon stick
5ml/1 tsp ground turmeric

1 fresh red chilli, seeded and finely chopped
1 medium potato, peeled and cut into 2.5cm/1in cubes
1 small aubergine (eggplant)
115g/4oz/1½ cups mushrooms, thickly sliced
115g/4oz/1 cup French beans, cut into 2.5cm/1in lengths
60ml/4 tbsp natural (plain) yogurt
150ml/¼ pint/⅔ cup double (heavy) cream
5ml/1 tsp garam masala
salt and ground black pepper
fresh coriander (cilantro) sprigs, to garnish
poppadums, to serve

1 Melt the butter in a heavy pan. Add the onions and cook for 5 minutes until soft. Add the garlic and ginger and cook for 2 minutes. Stir in the cumin, coriander, cardamoms, cinnamon, turmeric and chilli. Cook, stirring for 30 seconds.

2 Add the potato, aubergine and mushrooms and about 175ml/6fl oz/¾ cup water. Cover the pan, bring to the boil, then lower the heat and simmer for 15 minutes. Add the beans and cook, uncovered, for 5 minutes.

3 With a slotted spoon, remove the vegetables to a warmed serving dish and keep hot. Allow the cooking liquid to bubble until it reduces a little. Season with salt and pepper, then stir in the yogurt, cream and garam masala. Pour the sauce over the vegetables and garnish with coriander. Serve with poppadums.

Variation
Any combination of vegetables can be used for this korma, including carrots, cauliflower, broccoli, peas and chickpeas.

Spicy Chickpeas Energy 192kcal/809kJ; Protein 10.4g; Carbohydrate 24.6g, of which sugars 5.9g; Fat 6.6g, of which saturates 0.9g; Cholesterol 0mg; Calcium 126mg; Fibre 5.1g; Sodium 44mg.
Vegetable Korma Energy 381kcal/1577kJ; Protein 5.1g; Carbohydrate 20.9g, of which sugars 9.9g; Fat 31.4g, of which saturates 19.3g; Cholesterol 78mg; Calcium 95mg; Fibre 3.9g; Sodium 108mg.

Thai Vegetable Curry

This is a thin, soupy curry that is bursting with lots of fresh green vegetables and robust flavours. In the forested regions of Thailand, where this dish originated, it would be made using a variety of edible wild leaves and roots. Serve it with rice or noodles for a simple lunch or supper.

Serves 2

600ml/1 pint/2½ cups water
5ml/1 tsp Thai red curry paste
5cm/2in piece fresh galangal or
    fresh root ginger
90g/3½oz/scant 1 cup
    green beans
2 kaffir lime leaves, torn
8 baby corn cobs,
    halved widthways
2 heads Chinese broccoli, chopped
90g/3½oz/generous
    3 cups beansprouts
15ml/1 tbsp drained bottled
    green peppercorns, crushed
10ml/2 tsp sugar
5ml/1 tsp salt

1 Heat the water in a large pan. Add the red curry paste and stir until it has dissolved completely. Bring to the boil.

2 Meanwhile, using a sharp knife, peel and finely chop the fresh galangal or root ginger.

3 Add the galangal or ginger to the pan with the green beans, lime leaves, baby corn cobs, broccoli and beansprouts. Stir in the crushed peppercorns, sugar and salt.

4 Bring back to the boil, then reduce the heat to low and simmer for 2 minutes, so that the vegetables are hot but still crisp. Serve immediately.

> **Cook's Tips**
> • *The vegetables in this curry should taste fresh and retain their crispness: you can vary the ingredients depending on what is available, but choose vegetables that cook in a few minutes.*
> • *Galangal, used in South-east Asian cookery, resembles ginger but has a more earthy aroma and a resinous flavour.*

Pumpkin in Coconut Milk

Pumpkins, butternut squash and winter melons can all be cooked in this way. Throughout Vietnam and Cambodia, variations of this sweet, mellow dish are often served as an accompaniment to rice or as a side dish to offset the spicy flavours of a hot curry.

Serves 4

200ml/7fl oz/scant 1 cup
    coconut milk
15ml/1 tbsp mushroom ketchup
30ml/2 tbsp palm sugar (jaggery)
30ml/2 tbsp groundnut
    (peanut) oil
4 garlic cloves, peeled and
    finely chopped
25g/1oz fresh root ginger, peeled
    and finely shredded
675g/1½lb pumpkin, peeled,
    seeded and cubed
ground black pepper
handful of curry or basil leaves,
    to garnish
fried onion rings, to garnish
chilli oil, for drizzling
plain or coconut rice, to serve

1 In a bowl, beat the coconut milk and the mushroom ketchup with the sugar, until it has dissolved. Set aside.

2 Heat the oil in a wok or heavy pan and stir in the garlic and ginger. Stir-fry until they begin to colour, then stir in the pumpkin cubes, mixing well.

3 Pour in the coconut milk and mix well. Reduce the heat, cover and simmer for about 20 minutes, until the pumpkin is tender and the sauce has reduced.

4 Season with pepper and garnish with curry or basil leaves and fried onion rings. Serve hot with plain or coconut rice, drizzled with a little chilli oil.

> **Cook's Tip**
> *Vary the squash used to make this dish according to what is in season. As well as butternut squashes and winter melons, luffa squashes can be used. They are available in Asian stores and have a sweet and spongy flesh that absorbs spicy flavours.*

Vegetable Curry Energy 328kcal/1375kJ; Protein 10g; Carbohydrate 64.9g, of which sugars 11.1g; Fat 3.3g, of which saturates 0.6g; Cholesterol 0mg; Calcium 134mg; Fibre 3.9g; Sodium 535mg.
Pumpkin in Milk Energy 114Kcal/477kJ; Protein 1.5g; Carbohydrate 14g, of which sugars 13.4g; Fat 6g, of which saturates 1g; Cholesterol 0mg; Calcium 68mg; Fibre 1.7g; Sodium 323mg.

Luffa Squash with Coriander

All kinds of winter gourds, such as pumpkins, bitter melons, luffa squash and a variety of other squash that come under the kabocha umbrella, are popular ingredients in Vietnam and Cambodia for making comforting, nourishing soups and braised vegetable dishes like this one. All these vegetables have delicate, rather sweet flesh, so the spices and other flavourings used in such dishes tend to be mild and gentle.

Serves 4

750g/1lb 10oz luffa
  squash, peeled
30ml/2 tbsp groundnut (peanut)
  or sesame oil
2 shallots, halved and sliced
2 garlic cloves, finely chopped
115g/4oz/1½ cups button
  (white) mushrooms, quartered
15ml/1 tbsp mushroom sauce
10ml/2 tsp soy sauce
4 spring onions (scallions), cut into
  2cm/¾in pieces
fresh coriander (cilantro) leaves
  and thin strips of spring onion
  (scallion), to garnish

1 Cut the luffa squash diagonally into 2cm/¾in thick pieces.

2 Heat the oil in a large wok or heavy pan. Stir in the halved shallots and garlic, stir-fry until they begin to colour and turn golden, then add the mushrooms.

3 Add the mushroom and soy sauces, and the squash. Reduce the heat, cover and cook gently for a few minutes until the squash is tender.

4 Stir in the spring onion pieces, garnish with coriander and spring onion strips, and serve.

Cook's Tip
Squash lends itself to all types of flavours because the taste is quite bland. In Cambodia, squash is sometimes sweetened and cooked with coconut milk and served as a dessert. Luffa squash or ridged gourd, available from Asian markets, resembles a long courgette (zucchini) with ridges from one end to the other.

Spiced Aubergine Tagine

Spiced with coriander, cumin, cinnamon, turmeric and a dash of chilli sauce, this Moroccan-style stew makes a filling supper dish when served with couscous.

Serves 4

1 small aubergine (eggplant), cut
  into 1cm/½in dice
2 courgettes (zucchini),
  thickly sliced
60ml/4 tbsp olive oil
1 large onion, sliced
2 garlic cloves, chopped
150g/5oz/2 cups brown cap
  mushrooms, halved

15ml/1 tbsp ground coriander
10ml/2 tsp cumin seeds
15ml/1 tbsp ground cinnamon
10ml/2 tsp ground turmeric
225g/8oz new potatoes, quartered
600ml/1 pint/2½ cups passata
15ml/1 tbsp tomato purée (paste)
15ml/1 tbsp chilli sauce
75g/3oz/⅓ cup ready-to-eat
  unsulphured dried apricots
400g/14oz/3 cups canned
  chickpeas, drained and rinsed
salt and ground black pepper
15ml/1 tbsp chopped fresh
  coriander (cilantro), to garnish

1 Sprinkle salt over the aubergine and courgettes and leave for 30 minutes. Rinse and pat dry with a dish towel. Heat the grill to high. Arrange the courgettes and aubergine on a baking tray and toss in 30ml/2 tbsp of the olive oil. Grill for 20 minutes, turning occasionally, until tender and golden.

2 Meanwhile, heat the remaining oil in a large heavy pan and cook the onion and garlic for 5 minutes until softened, stirring occasionally. Add the mushrooms and sauté for 3 minutes until tender. Add the spices and cook for 1 minute more, stirring, to allow the flavours to mingle.

3 Add the potatoes and cook for about 3 minutes, stirring. Pour in the passata, tomato purée and 150ml/¼ pint/⅔ cup water. Cover and cook for 10 minutes to thicken the sauce.

4 Add the aubergine, courgettes, chilli sauce, apricots and chickpeas. Season and cook, partially covered, for about 15 minutes until the potatoes are tender. Add a little extra water if the tagine becomes too dry. Sprinkle with chopped fresh coriander to serve.

Squash with Coriander Energy 194Kcal/800kJ; Protein 3g; Carbohydrate 19g, of which sugars 3g; Fat 12g, of which saturates 2g; Cholesterol 0mg; Calcium 31mg; Fibre 5.1g; Sodium 100mg.
Aubergine Tagine Energy 359kcal/1509kJ; Protein 13.9g; Carbohydrate 45g, of which sugars 19.3g; Fat 15g, of which saturates 2.1g; Cholesterol 0mg; Calcium 123mg; Fibre 9.7g; Sodium 597mg.

Thai Vegetable Curry

This spicy curry made with coconut milk has a creamy richness that contrasts wonderfully with the heat of the chilli. Thai yellow curry paste is available in supermarkets, but you will really taste the difference when you make it yourself.

Serves 4
30ml/2 tbsp sunflower oil
200ml/7fl oz/scant 1 cup
   coconut cream
300ml/½ pint/1¼ cups
   coconut milk
150ml/¼ pint/⅔ cup
   vegetable stock
200g/7oz green beans, cut into
   2cm/¾in lengths
200g/7oz baby corn
4 baby courgettes
   (zucchini), sliced

1 small aubergine (eggplant),
   cubed or sliced
30ml/2 tbsp mushroom ketchup
10ml/2 tsp palm sugar (jaggery)
fresh coriander (cilantro) leaves,
   to garnish
noodles or rice, to serve

For the yellow curry paste
10ml/2 tsp hot chilli powder
10ml/2 tsp ground coriander
10ml/2 tsp ground cumin
5ml/1 tsp turmeric
15ml/1 tbsp chopped
   fresh galangal
10ml/2 tsp finely grated garlic
30ml/2 tbsp finely chopped
   lemon grass
4 red Asian shallots,
   finely chopped
5ml/1 tsp finely chopped
   lime rind

1 To make the curry paste, place all the ingredients in a food processor and blend with 30–45ml/2–3 tbsp of cold water to make a smooth paste. Add a little more water if the mixture seems too dry.

2 Heat a large wok over a medium heat and add the sunflower oil. When hot add 30–45ml/2–3 tbsp of the curry paste and stir-fry for 1–2 minutes. Add the coconut cream and cook gently for 8–10 minutes, or until the mixture starts to separate.

3 Add the coconut milk, stock and vegetables and cook gently for 8–10 minutes, until the vegetables are just tender. Stir in the mushroom ketchup and palm sugar, garnish with coriander leaves and serve with noodles or rice.

Richly Spiced Dhal

Flavoured with spices, coconut milk and tomatoes, this lentil dish makes a filling supper. Warm naan bread and natural yogurt are all that are needed as accompaniments.

Serves 4
30ml/2 tbsp vegetable oil
1 large onion, finely chopped
3 garlic cloves, chopped
1 carrot, diced
10ml/2 tsp cumin seeds
10ml/2 tsp yellow mustard seeds
2.5cm/1in piece fresh root
   ginger, grated

10ml/2 tsp ground turmeric
5ml/1 tsp mild chilli powder
5ml/1 tsp garam masala
225g/8oz/1 cup split red lentils
400ml/14fl oz/1⅔ cups water
400ml/14fl oz/1⅔ cups
   coconut milk
5 tomatoes, peeled, seeded
   and chopped
juice of 2 limes
60ml/4 tbsp chopped fresh
   coriander (cilantro)
salt and ground black pepper
25g/1oz/¼ cup flaked almonds,
   toasted, to garnish

1 Heat the oil in a large heavy pan. Sauté the onion for 5 minutes until softened, stirring occasionally. Stir in the garlic, carrot, cumin and mustard seeds, and ginger. Cook for 5 minutes, stirring, until the seeds begin to pop and the carrot softens slightly.

2 Stir in the ground turmeric, chilli powder and garam masala, and cook for 1 minute or until the flavours begin to mingle, stirring to prevent the spices burning.

3 Add the lentils, water, coconut milk and tomatoes, and season well. Bring to the boil, then reduce the heat and simmer, covered, for about 45 minutes, stirring occasionally to prevent the lentils sticking.

4 Stir in the lime juice and 45ml/3 tbsp of the fresh coriander, then check the seasoning.

5 Cook for a further 15 minutes until the lentils soften and become tender. To serve, sprinkle with the remaining coriander and the flaked almonds.

Richly Spiced Dhal Energy 295kcal/1242kJ; Protein 16.1g; Carbohydrate 43.7g, of which sugars 8.5g; Fat 7.6g, of which saturates 1g; Cholesterol 0mg; Calcium 71mg; Fibre 4.7g; Sodium 30mg.
Thai Curry Energy 279kcal/1161kJ; Protein 9.8g; Carbohydrate 17.4g, of which sugars 13.3g; Fat 19.4g, of which saturates 3.6g; Cholesterol 5mg; Calcium 99mg; Fibre 3.3g; Sodium 824mg.

Pumpkin and Peanut Curry

This is a hearty, soothing Thai curry that is perfect for autumn or winter evenings. Its cheerful colour alone will brighten you up – and it tastes terrific.

Serves 4

30ml/2 tbsp vegetable oil
4 garlic cloves, crushed
4 shallots, finely chopped
30ml/2 tbsp Thai yellow
   curry paste
600ml/1 pint/2¹/₂ cups
   vegetable stock
2 kaffir lime leaves, torn

15ml/1 tbsp chopped galangal
450g/1lb pumpkin, peeled, seeded
   and diced
225g/8oz sweet potatoes, diced
90g/3¹/₂oz/scant 1 cup peanuts,
   roasted and chopped
300ml/¹/₂ pint/1¹/₄ cups
   coconut milk
90g/3¹/₂oz/1¹/₂ cups chestnut
   mushrooms, sliced
15ml/1 tbsp soy sauce
30ml/2 tbsp Thai
   mushroom ketchup
50g/2oz/¹/₃ cup pumpkin seeds,
   toasted, and fresh green chilli
   flowers, to garnish

1 Heat the oil in a large pan. Add the garlic and shallots and cook over a medium heat, stirring occasionally, for 10 minutes, until softened and golden. Do not let them burn.

2 Add the yellow curry paste and stir-fry over a medium heat for 30 seconds, until the mixture is fragrant.

3 Add the stock, lime leaves, galangal, pumpkin and sweet potatoes. Bring to the boil, stirring frequently, then reduce the heat to low and simmer gently for 15 minutes.

4 Add the peanuts, coconut milk and mushrooms. Stir in the soy sauce and mushroom ketchup and simmer for 5 minutes more. Spoon into warmed individual serving bowls, garnish with the pumpkin seeds and chilli flowers and serve.

> **Cook's Tip**
> *The well-drained vegetables from a curry of this kind would make a very tasty filling for a pastry or pie. This may not be a Thai tradition, but it is a good example of fusion food.*

Corn and Nut Curry

A substantial curry, this dish combines all the essential flavours of southern Thailand. It is deliciously aromatic, but the flavour is fairly mild.

Serves 4

30ml/2 tbsp vegetable oil
4 shallots, chopped
90g/3¹/₂oz/scant 1 cup
   cashew nuts
5ml/1 tsp Thai red curry paste
400g/14oz potatoes, peeled and
   cut into chunks
1 lemon grass stalk,
   finely chopped

200g/7oz can chopped tomatoes
600ml/1 pint/2¹/₂ cups
   boiling water
200g/7oz/generous 1 cup drained
   canned whole kernel corn
4 celery sticks, sliced
2 kaffir lime leaves, rolled into
   cylinders and thinly sliced
   into ribbons
15ml/1 tbsp tomato ketchup
15ml/1 tbsp light soy sauce
5ml/1 tsp palm sugar or light
   muscovado (brown) sugar
5ml/1 tsp mushroom ketchup
4 spring onions (scallions),
   thinly sliced
small bunch fresh basil, chopped

1 Heat the oil in a large, heavy pan or wok. Add the shallots and stir-fry over a medium heat for 2–3 minutes, until softened. Add the cashew nuts and stir-fry for a few minutes until golden.

2 Stir in the red curry paste. Stir-fry for 1 minute, then add the potatoes, lemon grass, tomatoes and boiling water. Bring back to the boil, then reduce the heat to low, cover and simmer gently for 15–20 minutes, or until the potatoes are tender.

3 Stir the corn, celery, lime leaves, tomato ketchup, soy sauce, sugar and mushroom ketchup into the pan or wok. Simmer for a further 5 minutes, until heated through, then spoon into warmed serving bowls. Sprinkle with the sliced spring onions and basil and serve.

> **Cook's Tip**
> *Rolling the lime leaves into cylinders before slicing produces very fine strips – a technique known as cutting en chiffonnade. Remove the central rib from the leaves before cutting them.*

Pumpkin Curry Energy 306kcal/1279kJ; Protein 9.6g; Carbohydrate 24.5g, of which sugars 11.4g; Fat 19.6g, of which saturates 3.3g; Cholesterol 0mg; Calcium 160mg; Fibre 6.4g; Sodium 409mg.
Corn and Nut Curry Energy 298kcal/1245kJ; Protein 8.8g; Carbohydrate 27.6g, of which sugars 8.9g; Fat 17.7g, of which saturates 3.1g; Cholesterol 0mg; Calcium 33mg; Fibre 3.5g; Sodium 981mg.

Tofu and Green Bean Curry

This Thai curry is one of those versatile recipes that should be in every cook's repertoire. This version uses green beans, but other types of vegetable work equally well. The tofu takes on the flavour of the spice paste and also boosts the nutritional value of the dish.

Serves 4–6
600ml/1 pint/2½ cups canned coconut milk
15ml/1 tbsp Thai red curry paste
45ml/3 tbsp mushroom ketchup
10ml/2 tsp palm sugar (jaggery) or light muscovado (brown) sugar
225g/8oz/3¼ cups button (white) mushrooms
115g/4oz/scant 1 cup green beans, trimmed
175g/6oz firm tofu, rinsed, drained and cut into 2cm/¾in cubes
4 kaffir lime leaves, torn
2 fresh red chillies, seeded and sliced
fresh coriander (cilantro) leaves, to garnish

1 Pour about one-third of the coconut milk into a wok or pan and cook until it starts to separate and an oily sheen appears on the surface.

2 Add the red curry paste, mushroom ketchup and sugar to the coconut milk. Mix thoroughly, then add the mushrooms. Stir and cook for 1 minute.

3 Stir in the remaining coconut milk. Bring back to the boil, then add the green beans and tofu cubes. Simmer gently for 4–5 minutes more.

4 Stir in the kaffir lime leaves and sliced red chillies. Spoon the curry into a serving dish, garnish with the coriander leaves and serve immediately.

Cook's Tip
The Kaffir lime is a native of Indonesia but is grown in many other parts of the world. The leaves are a popular flavouring in the cooking of Thailand, Cambodia and Laos, and are widely available fresh, frozen or dried.

Parsnip Curry

The sweet flavour of parsnips goes very well with the spices in this Indian-style vegetable stew.

Serves 4
200g/7oz dried chickpeas, soaked overnight in cold water, then drained
7 garlic cloves, finely chopped
1 small onion, chopped
5cm/2in piece fresh root ginger, chopped
2 green chillies, seeded and chopped
75ml/5 tbsp water
450ml/¾ pint/scant 2 cups water
60ml/4 tbsp groundnut oil
5ml/1 tsp cumin seeds
10ml/2 tsp ground coriander
5ml/1 tsp ground turmeric
2.5–5ml/½–1 tsp chilli powder
50g/2oz cashew nuts, toasted and ground
250g/9oz tomatoes, peeled and chopped
900g/2lb parsnips, cut in chunks
5ml/1 tsp ground cumin seeds
juice of 1 lime, to taste
salt and ground black pepper
fresh coriander (cilantro) leaves and toasted cashew nuts, to garnish

1 Put the soaked chickpeas in a pan, cover with cold water and bring to the boil. Boil vigorously for 10 minutes, then reduce the heat so that the water boils steadily. Cook for 1–1½ hours, or until the chickpeas are tender. Drain.

2 Set 10ml/2 tsp of the garlic aside, then place the rest in a food processor or blender with the onion, ginger and half the chillies. Add the 75ml/5 tbsp water, and process until smooth.

3 Heat the oil in a large, deep, frying pan and cook the cumin seeds for 30 seconds. Stir in the coriander seeds, turmeric, chilli powder and the ground cashew nuts. Add the ginger and chilli paste and cook, stirring frequently. Add the tomatoes and stir-fry until the mixture begins to turn red-brown. Mix in the chickpeas and parsnips with the main batch of water, 5ml/1 tsp salt and plenty of black pepper. Bring to the boil then simmer, uncovered, for 15–20 minutes.

4 Reduce the liquid, if necessary, by boiling fiercely. Add the ground cumin with more salt and lime juice to taste. Stir in the reserved garlic and green chilli. Sprinkle the coriander leaves and toasted cashew nuts over and serve straight away.

Parsnip Curry Energy 506kcal/2124kJ; Protein 18.4g; Carbohydrate 60.1g, of which sugars 18.2g; Fat 23.1g, of which saturates 3.4g; Cholesterol 0mg; Calcium 192mg; Fibre 17.1g; Sodium 86mg.
Tofu and Bean Curry Energy 79kcal/333kJ; Protein 3.9g; Carbohydrate 8.2g, of which sugars 7.8g; Fat 3.6g, of which saturates 0.6g; Cholesterol 0mg; Calcium 189mg; Fibre 0.8g; Sodium 647mg.

Aubergine and Sweet Potato Stew

Inspired by Thai cooking, this aubergine and sweet potato stew is cooked in a coconut sauce and scented with fragrant lemon grass, ginger and lots of garlic.

Serves 6
60ml/4 tbsp groundnut (peanut) oil
2 aubergines (eggplants), cut into chunks
225g/8oz Thai red shallots or other shallots
5ml/1 tsp fennel seeds, lightly crushed
4–5 garlic cloves, thinly sliced
25ml/1½ tbsp finely chopped fresh root ginger
475ml/16fl oz/2 cups vegetable stock

2 stems lemon grass, outer layers discarded, finely chopped
15g/½oz fresh coriander (cilantro), stalks and leaves chopped separately
3 kaffir lime leaves, lightly bruised
2–3 small red chillies
45–60ml/3–4 tbsp Thai green curry paste
675g/1½lb sweet potatoes, cut into thick chunks
400ml/14fl oz/1⅔ cups coconut milk
2.5–5ml/½–1 tsp light muscovado (brown) sugar
250g/9oz mushrooms, sliced
juice of 1 lime, to taste
salt and ground black pepper
18 fresh Thai basil leaves or ordinary basil, to garnish

1 Heat half the oil in a lidded frying pan. Add the aubergines and cook over a medium heat, stirring occasionally, until lightly browned on all sides. Remove from the pan and set aside.

2 Slice 4–5 of the shallots and set aside. Fry the remaining whole shallots in the pan, adding more oil if necessary, until browned. Set aside. Add the remaining oil to the pan and cook the sliced shallots, fennel, garlic and ginger until soft but not browned. Add the vegetable stock, lemon grass, coriander stalks, lime leaves and whole chillies. Cover and simmer for 5 minutes.

3 Stir in 30ml/2 tbsp of the curry paste and the sweet potatoes. Simmer for 10 minutes, return the aubergines and shallots to the pan and cook for a further 5 minutes. Stir in the coconut milk and sugar. Season to taste, then add the mushrooms and simmer for 5 minutes. Stir in more curry paste and lime juice to taste, followed by the chopped coriander leaves. Sprinkle with basil and serve.

Malay Curry with Cumin

Originally from southern India, this delicious spicy dish is cooked in many Malay homes. It is substantial and flexible – choose your own favourite assortment of vegetables, such as pumpkin, butternut squash, winter melon, yams, aubergines or beans.

Serves 4
2–3 green chillies, seeded and chopped
25g/1oz fresh root ginger, peeled and chopped
5–10ml/1–2 tsp roasted cumin seeds
10ml/2 tsp sugar
5–10ml/1–2 tsp ground turmeric
1 cinnamon stick

5ml/1 tsp salt
2 carrots, cut into bitesize sticks
2 sweet potatoes, cut into bitesize sticks
2 courgettes (zucchini), partially peeled in strips, seeded and cut into bitesize sticks
1 green plantain, peeled and cut into bitesize sticks
small coil of long (snake) beans or a handful of green beans, cut into bitesize sticks
handful fresh curry leaves
1 fresh coconut, grated
250ml/8fl oz/1 cup natural (plain) yogurt
salt and ground black pepper

1 Using a mortar and pestle or a food processor, grind the chillies, ginger, roasted cumin seeds and sugar to a paste.

2 In a heavy pan, bring 450ml/15fl oz/scant 2 cups water to the boil. Stir in the turmeric, cinnamon stick and salt. Add the carrots and cook for 1 minute. Add the sweet potatoes and cook for 2 minutes. Add the courgettes, plantain and beans and cook for a further 2 minutes. Reduce the heat, stir in the spice paste and curry leaves, and cook gently for 4–5 minutes, or until the vegetables are tender but not soft and mushy, and the liquid has greatly reduced.

3 Gently stir in half the coconut. Take the pan off the heat and fold in the yogurt. Season to taste with salt and pepper. Quickly roast the remaining coconut in a heavy pan over a high heat, until nicely browned. Sprinkle a little over the vegetables, and serve the rest separately.

Aubergine Stew Energy 228kcal/960kJ; Protein 4.3g; Carbohydrate 34g, of which sugars 13.4g; Fat 9.3g, of which saturates 1.2g; Cholesterol 0mg; Calcium 130mg; Fibre 7.2g; Sodium 159mg.
Malay Curry Energy 419Kcal/1753kJ; Protein 9.9g; Carbohydrate 47.7g, of which sugars 19.4g; Fat 23g, of which saturates 16.9g; Cholesterol 0mg; Calcium 176mg; Fibre 9g; Sodium 104mg.

Leek Terrine with Peppers

This pressed leek terrine looks very pretty when sliced and served on individual plates with the dressing drizzled over.

Serves 6–8
1.8kg/4lb slender leeks
4 red (bell) peppers, halved
15ml/1 tbsp extra virgin olive oil
10ml/2 tsp balsamic vinegar
5ml/1 tsp ground roasted cumin seeds
salt and ground black pepper

For the dressing
120ml/4fl oz/½ cup extra virgin olive oil
1 garlic clove, bruised and peeled
5ml/1 tsp Dijon mustard
5ml/1 tsp soy sauce
15ml/1 tbsp balsamic vinegar
pinch of caster (superfine) sugar
2.5–5ml/½–1 tsp ground roasted cumin seeds
15–30ml/1–2 tbsp chopped mixed fresh basil and flat leaf parsley

1 Line a 23cm/9in long terrine or loaf tin (pan) with clear film (plastic wrap), leaving the ends overhanging the tin. Cut the leeks to the same length as the tin. Cook the leeks in boiling salted water for 5–7 minutes, until just tender. Drain and allow to cool, then squeeze out as much water as possible and leave to drain.

2 Grill the peppers with the skin-side uppermost, until the skin blisters and blackens. Place in a bowl, cover and leave for 10 minutes until cool enough to handle. Peel, cut the flesh into long strips and place in a bowl. Mix in the oil, balsamic vinegar and roasted cumin. Season.

3 Layer the leeks and strips of red pepper in the lined tin, alternating the layers. Season the leeks with a little more salt and pepper. Cover with the overhanging clear film. Top with a plate and weigh it down with heavy food cans or scale weights. Chill for several hours or overnight.

4 To make the dressing, place the oil, garlic, mustard, soy sauce and vinegar in a jar and shake. Season and add the caster sugar. Add ground cumin to taste and leave to stand for several hours. Discard the garlic, and add the fresh herbs. Unmould the terrine and cut it into slices to serve with the dressing.

Fried Seeds and Vegetables

The contrast between the crunchy seeds and vegetables and the rich, savoury sauce is what makes this dish so delicious. Serve it alone, or with rice or noodles.

Serves 4
30ml/2 tbsp vegetable oil
30ml/2 tbsp sesame seeds
30ml/2 tbsp sunflower seeds
30ml/2 tbsp pumpkin seeds
2 garlic cloves, finely chopped
2.5cm/1in piece fresh root ginger, finely chopped
2 large carrots, cut into batons
2 large courgettes (zucchini), cut into batons
90g/3½oz/1½ cups oyster mushrooms, torn in pieces
150g/5oz watercress or spinach leaves, coarsely chopped
small bunch fresh mint or coriander (cilantro), leaves and stems chopped
60ml/4 tbsp black bean sauce
30ml/2 tbsp light soy sauce
15ml/1 tbsp palm sugar (jaggery) or light muscovado (brown) sugar
30ml/2 tbsp rice vinegar

1 Heat the oil in a wok or large frying pan. Add the seeds and toss over a medium heat for 1 minute, then add the garlic and ginger and continue to stir-fry until the ginger is aromatic and the garlic is golden. Do not let the garlic burn or the dish will taste bitter.

2 Add the carrot and courgette batons and the sliced mushrooms to the wok or pan and stir-fry over a medium heat for a further 5 minutes, or until all the vegetables are crisp-tender and are golden at the edges.

3 Add the watercress or spinach with the fresh herbs. Toss over the heat for 1 minute, then stir in the black bean sauce, soy sauce, sugar and vinegar. Stir-fry for 1–2 minutes, until combined and hot. Serve immediately.

Cook's Tip
Oyster mushrooms have acquired their name because of their texture, rather than flavour, which is quite superb. They are delicate, so it is usually better to tear them into pieces along the lines of the gills, rather than slicing them with a knife.

Leek Terrine Energy 171kcal/710kJ; Protein 4.6g; Carbohydrate 12.4g, of which sugars 10.5g; Fat 11.7g, of which saturates 1.8g; Cholesterol 0mg; Calcium 66mg; Fibre 6.4g; Sodium 161mg.
Seeds and Vegetables Energy 205kcal/849kJ; Protein 6.9g; Carbohydrate 9.7g, of which sugars 7.7g; Fat 15.6g, of which saturates 2g; Cholesterol 0mg; Calcium 159mg; Fibre 3.4g; Sodium 294mg.

Vegetables with Chilli Salsa

Use a double layer of coals on the barbecue so they will be deep enough to make a bed for the foil-wrapped vegetables. While they are cooking, make the salsa on the grill rack above.

Serves 4–6
2 small whole heads of garlic
2 butternut squash, about 450g/1lb each, halved lengthways and seeded
4–6 onions, about 115g/4oz each, with a cross cut in the top of each
4–6 baking potatoes, about 175g/6oz each

4–6 sweet potatoes, about 175g/6oz each
45ml/3 tbsp olive oil
fresh thyme, bay leaf and rosemary sprigs
salt and ground black pepper

For the chilli salsa
500g/1¼lb tomatoes, quartered and seeded
2.5ml/½ tsp sugar
a pinch of chilli flakes
1.5ml/¼ tsp smoked chilli powder
30ml/2 tbsp tomato chutney

1 Prepare a barbecue with plenty of coals. Sit the garlic, squash and onions separately in double layers of foil, leaving them open. Wrap the potatoes in pairs of one sweet and one ordinary potato. Drizzle a little oil over the contents of each packet, season well and add a herb sprig. Spray with a little water and scrunch up the foil to secure the parcels.

2 Once the flames have died down and the coals are hot, place the parcels on top of them. The garlic will take 20 minutes to cook, the squash 30 minutes, the onions 45 minutes and the potatoes 1 hour. As each vegetable cooks, remove the parcel and wrap in an extra layer of foil to keep warm. Set aside.

3 Meanwhile, make the salsa. Put a lightly oiled grill rack in place to heat. Sprinkle the tomatoes with sugar, chilli flakes and seasoning. Place them on the grill rack above the vegetables and cook, covered for around 15 minutes. Remove the tomatoes from the rack and spoon the flesh from the charred skins into a bowl, crush with a fork and mix in the other ingredients. Serve with the vegetables.

Vegetable Kebabs with Harissa

This simple and tasty vegetarian dish is delicious served with couscous and a fresh, crispy green salad. It also makes an excellent side dish to accompany meat-based main courses. Vegetable and fish kebabs are becoming increasingly popular in Morocco.

Serves 4
2 aubergines (eggplants), part-peeled and cut into chunks
2 courgettes (zucchini), cut into chunks
2–3 red or green (bell) peppers, cut into chunks
12–16 cherry tomatoes
4 small red onions, quartered
60ml/4 tbsp olive oil

juice of ½ lemon
1 garlic clove, crushed
5ml/1 tsp ground coriander
5ml/1 tsp ground cinnamon
10ml/2 tsp clear honey
5ml/1 tsp salt

For the harissa and yogurt dip
450g/1lb/2 cups natural (plain) yogurt
30–60ml/2–4 tbsp harissa
small bunch of fresh coriander (cilantro), finely chopped
small bunch of mint, finely chopped
salt and ground black pepper

1 Preheat the grill (broiler) on the hottest setting. Put all the vegetables in a bowl.

2 Mix the olive oil, lemon juice, garlic, ground coriander, cinnamon, honey and salt and pour the mixture over the vegetables. Turn the vegetables gently in the marinade, then thread them on to metal skewers. Cook the kebabs under the grill, turning them occasionally until the vegetables are nicely browned all over.

3 To make the dip, put the yogurt in a bowl and beat in the harissa, making it as fiery as you like by adding more harissa.

4 Add most of the coriander and mint, reserving a little to garnish, and season well with salt and pepper. While they are still hot, slide the vegetables off the skewers. Garnish with the reserved herbs and serve with the yogurt dip.

Vegetables with Salsa Energy 244kcal/1029kJ; Protein 6.2g; Carbohydrate 42.4g, of which sugars 13g; Fat 6.7g, of which saturates 1.1g; Cholesterol 0mg; Calcium 65mg; Fibre 5.4g; Sodium 54mg.
Vegetable Kebabs Energy 274kcal/1144kJ; Protein 11.1g; Carbohydrate 28.8g, of which sugars 26.2g; Fat 13.7g, of which saturates 2.5g; Cholesterol 1mg; Calcium 303mg; Fibre 5.9g; Sodium 111mg.

Stuffed Aubergines

This Ligurian dish is spiked with paprika and allspice, a legacy from the days when spices from the East came into northern Italy via the port of Genoa.

Serves 4

2 aubergines (eggplants), about
   225g/8oz each, stalks removed
275g/10oz potatoes, peeled
   and diced
30ml/2 tbsp olive oil
1 small onion, finely chopped
1 garlic clove, finely chopped
good pinch each of ground
   allspice and paprika
1 egg, beaten
40g/1½oz/½ cup grated
   Parmesan cheese
15ml/1 tbsp fresh white
   breadcrumbs
salt and ground black pepper
fresh mint sprigs, to garnish
salad leaves, to serve

1 Bring a large pan of lightly salted water to the boil. Add the aubergines and cook for 5 minutes, turning often. Remove and set aside. Cook the potatoes for 20 minutes, until tender.

2 Meanwhile, cut the aubergines in half lengthways and gently scoop out the flesh with a small sharp knife and a spoon, leaving a shell 5mm/¼in thick. Select a baking dish that will hold the aubergine shells snugly in a single layer. Brush it lightly with oil and arrange the shells in the dish. Chop the scooped-out aubergine flesh roughly.

3 Heat the oil in a frying pan, add the onion and cook gently, stirring frequently, until softened. Add the chopped aubergine flesh and the garlic. Cook, stirring frequently, for 6–8 minutes. Tip into a bowl. Preheat the oven to 190°C/375°F/Gas 5.

4 Drain and mash the potatoes. Add to the aubergine with the spices and egg. Set aside 15ml/1 tbsp of the Parmesan and add the rest to the aubergine mixture. Season to taste.

5 Spoon the mixture into the prepared aubergine shells. Mix the breadcrumbs with the reserved Parmesan cheese and sprinkle over the aubergines. Bake for 40–45 minutes until the topping is crisp. Garnish with sprigs of mint and serve with salad leaves.

Bean-stuffed Mushrooms with Garlic

These bean and lemon-stuffed mushrooms are beautifully fragrant. The garlic and pine nut paste is a traditional Middle Eastern accompaniment.

Serves 4

200g/7oz/1 cup dried aduki beans
45ml/3 tbsp olive oil
1 onion, finely chopped
2 garlic cloves, crushed
30ml/2 tbsp fresh thyme leaves
8 large field (portabello)
   mushrooms, stalks chopped
50g/2oz/1 cup fresh wholemeal
   (whole-wheat) breadcrumbs
juice of 1 lemon
185g/6½oz/generous ¾ cup
   crumbled goat's cheese
salt and ground black pepper
steamed spinach leaves, to serve

For the pine nut paste
50g/2oz/½ cup pine nuts, toasted
50g/2oz/1 cup cubed white bread
2 garlic cloves, chopped
200ml/7fl oz/scant 1 cup milk
45ml/3 tbsp olive oil

1 Soak the beans overnight, then drain and rinse well. Place in a pan, add enough water to cover and bring to the boil. Boil rapidly for 10 minutes, then reduce the heat, cook for 30 minutes, or until tender, then drain.

2 Preheat the oven to 200°C/400°F/Gas 6. Heat the oil in a large, heavy frying pan, add the onion and garlic and cook over a low heat, stirring frequently, for 5 minutes, or until softened. Add the thyme and the mushroom stalks and cook for a further 3 minutes, stirring occasionally, until tender.

3 Stir in the aduki beans, breadcrumbs and lemon juice, season to taste with salt and pepper, then cook gently for 2–3 minutes. Mash about two-thirds of the beans with a fork or potato masher, leaving the remaining beans whole, then mix together.

4 Oil an ovenproof dish and the base of the mushrooms. Top each with a spoonful of the bean mixture, place in the dish, cover with foil and bake for 20 minutes. Remove the foil, top each mushroom with cheese and bake until the cheese melts.

5 To make the pine nut paste, process all the ingredients until smooth. Serve with the mushrooms, with steamed spinach.

Stuffed Aubergines Energy 94kcal/396kJ; Protein 3.8g; Carbohydrate 12.2g, of which sugars 3.1g; Fat 3.8g, of which saturates 1.3g; Cholesterol 4mg; Calcium 73mg; Fibre 2.3g; Sodium 74mg.
Stuffed Mushrooms Energy 350kcal/1469kJ; Protein 21.3g; Carbohydrate 30.6g, of which sugars 1.2g; Fat 16.7g, of which saturates 8.9g; Cholesterol 43mg; Calcium 115mg; Fibre 6.3g; Sodium 331mg.

Sweet Potato Turnovers

The subtle sweetness of the potatoes makes a great filling when flavoured with a selection of light spices.

Serves 4
1 sweet potato, about 225g/8oz
30ml/2 tbsp vegetable oil
2 shallots, finely chopped
10ml/2 tsp coriander
   seeds, crushed
5ml/1 tsp ground cumin
5ml/1 tsp garam masala
115g/4oz/1 cup frozen peas
15ml/1 tbsp chopped fresh mint
salt and ground black pepper
mint sprigs, to garnish

For the pastry
15ml/1 tbsp olive oil
1 small egg
150ml/¼ pint/⅔ cup natural
   (plain) yogurt
115g/4oz/8 tbsp butter, melted
275g/10oz/2½ cups plain
   (all-purpose) flour
1.5ml/¼ tsp bicarbonate of soda
10ml/2 tsp paprika
5ml/1 tsp salt
beaten egg, to glaze

1 Cook the sweet potato in boiling salted water for 15–20 minutes, until tender. Drain well and leave to cool. When cool enough to handle, peel the potato and cut into 1cm/½in cubes.

2 Heat the oil in a frying pan, add the shallots and cook until softened. Add the sweet potato and fry until it browns at the edges. Add the spices and fry, for a few seconds. Remove from the heat and add the peas, mint and seasoning. Leave to cool.

3 Preheat the oven to 200°C/400°F/Gas 6. Grease a baking sheet. To make the pastry, whisk together the oil and egg, stir in the yogurt, then add the melted butter. Sift the flour, bicarbonate of soda, paprika and salt into a bowl, then stir into the yogurt mixture to form a soft dough. Turn out the dough, and knead gently. Roll it out, then stamp it out into rounds.

4 Spoon about 10ml/2 tsp of the filling on to one side of each round, then fold over and seal the edges. Re-roll the trimmings and stamp out more rounds until the filling is used up.

5 Arrange the turnovers on the prepared baking sheet and brush the tops with beaten egg. Bake in the oven for about 20 minutes until crisp and golden brown. Serve hot with mint.

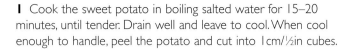

Eggs in Remoulade Sauce

There are as many recipes for remoulade sauce as there are cooks in Louisiana. This one comes from the McIlhenny family, makers of Tabasco sauce, and naturally they splash some of the hot stuff into their remoulade.

Serves 4
45ml/3 tbsp coarse-ground
   mustard
10ml/2 tsp paprika
5ml/1 tsp Tabasco sauce
5ml/1 tsp salt
2.5ml/½ tsp ground black pepper
45ml/3 tbsp tarragon vinegar
250ml/8fl oz/1 cup olive oil
3 spring onions
   (scallions), shredded
1 celery stick, shredded
45ml/3 tbsp finely chopped
   fresh parsley
6 hard-boiled eggs
a handful of mustard and cress,
   to garnish

1 Whisk together the mustard, paprika, Tabasco sauce, salt and pepper, then beat in the vinegar.

2 Beating constantly, add the oil in a slow thin trickle, continuing to beat until the sauce becomes thick and smooth.

3 Stir in the spring onions, celery and parsley and mix well. Cover the bowl and leave to stand for at least 2 hours to allow the flavours to blend.

4 Meanwhile, shell the hard-boiled eggs and halve them lengthways. To serve, arrange three half eggs on each of four small plates. Spoon the remoulade sauce over the eggs, then sprinkle lightly with mustard and cress to garnish.

Cook's Tip
• *Reduce the quantity of Tabasco if you want to make a less fiery sauce: it will still have plenty of flavour.*
• *This is an easy dish to make in a larger quantity for a buffet table. Leave the final assembly as late as you can before serving it.*

Sweet Potato Turnovers Energy 660kcal/2760kJ; Protein 13.9g; Carbohydrate 75.8g, of which sugars 9.3g; Fat 35.9g, of which saturates 17g; Cholesterol 105mg; Calcium 216mg; Fibre 5.2g; Sodium 740mg.
Eggs in Remoulade Sauce Energy 530kcal/2185kJ; Protein 10.8g; Carbohydrate 2.3g, of which sugars 1.2g; Fat 53.4g, of which saturates 8.7g; Cholesterol 285mg; Calcium 66mg; Fibre 0.3g; Sodium 444mg.

Eggs in Hot Red Sauce

Popular at street stalls in Malaysia and Singapore, this spicy egg dish originally comes from Indonesia. It is usually served wrapped in a banana leaf. The Malays often eat it with plain steamed rice, sliced chillies, onion and fresh coriander, and it is ideal for a quick, tasty meal.

Serves 4
vegetable oil, for deep-frying
8 eggs, hard-boiled and shelled
1 lemon grass stalk, trimmed, quartered and crushed
2 large tomatoes, skinned, seeded and chopped to a pulp
5–10ml/1–2 tsp sugar
30ml/2 tbsp dark soy sauce
juice of 1 lime
fresh coriander (cilantro) and mint leaves, coarsely chopped, to garnish

For the spice paste
4–6 red chillies, seeded and chopped
4 shallots, chopped
2 garlic cloves, peeled and chopped

1 Using a mortar and pestle or a food processor, grind the chillies, shallots and garlic cloves for the spice paste until a smooth mixture is reached. Set the paste aside and prepare the eggs.

2 Heat enough oil for deep-frying in a wok or heavy pan and deep-fry the whole boiled eggs until they are golden brown. Lift them out and drain.

3 Reserve 15ml/1 tbsp of the oil in the wok or pan and discard the rest. Heat the oil in the wok or a large heavy pan and stir in the spice paste. Cook, stirring, until it becomes fragrant.

4 Add the lemon grass, followed by the tomatoes and sugar. Cook for 2–3 minutes, until it forms a thick paste.

5 Reduce the heat and stir in the soy sauce and lime juice. Add 30ml/2 tbsp water to thin the sauce. Toss in the eggs, making sure they are thoroughly coated, and serve hot, garnished with chopped coriander and mint leaves.

Peppers with Spiced Vegetables

Indian spices season the potato and aubergine stuffing in these colourful baked peppers.

Serves 6
6 large, evenly shaped red or yellow (bell) peppers
500g/1¼lb waxy potatoes
1 small onion, chopped
4–5 garlic cloves, chopped
5cm/2in piece fresh root ginger, chopped
2 green chillies, seeded and sliced
105ml/7 tbsp water
90–105ml/6–7 tbsp groundnut (peanut) oil
1 aubergine (eggplant), diced
10ml/2 tsp cumin seeds
5ml/1 tsp kalonji seeds
2.5ml/½ tsp ground turmeric
5ml/1 tsp ground coriander
5ml/1 tsp ground cumin seeds
pinch of cayenne pepper
about 30ml/2 tbsp lemon juice
salt and ground black pepper
30ml/2 tbsp chopped fresh coriander (cilantro), to garnish

1 Cut the tops off the peppers and discard the seeds. Cut a thin slice off the base. Cook the peppers in boiling water for 5–6 minutes. Drain and leave upside down in a colander.

2 Cook the potatoes for 10–12 minutes. Drain, cool and peel them, then cut into 1cm/½in dice. Blend the onion, garlic, ginger and green chillies with 60ml/4 tbsp of the water and process to a purée.

3 Heat 45ml/3 tbsp of the oil and stir-fry the aubergine, until browned. Remove from the pan and set aside. Add 30ml/2 tbsp of the oil to the pan and cook the potatoes until browned. Remove and set aside.

4 Fry the cumin and kalonji seeds briefly, add the turmeric, coriander and cumin. Stir in the onion and garlic purée and fry until it begins to brown. Return the potatoes and aubergines to the pan, add salt, pepper and 2 pinches of cayenne. Add the remaining water and 15ml/1 tbsp lemon juice and cook until the liquid evaporates. Preheat the oven to 190°C/375°F/Gas 5.

5 Stuff the peppers with the potato mixture. Place on a lightly greased baking tray and bake for 30–35 minutes, until the peppers are cooked. Garnish with coriander and serve.

Spiced Vegetables Energy 234kcal/976kJ; Protein 4.2g; Carbohydrate 28.1g, of which sugars 14.8g; Fat 12.4g, of which saturates 2.4g; Cholesterol 0mg; Calcium 45mg; Fibre 5.5g; Sodium 21mg.
Eggs in Hot Sauce Energy 271Kcal/1125kJ; Protein 13.3g; Carbohydrate 5.5g, of which sugars 5g; Fat 22.3g, of which saturates 4.4g; Cholesterol 381mg; Calcium 67mg; Fibre 0.7g; Sodium 679mg.

Cheese and Leek Rissoles

These rissoles are based on the Welsh speciality, Glamorgan sausages, which are made with cheese and leeks. They are usually made with breadcrumbs alone, but mashed potato lightens the mix and makes them easier to shape into rissoles. Here they are served with a lively tomato sauce.

Serves 4
25g/1oz/2 tbsp butter
175g/6oz leeks, finely chopped
90ml/6 tbsp cold mashed potato
115g/4oz/2 cups fresh white or
   wholemeal (whole-wheat)
   breadcrumbs
150g/5oz/1¼ cups grated
   Caerphilly or Lancashire cheese
30ml/2 tbsp chopped fresh parsley
5ml/1 tsp chopped fresh sage

2 large eggs, beaten
cayenne pepper
65g/2½oz/1 cup dry white
   breadcrumbs
oil for shallow frying

For the sauce
30ml/2 tbsp olive oil
2 garlic cloves, thinly sliced
1 fresh red chilli, seeded and
   finely chopped, or a good pinch
   of dried red chilli flakes
1 small onion, finely chopped
500g/1¼lb tomatoes, peeled,
   seeded and chopped
few fresh thyme sprigs
10ml/2 tsp balsamic vinegar or
   red wine vinegar
pinch of light brown sugar
15–30ml/1–2 tbsp chopped
   fresh oregano
salt and ground black pepper

1 Melt the butter and fry the leeks for 4–5 minutes, until softened. Mix with the mashed potato, fresh breadcrumbs, cheese, parsley and sage. Add sufficient beaten egg (about two-thirds) to bind. Season well and add a good pinch of cayenne. Shape the mixture into 12 rissoles. Dip in the remaining egg, then coat with the dry breadcrumbs. Chill the coated rissoles.

2 To make the sauce, heat the oil over a low heat in a pan, add the garlic, chilli and onion and cook for 3–4 minutes. Add the tomatoes, thyme and vinegar. Add salt, pepper and sugar. Cook for 40–50 minutes, until reduced. Remove the thyme and purée in a blender. Reheat with the oregano, and adjust the seasoning.

3 Fry the rissoles in shallow oil until golden brown on all sides. Drain on kitchen paper and serve with the sauce.

Vegetables and Spicy Sauce

Served as a vegetable side dish or as a main course, a selection of roasted vegetables in a peanut sauce, enhanced by chillies and soy sauce, is a favourite throughout South-east Asia.

Serves 4
1 aubergine (eggplant), partially
   peeled and cut into long strips
2 courgettes (zucchini), partially
   peeled and cut into long strips
1 thick, long sweet potato, cut into
   long strips
2 leeks, trimmed, halved
   and sliced
2 garlic cloves, chopped
25g/1oz fresh root ginger, peeled
   and chopped

60ml/4 tbsp vegetable or oil
salt
45ml/3 tbsp roasted peanuts,
   ground, to garnish
fresh crusty bread, to serve

For the sauce
4 garlic cloves, chopped
2–3 red chillies, seeded
   and chopped
115g/4oz/1 cup roasted
   peanuts, crushed
15–30ml/1–2 tbsp dark soy sauce
juice of 1 lime
5–10ml/1–2 tsp Chinese
   rice vinegar
10ml/2 tsp palm sugar (jaggery)
   or honey
salt and ground black pepper

1 Preheat the oven to 200°C/400°F/Gas 6. Arrange the vegetables in a roasting pan. Using a mortar and pestle or food processor, grind the garlic and ginger to a paste, and smear it over the vegetables. Sprinkle with salt and pour over the oil.

2 Place the pan in the oven for about 45 minutes, until the vegetables are lightly browned, tossing halfway through cooking.

3 Meanwhile, make the sauce. Using a mortar and pestle or food processor, grind the garlic and chillies to a paste. Beat in the peanuts. Stir in the soy sauce, lime juice, vinegar and sugar or honey, and blend with a little water so that the sauce is the consistency of pouring cream. Season with salt and pepper and adjust the balance of sweet and sour to taste.

4 Arrange the roasted vegetables on a plate. Drizzle the sauce over them, or serve it separately in a bowl. Sprinkle the ground peanuts over the top and serve with bread.

Cheese Rissoles Energy 580kcal/2416kJ; Protein 19.2g; Carbohydrate 35.5g, of which sugars 6.9g; Fat 40.3g, of which saturates 15.2g; Cholesterol 164mg; Calcium 361mg; Fibre 3.6g; Sodium 604mg.
Vegetables and Spicy Sauce Energy 361Kcal/1502kJ; Protein 11.9g; Carbohydrate 22.7g, of which sugars 11.1g; Fat 25.4g, of which saturates 4.1g; Cholesterol 0mg; Calcium 76mg; Fibre 6.9g; Sodium 292mg.

Lentil Salad with Cumin

This wonderful, earthy salad is great with barbecued food. It is best served at room temperature.

Serves 6
225g/8oz/1 cup Puy lentils
1 fresh bay leaf
1 celery stick
fresh thyme sprig
30ml/2 tbsp olive oil
1 onion or 3–4 shallots, chopped
10ml/2 tsp crushed toasted
   cumin seeds

400g/14oz young spinach
salt and ground black pepper
30–45ml/2–3 tbsp chopped fresh
   parsley, plus a few extra sprigs
French bread rounds, to serve

For the dressing
75ml/5 tbsp extra virgin olive oil
5ml/1 tsp Dijon mustard
15–25ml/1–1½ tbsp red
   wine vinegar
1 small garlic clove, chopped
2.5ml/½ tsp finely grated
   lemon rind

1 Rinse the lentils and place in a large pan. Add water to cover. Tie the bay leaf, celery and thyme into a bundle and add to the pan, then bring to the boil. Reduce the heat. Cook the lentils for 30 minutes, until just tender. Drain and turn into a bowl.

2 Meanwhile, to make the dressing, mix the oil, mustard, 15ml/1 tbsp vinegar, the garlic and lemon rind, and season well with salt and pepper. Add most of the dressing to the lentils and toss well, then set aside.

3 Heat the oil in a deep pan and cook the onion or shallots over a low heat for about 4–5 minutes, stirring occasionally, until they are beginning to soften. Add the cumin and cook for 1 minute. Add the spinach and season to taste, cover and cook for 2 minutes. Stir, then cook again briefly until wilted.

4 Stir the spinach into the lentils and leave the salad to cool. Bring back to room temperature if necessary. Stir in the remaining dressing and chopped parsley. Adjust the seasoning, adding extra red wine vinegar if necessary.

5 Brush the rounds of French bread with olive oil and toast under the grill (broiler). Turn the salad on to a serving platter, sprinkle over some parsley sprigs and serve with the toast.

Leek and Fennel Salad

This is an excellent salad to make in the early autumn when young leeks are tender and at their best. Serve with bread.

Serves 2
2 large fennel bulbs
675g/1½lb leeks, trimmed
120ml/4fl oz/½ cup olive oil
2 shallots, chopped
150ml/¼ pint/⅔ cup dry white
   wine or white vermouth

5ml/1 tsp fennel
   seeds, crushed
6 fresh thyme sprigs
2–3 bay leaves
pinch of dried red chilli flakes
350g/12oz tomatoes, peeled,
   seeded and diced
5ml/1 tsp sun-dried tomato paste
good pinch of caster
   (superfine) sugar
75g/3oz/¾ cup small
   black olives
salt and ground black pepper

1 Trim the fennel bulbs, reserving any feathery tops for the garnish and cut the bulbs into wedges. Cook the fennel with the leeks in boiling salted water for 4–5 minutes. Drain thoroughly and cool. Squeeze out excess water from the leeks and cut into 7.5cm/3in lengths. Toss the fennel pieces with 30ml/2 tbsp of the olive oil. Season to taste with black pepper.

2 Heat a ridged cast-iron griddle. Arrange the leeks and fennel on the griddle and cook until tinged deep brown, turning once. Remove the vegetables from the griddle, place in a large shallow dish and set aside.

3 Place the remaining olive oil, the shallots, white wine or vermouth, crushed fennel seeds, thyme, bay leaves and chilli flakes in a large pan and bring to the boil. Lower the heat and simmer for 10 minutes. Add the diced tomatoes and cook briskly for 5–8 minutes, or until reduced and thickened.

4 Add the tomato paste, and adjust the seasoning, adding a good pinch of caster sugar if you think the dressing needs it.

5 Pour the dressing over the leeks and fennel, toss to mix and leave to cool. When ready to serve, stir the salad then sprinkle the chopped fennel tops and black olives over the top.

Lentil Salad Energy 192kcal/816kJ; Protein 14.2g; Carbohydrate 30.2g, of which sugars 3.1g; Fat 2.5g, of which saturates 0.4g; Cholesterol 0mg; Calcium 47mg; Fibre 5.7g; Sodium 12mg.
Leek and Fennel Salad Energy 194kcal/801kJ; Protein 2.8g; Carbohydrate 6.8g, of which sugars 5.9g; Fat 14.7g, of which saturates 2.2g; Cholesterol 0mg; Calcium 53mg; Fibre 4.6g; Sodium 297mg.

Pumpkin and Pistachio Risotto

Vegetarians will love this elegant combination of creamy, golden saffron rice and orange pumpkin, and so will everyone else. It would look impressive served in the hollowed-out pumpkin shell.

Serves 4
1.2 litres/2 pints/5 cups vegetable stock or water
generous pinch of saffron strands
30ml/2 tbsp olive oil
1 onion, chopped
2 garlic cloves, crushed

900g/2lb pumpkin, peeled, seeded and cut into 2cm/³⁄₄in cubes (about 7 cups)
400g/14oz/2 cups risotto rice
200ml/7fl oz/scant 1 cup dry white wine
30ml/2 tbsp freshly grated Parmesan cheese
50g/2oz/¹⁄₂ cup pistachios, coarsely chopped
45ml/3 tbsp chopped fresh marjoram or oregano, plus leaves to garnish
salt, freshly grated nutmeg and ground black pepper

1 Bring the stock or water to the boil and reduce to a low simmer. Ladle a little of it into a small bowl. Add the saffron strands and leave to infuse.

2 Heat the oil in a large, heavy pan or deep frying pan. Add the onion and garlic and cook gently for 5 minutes until softened. Add the pumpkin and rice and stir to coat everything in oil. Cook for a few more minutes until the rice looks transparent.

3 Pour in the wine and allow it to bubble hard. When it has been absorbed, add a quarter of the hot stock or water and the saffron liquid. Stir until all the liquid has been absorbed. Gradually add the remaining stock or water, a little at a time, allowing the rice to absorb the liquid before adding more, and stirring constantly.

4 After 20–30 minutes the rice should be golden yellow, creamy and al dente. Stir in the Parmesan cheese, cover the pan and leave to stand for 5 minutes. To finish, stir in the pistachios and marjoram or oregano. Season to taste with a little salt, nutmeg and pepper, sprinkle over a few marjoram or oregano leaves and serve.

Pumpkin with Saffron Pilaff

A pumpkin makes an ideal cooking vessel, whether filled with an aromatic pilaff as in this recipe, with vegetables and rice, or soup.

Serves 4–6
1 medium-sized pumpkin, weighing about 1.2kg/2¹⁄₂lb
225g/8oz/generous 1 cup long grain rice, well rinsed
30–45ml/2–3 tbsp olive oil
15ml/1 tbsp butter
pinch of saffron threads
5ml/1 tsp coriander seeds
2–3 strips of orange peel, sliced

45–60ml/3–4 tbsp shelled pistachio nuts
30–45ml/2–3 tbsp dried cranberries, soaked in boiling water for 5 minutes and drained
175g/6oz/³⁄₄ cup dried apricots, sliced or chopped
1 bunch of fresh basil, leaves
1 bunch each of fresh coriander (cilantro), mint and flat leaf parsley, coarsely chopped
salt and ground black pepper
lemon wedges and thick natural (plain) yogurt, to serve

1 Preheat the oven to 200°C/400°F/Gas 6. Wash the pumpkin and cut off the top to use as a lid. Scoop the seeds out of the middle with a metal spoon, and pull out the stringy bits. Replace the lid, put the pumpkin on a baking tray and bake for 1 hour.

2 Meanwhile, tip the rice into a pan and pour in just enough water to cover. Add a pinch of salt and bring to the boil, then lower the heat and partially cover the pan. Simmer for 10–12 minutes, until all the water has been absorbed and the grains of rice are cooked but still have a bite.

3 Heat the oil and butter in a wide, heavy pan. Stir in the saffron, coriander seeds, orange peel, pistachios, cranberries, apricots, and rice, season with salt and pepper, and mix. Turn off the heat, cover the pan with a dish towel and press the lid on top. Leave to steam for 10 minutes, then toss in the herbs.

4 Take the pumpkin out of the oven. Lift off the lid and spoon the pilaff inside. Replace the lid and cook for 20 minutes. To serve, remove the lid, slice off the top of the pumpkin, place on a plate and spoon pilaff in the middle. Continue until everyone is served. Serve with lemon wedges and a bowl of yogurt.

Pumpkin Risotto Energy 585kcal/2441kJ; Protein 14.4g; Carbohydrate 87.3g, of which sugars 5.7g; Fat 15.9g, of which saturates 3.5g; Cholesterol 8mg; Calcium 196mg; Fibre 3.2g; Sodium 151mg.
Pumpkin Pilaff Energy 345kcal/1443kJ; Protein 9.9g; Carbohydrate 50.1g, of which sugars 18.6g; Fat 12g, of which saturates 2.6g; Cholesterol 5mg; Calcium 299mg; Fibre 9.6g; Sodium 93mg.

Chilli Courgette Pilaff

This is a recipe from the Balkans, but it bears testimony to the influence of Italy, just on the other side of the Adriatic Sea, on the region's cuisine.

Serves 4

1kg/2¼lb small or medium
   courgettes (zucchini)
60ml/4 tbsp olive oil
3 onions, finely chopped
3 garlic cloves, crushed
5ml/1 tsp chilli powder
400g/14oz can
   chopped tomatoes
200g/7oz/1 cup risotto or round
   grain rice
600–750ml/1–1¼ pints/
   2½–3 cups vegetable stock
30ml/2 tbsp chopped
   fresh parsley
30ml/2 tbsp chopped fresh dill
salt and ground white pepper
sprigs of dill and olives, to garnish
thick natural (plain) yogurt, to serve

1 Preheat the oven to 190°C/375°F/Gas 5. Top and tail the courgettes and slice into large chunks.

2 Heat half the olive oil in a large pan and gently fry the onions and garlic until just soft. Stir in the chilli powder and tomatoes and simmer for about 5–8 minutes before adding the courgettes and salt to taste.

3 Cook over a gentle to medium heat for 10–15 minutes, before stirring the rice into the pan. Add the stock to the pan, cover and simmer for about 45 minutes or until the rice is tender. Stir the mixture occasionally.

4 Remove from the heat and stir in pepper to taste, parsley and dill. Spoon into an ovenproof dish and bake for about 45 minutes. Halfway through cooking, brush the remaining oil over the courgette mixture. Garnish with the dill and olives. Serve with the yogurt.

> **Cook's Tip**
> Add extra liquid if necessary, during baking, to prevent the mixture from sticking.

Cuban-style Rice

Arroz a la cubana, garnished with fried eggs and bananas, is a Spanish dish popular in the Canary Islands and Catalonia. It makes a simple, tasty meal.

Serves 4

3 garlic cloves
120ml/4fl oz/½ cup olive oil
300g/11oz/1½ cups long
   grain rice
15g/½oz/1 tbsp butter
4 small bananas or
   2 large bananas
4 eggs
salt and paprika

For the tomato sauce
30ml/2 tbsp olive oil
1 onion, chopped
2 garlic cloves, finely chopped
800g/1lb 12oz can tomatoes
4 thyme or oregano sprigs
salt and ground black pepper

1 To make the tomato sauce, heat the oil in a pan, add the onion and garlic and fry gently, stirring, until soft. Stir in the tomatoes and thyme or oregano sprigs and simmer gently for 5 minutes. Add seasoning to taste. Remove the herb sprigs and keep the sauce warm.

2 Put 850ml/1 pint 8fl oz/3½ cups water in a pan with two whole garlic cloves and 15ml/1 tbsp oil. Bring to the boil, add the rice and cook for 18 minutes until it is tender and the liquid has been absorbed.

3 Heat a pan with 30ml/2 tbsp oil and gently fry one chopped garlic clove. Tip in the rice, stir, season well, then turn off the heat and cover the pan.

4 Heat the butter in a frying pan with 15ml/1 tbsp oil. Halve the bananas lengthways and fry briefly on both sides. Remove from the pan and keep warm.

5 Add 60ml/4 tbsp oil to the pan and fry the eggs over a medium-high heat, so that the edges turn golden. Season with salt and paprika.

6 Serve the rice surrounded by tomato sauce and the fried bananas and eggs.

Sweet Rice with Chickpeas and Lemon

Lemon adds piquancy to this spicy dish perfumed with cloves and cardamom.

Serves 6
225g/8oz tomatoes, skinned
350g/12oz/2 cups dried
   chickpeas, soaked overnight
60ml/4 tbsp vegetable oil
1 large onion, very finely chopped
15ml/1 tbsp ground coriander
15ml/1 tbsp ground cumin
5ml/1 tsp ground fenugreek
5ml/1 tsp ground cinnamon
1–2 fresh green chillies, seeded
   and thinly sliced
2.5cm/1in piece fresh root ginger,
   peeled and grated
60ml/4 tbsp lemon juice
15ml/1 tbsp chopped fresh
   coriander (cilantro)
salt and ground black pepper

For the rice
40g/1½oz/3 tbsp butter
4 green cardamom pods
4 cloves
650ml/22fl oz/2¾ cups
   boiling water
350g/12oz/1¾ cups basmati
   rice, soaked for 30 minutes
   and drained
5–10ml/1–2 tsp granulated sugar
5–6 saffron threads, soaked in
   warm water

1 Chop the tomatoes. Set aside. Drain the chickpeas, cover with water, bring to the boil, cover and simmer, for 1–1¼ hours. Drain, reserving the cooking liquid.

2 Heat the oil in a pan. Reserve 30ml/2 tbsp of the onion and add the rest to the pan. Cook for 4–5 minutes. Add the tomatoes and cook over a low heat for 5 minutes. Add the ground spices, then add the chickpeas and 350ml/12fl oz/1½ cups of the reserved cooking liquid. Season, then cover and simmer gently for 15–20 minutes. Add more liquid if needed.

3 Melt the butter and fry the cardamom pods and cloves for 30 seconds. Add the rice, stir well, then add the boiling water. Cover and simmer for 10 minutes, then turn off the heat and stir in the sugar and saffron liquid. Cover.

4 Add the reserved chopped onion, chillies, ginger, lemon juice, and coriander to the chickpeas. Serve with the rice.

Lentils and Rice with Spiced Onions

This dish of rice and lentils is a classic Middle Eastern meal, popular from Egypt and Libya to Galilee and Greece. It is often eaten with a bowl of vegetables, accompanied by yogurt and a plate of crisp salad.

Serves 6–8
400g/14oz/1¾ cups large brown
   or green lentils
45ml/3 tbsp olive oil
3–4 onions, 1 chopped and
   2–3 thinly sliced
5ml/1 tsp ground cumin
2.5ml/½ tsp ground cinnamon
6 cardamom pods
300g/11oz/1½ cups long grain
   rice, rinsed
about 250ml/8fl oz/1 cup
   vegetable stock
salt and ground black pepper
natural (plain) yogurt, to serve

1 Put the lentils in a saucepan with enough water to cover generously. Bring to the boil, then simmer for about 30 minutes, or until tender. Skim off any scum that forms on top.

2 Meanwhile, heat half the oil in a pan, add the chopped onion and fry for 10 minutes, or until softened and golden brown. Stir in half the cumin and half the cinnamon.

3 When the lentils are cooked, add the spicy fried onions to the pan, together with the cardamom pods, rice and stock. Stir well and bring to the boil, then reduce the heat, cover the pan and simmer gently until the rice is tender and all the liquid has been absorbed. If the mixture appears to be getting a little too dry, add some extra water or stock. Season with salt and pepper to taste.

4 Meanwhile, heat the remaining oil in a pan, add the sliced onions and fry for about 10 minutes, until dark brown, caramelized and crisp. Sprinkle in the remaining cumin and cinnamon just before the end of cooking.

5 To serve, pile the rice and lentil mixture on to a serving dish, then top with the browned, caramelized onions. Serve immediately, with yogurt.

Rice with Chickpeas Energy 556kcal/2327kJ; Protein 18.2g; Carbohydrate 84.6g, of which sugars 8.2g; Fat 16.8g, of which saturates 4.7g; Cholesterol 14mg; Calcium 130mg; Fibre 7.6g; Sodium 70mg.
Lentils and Rice Energy 394kcal/1656kJ; Protein 17.5g; Carbohydrate 68g, of which sugars 5.1g; Fat 6.6g, of which saturates 0.9g; Cholesterol 0mg; Calcium 54mg; Fibre 3.8g; Sodium 23mg.

Jewelled Vegetable Rice with Crispy Deep-fried Eggs

Inspired by the traditional Indonesian dish *nasi goreng*, this vibrant, colourful stir-fry makes a tasty vegetarian meal. For an extra healthy version, you could use brown basmati rice in place of the white rice.

Serves 4
30ml/2 tbsp sunflower oil
2 garlic cloves, finely chopped
4 red Asian shallots, thinly sliced
1 small red chilli, finely sliced
90g/3½oz carrots, cut into
   thin matchsticks
90g/3½oz fine green beans, cut
   into 2cm/¾in lengths
90g/3½oz fresh
   sweetcorn kernels
1 red (bell) pepper, diced
90g/3½oz baby button
   (white) mushrooms
500g/1¼lb cooked, cooled long
   grain rice
45ml/3 tbsp light soy sauce
10ml/2 tsp green Thai curry paste
4 crispy fried eggs, to serve
crisp green salad leaves and lime
   wedges, to garnish

1 Heat the sunflower oil in a wok over a high heat. When hot, add the garlic, shallots and chilli. Stir-fry for about 2 minutes.

2 Add the carrots, green beans, sweetcorn, red pepper and mushrooms to the wok and stir-fry for 3–4 minutes. Add the cooked, cooled rice and stir-fry for a further 4–5 minutes.

3 Mix together the light soy sauce and curry paste and add to the wok. Toss to mix well and stir-fry for 2–3 minutes until piping hot. Ladle the rice into four bowls or plates and top each portion with a crispy fried egg. Serve with crisp green salad leaves and wedges of lime to squeeze over.

Cook's Tip
For this dish, it is important to use cold cooked rice rather than hot, freshly cooked rice. Hot boiled rice tends to clump together when it is stir-fried, whereas the grains of cooled rice will remain separate.

Moroccan Aubergine Pilaff with Cinnamon and Mint

This North African rice dish varies from region to region, but all recipes include meaty chunks of aubergine.

Serves 4–6
2 large aubergines (eggplants)
30–45ml/2–3 tbsp olive oil
30–45ml/2–3 tbsp pine nuts
1 large onion, finely chopped
5ml/1 tsp coriander seeds
30ml/2 tbsp currants, soaked for
   5–10 minutes and drained
10–15ml/2–3 tsp sugar
15–30ml/1–2 tbsp
   ground cinnamon
15–30ml/1–2 tbsp dried mint
1 small bunch of fresh dill,
   finely chopped
3 tomatoes, skinned, seeded and
   finely chopped
350g/12oz/generous 1¾ cups
   long or short grain rice, well
   rinsed and drained
sunflower oil, for deep-frying
juice of ½ lemon
salt and ground black pepper
fresh mint and lemon, to serve

1 Quarter the aubergines lengthways, then slice each quarter into chunks and place in a bowl of salted water. Leave to soak for at least 30 minutes.

2 Meanwhile, heat the olive oil in a heavy pan, stir in the pine nuts and cook until they turn golden. Add the onion and cook until soft, then stir in the coriander seeds and currants. Add the sugar, cinnamon, mint and dill and stir in the tomatoes.

3 Toss in the rice, stirring until well coated, then pour in 900ml/1½ pints/3¾ cups water, season with salt and pepper and bring to the boil. Lower the heat, partially cover the pan, and simmer for 10–12 minutes, until almost all the liquid has been absorbed. Turn off the heat, cover with a dish towel and the lid and leave the rice to steam for about 15 minutes.

4 Heat enough sunflower oil for deep-frying in a wok. Drain the aubergines and squeeze them dry, then fry them in batches. When they are golden brown, lift out and drain on paper towels. Tip the rice into a serving bowl and toss the aubergine chunks through it with the lemon juice. Garnish with fresh mint and serve warm or cold, with lemon wedges for squeezing.

Rice with Eggs Energy 392kcal/1648kJ; Protein 13.6g; Carbohydrate 51.4g, of which sugars 8.2g; Fat 16.1g, of which saturates 3.6g; Cholesterol 261mg; Calcium 79mg; Fibre 2.2g; Sodium 968mg.
Aubergine Pilaff Energy 369kcal/1539kJ; Protein 6.1g; Carbohydrate 52.2g, of which sugars 11g; Fat 15.2g, of which saturates 1.8g; Cholesterol 0mg; Calcium 38mg; Fibre 2.7g; Sodium 8mg.

Noodles with Yellow Bean Sauce

Served solo, steamed leeks, courgettes and peas can be rather bland, but the addition of a punchy mixture of yellow bean and sweet chilli sauces adds deliciously hot and aromatic flavours.

Serves 4
150g/5oz thin egg noodles
200g/7oz baby leeks,
  sliced lengthways
200g/7oz baby courgettes
  (zucchini), halved lengthways
200g/7oz sugar snap
  peas, trimmed
200g/7oz/1¾ cups fresh
  or frozen peas
15ml/1 tbsp vegetable oil
5 garlic cloves, sliced
45ml/3 tbsp yellow bean sauce
45ml/3 tbsp sweet chilli sauce
30ml/2 tbsp sweet soy sauce
50g/2oz/½ cup cashew nuts,
  to garnish

1 Cook the noodles according to the packet instructions, drain and set aside.

2 Line a large bamboo steamer with some perforated baking parchment and add the leeks, courgettes, sugar snaps and peas. Cover and stand over a wok of simmering water. Steam the vegetables for about 5 minutes, then remove and set aside. Drain and dry the wok.

3 Heat the vegetable oil in the wok and stir-fry the sliced garlic for 1–2 minutes.

4 In a separate bowl, mix together the yellow bean, sweet chilli and soy sauces, then pour into the wok. Stir to mix with the garlic, then add the steamed vegetables and the noodles and toss together to combine.

5 Cook the vegetables and noodles for 2–3 minutes, stirring frequently, until heated through.

6 Divide the vegetable noodles among four warmed serving bowls and sprinkle over the cashew nuts to garnish.

Sweet Vegetable Noodles in Plum Sauce

Ginger and plum sauce give this noodle dish its mild, fruity flavour.

Serves 4
130g/4½oz dried rice noodles
30ml/2 tbsp groundnut
  (peanut) oil
2.5cm/1in piece fresh root ginger,
  sliced into thin batons
1 garlic clove, crushed
130g/4½oz drained canned
  bamboo shoots, sliced in batons
2 medium carrots, sliced in batons
130g/4½oz/1½ cups beansprouts
1 small white cabbage, shredded
30ml/2 tbsp soy sauce
30ml/2 tbsp plum sauce
10ml/2 tsp sesame oil
15ml/1 tbsp palm sugar (jaggery)
juice of ½ lime
90g/3½oz mooli (daikon), sliced
  into thin batons
small bunch fresh coriander
  (cilantro), chopped
60ml/4 tbsp sesame seeds,
  toasted

1 Cook the noodles in a large pan of boiling water, following the instructions on the packet. Meanwhile, heat the oil in a wok or large frying pan and stir-fry the ginger and garlic together for 2–3 minutes over a medium heat, until golden.

2 Drain the noodles and keep warm. Add the bamboo shoots to the wok, increase the heat to high and stir-fry for 5 minutes. Add the carrots, beansprouts and cabbage and stir-fry for a further 5 minutes, until they are beginning to char at the edges.

3 Stir in the sauces, sesame oil, sugar and lime juice. Add the mooli and coriander, toss to mix, and serve with the noodles in warmed bowls, sprinkled with toasted sesame seeds.

Cook's Tip
Use a large, sharp knife for shredding cabbage. Remove any tough outer leaves, if necessary, then cut the cabbage into quarters. Cut off and discard the hard core from each quarter, place flat side down, then slice the cabbage very thinly to make fine shreds.

Sweet Noodles Energy 368kcal/1530kJ; Protein 8.8g; Carbohydrate 45.8g, of which sugars 17.6g; Fat 16.5g, of which saturates 2.3g; Cholesterol 0mg; Calcium 200mg; Fibre 6.2g; Sodium 650mg.
Noodles with Bean Sauce Energy 296kcal/1241kJ; Protein 14.2g; Carbohydrate 44.9g, of which sugars 7.4g; Fat 7.8g, of which saturates 1.6g; Cholesterol 11mg; Calcium 61mg; Fibre 8.2g; Sodium 209mg.

Crispy Chilli Noodles

This Thai dish is a stunning combination of sweet and hot, salty and sour, while the texture contrives to be both crisp and chewy.

Serves 1
vegetable oil, for deep-frying
130g/4½oz rice vermicelli noodles

For the sauce
30ml/2 tbsp vegetable oil
130g/4½oz fried tofu, cut into thin strips
2 garlic cloves, finely chopped
2 small shallots, finely chopped
15ml/1 tbsp light soy sauce

30ml/2 tbsp palm sugar (jaggery) or light muscovado (brown) sugar
60ml/4 tbsp vegetable stock
juice of 1 lime
2.5ml/½ tsp dried chilli flakes

For the garnish
15ml/1 tbsp vegetable oil
1 egg, lightly beaten with 15ml/1 tbsp cold water
25g/1oz/⅓ cup beansprouts
1 spring onion (scallion), thinly shredded
1 fresh red chilli, seeded and finely chopped
1 whole head pickled garlic, sliced across to resemble a flower

1 Heat the oil for deep-frying in a wok or large pan to 190°C/375°F, or until a cube of bread, added to the oil, browns in about 45 seconds. Add the noodles and deep-fry until golden and crisp. Drain on kitchen paper and set aside.

2 Make the sauce. Heat the oil in a wok, add the fried tofu and cook over a medium heat until crisp. Using a slotted spoon, transfer it to a plate.

3 Add the garlic and shallots to the pan and cook until golden brown. Stir in the soy sauce, sugar, stock, lime juice and chilli flakes. Cook, stirring, until the mixture caramelizes. Add the reserved tofu and stir. Remove the wok from the heat and set aside.

4 Prepare the egg garnish. Heat the oil in a wok or frying pan. Pour in the egg in a thin stream to form trails. As soon as it sets, lift it out with a metal spatula and place on a plate.

5 Crumble the noodles into the tofu sauce, mix well, then spoon into serving bowls. Sprinkle with the beansprouts, spring onion, fried egg strips, chilli and pickled garlic and serve.

Noodles and Vegetables in Coconut Sauce with Fresh Red Chillies

When everyday vegetables are given the Thai treatment, the result is a delectable dish which everyone is certain to enjoy.

Serves 4 to 6
30ml/2 tbsp sunflower oil
1 lemon grass stalk, finely chopped
15ml/1 tbsp Thai red curry paste
1 onion, thickly sliced
3 courgettes (zucchini), thickly sliced
115g/4oz Savoy cabbage, thickly sliced
2 carrots, thickly sliced

150g/5oz broccoli, stem sliced and head separated into florets
2 X 400ml/14fl oz cans coconut milk
475ml/16fl oz vegetable stock
150g/5oz dried egg noodles
30ml/2 tbsp soy sauce
60ml/4 tbsp chopped fresh coriander (cilantro)

For the garnish
2 lemon grass stalks
1 bunch fresh coriander (cilantro)
8–10 small fresh red chillies

1 Heat the oil in a large pan or wok. Add the lemon grass and red curry paste and stir-fry for 2–3 seconds. Add the onion and cook over a medium heat, stirring occasionally, for about 5–10 minutes, until the onion has softened but not browned.

2 Add the courgettes, cabbage, carrots and slices of broccoli stem. Toss the vegetables with the onion mixture. Reduce the heat and cook gently, stirring occasionally, for 5 minutes.

3 Increase the heat to medium, stir in the coconut milk and vegetable stock and bring to the boil. Add the broccoli florets and the noodles, then simmer gently for 20 minutes.

4 Meanwhile, make the garnish. Split the lemon grass stalks lengthways. Gather the coriander into a small bouquet and lay it on a platter, following the curve of the rim. Tuck the lemon grass halves into the bouquet and add chillies to resemble flowers.

5 Stir the fish sauce, soy sauce and chopped coriander into the noodle mixture. Spoon on to the platter, taking care not to disturb the herb bouquet, and serve immediately.

Crispy Noodles Energy 1293kcal/5362kJ; Protein 28.8g; Carbohydrate 109.1g, of which sugars 5.2g; Fat 80.5g, of which saturates 10.6g; Cholesterol 509mg; Calcium 733mg; Fibre 0.4g; Sodium 1180mg.
Noodles with Chillies Energy 293kcal/1235kJ; Protein 8.9g; Carbohydrate 44.7g, of which sugars 17.3g; Fat 10g, of which saturates 2.1g; Cholesterol 11mg; Calcium 131mg; Fibre 4.2g; Sodium 1007mg.

Potato Skins with Cajun Dip

These crisp potato skins are served with a chilli dip.

Serves 2
2 large potatoes, baked
vegetable oil for deep-frying

120ml/4fl oz/½ natural
  (plain) yogurt
1 garlic clove, crushed
½ fresh green chilli, seeded
  and chopped
salt and ground black pepper

1 Cut the baked potatoes in half, scoop out the flesh, leaving a thin layer on the skins. Cut in half again. Mix together the yoghurt, garlic, chilli and salt and pepper in a small bowl.

2 Deep-fry the potato skins until crisp and golden. Drain and serve immediately with the yogurt and chilli dip.

Spicy Spanish Potatoes

There are many variations on this popular potato and chilli dish, but the most important thing is the spice mix, sharpened with vinegar.

Serves 4
675g/1½lb small new potatoes
75ml/5 tbsp olive oil
2 garlic cloves, sliced

3 dried red chillies, seeded
  and chopped
2.5ml/½ tsp ground cumin
10ml/2 tsp paprika
30ml/2 tbsp red or white
  wine vinegar
1 red or green (bell)
  pepper, sliced
coarse sea salt, for
  sprinkling (optional)

1 Scrub the potatoes and put them into a pan of salted water. Bring to the boil and cook for 10 minutes, or until almost tender. Drain and leave to cool slightly. Cut into chunks. Heat the oil in a large pan and fry the potatoes, turning, until golden.

2 Meanwhile, crush together the garlic, chillies and cumin using a mortar and pestle. Mix the paste with the paprika and wine vinegar, then add to the potatoes with the sliced pepper and cook, stirring, for 2 minutes. Sprinkle with salt, if using, and serve hot as a tapas dish or cold as a side dish.

Spicy Potato Wedges with Chilli Dip

For a healthy snack with a superb flavour, try these dry-roasted potato wedges. The crisp spice crust makes them taste irresistible, especially when they are served with a vibrant chilli dip.

Serves 2
2 baking potatoes, about 225g/
  8oz each
30ml/2 tbsp olive oil
2 garlic cloves, crushed
5ml/1 tsp ground allspice

5ml/1 tsp ground coriander
15ml/1 tbsp paprika
salt and ground black pepper

For the chilli dip
15ml/1 tbsp olive oil
1 small onion, finely chopped
1 garlic clove, crushed
200g/7oz can chopped tomatoes
1 fresh red chilli, seeded and
  finely chopped
15ml/1 tbsp balsamic vinegar
15ml/1 tbsp chopped fresh
  coriander (cilantro), plus extra
  to garnish

1 Preheat the oven to 200°C/400°F/Gas 6. Cut the potatoes in half, then cut each half lengthways into eight wedges.

2 Place the wedges in a pan of cold water. Bring to the boil, then lower the heat and simmer gently for 10 minutes or until the potatoes have softened slightly. Drain well and pat dry on kitchen paper.

3 Mix the oil, garlic, allspice, coriander and paprika in a roasting pan and add salt and pepper to taste. Add the potatoes to the pan and shake to coat them thoroughly in the spicy oil. Roast for 20 minutes, turning the potato wedges occasionally, or until they are browned, crisp and fully cooked.

4 Meanwhile, to make the chilli dip, heat the oil in a pan and add the onion and garlic. Cook over a medium heat for 5–10 minutes until softened. Add the tomatoes, with their juice. Stir in the chilli and vinegar.

5 Cook gently for 10 minutes until the mixture has reduced and thickened, then check the seasoning. Stir in the fresh coriander and serve hot, with the potato wedges, garnished with salt and fresh coriander.

Potato Skins with Dip Energy 211kcal/873kJ; Protein 2.7g; Carbohydrate 12.5g, of which sugars 3.3g; Fat 17g, of which saturates 2.2g; Cholesterol 0mg; Calcium 62mg; Fibre 0.7g; Sodium 35mg.
Spicy Spanish Potatoes Energy 273kcal/1148kJ; Protein 4.6g; Carbohydrate 39.5g, of which sugars 5.9g; Fat 11.9g, of which saturates 1.9g; Cholesterol 0mg; Calcium 22mg; Fibre 3.1g; Sodium 39mg.
Potato Wedges Energy 239kcal/1001kJ; Protein 4g; Carbohydrate 30.8g, of which sugars 4.9g; Fat 11.9g, of which saturates 1.9g; Cholesterol 0mg; Calcium 23mg; Fibre 2.6g; Sodium 28mg.

Aloo Saag

Traditional Indian spices – mustard seed, ginger and chilli – give a really good kick to potatoes and spinach in this delicious and authentic curry.

Serves 4

450g/1lb spinach
30ml/2 tbsp vegetable oil
5ml/1 tsp black mustard seeds
1 onion, thinly sliced
2 garlic cloves, crushed
2.5cm/1in piece root ginger, finely chopped
675g/1½lb firm potatoes, cut into 2.5cm/1in chunks
5ml/1 tsp chilli powder
5ml/1 tsp salt
120ml/4fl oz/½ cup water

1 Wash the spinach in several changes of water then blanch it in a little boiling water for 3–4 minutes.

2 Drain the spinach thoroughly and leave to cool. When it is cool enough to handle, use your hands to squeeze out any remaining liquid.

3 Heat the oil in a large pan and fry the mustard seeds for 2 minutes, stirring, until they begin to splutter.

4 Add the onion, garlic and ginger to the pan and fry for 5 minutes, stirring.

5 Stir in the potatoes, chilli powder, salt and water and cook for about 8 minutes, stirring occasionally.

6 Finally, add the spinach to the pan. Cover and simmer for 10–15 minutes until the spinach is very soft and the potatoes are tender. Serve hot.

Cook's Tip
To make certain that the spinach is dry before adding it to the potatoes, put it in a clean dish towel, roll up tightly and squeeze gently to remove any excess liquid. Choose a firm waxy variety of potato or a salad potato so the pieces do not break up during cooking.

Cumin and Fennel Spiced Potatoes

If you like chillies, you'll love these potatoes. However, if you're not a fan of very fiery flavours, simply leave out the chilli seeds, from both the dried and fresh chillies, and use the flesh by itself.

Serves 4

12–14 small new or salad potatoes, halved
30ml/2 tbsp vegetable oil
2.5ml/½ tsp dried red chillies, crushed
2.5ml/½ tsp white cumin seeds
2.5ml/½ tsp fennel seeds
2.5ml/½ tsp crushed coriander seeds
5ml/1 tsp salt
1 onion, sliced
1–4 fresh red chillies, chopped
15ml/1 tbsp chopped fresh coriander (cilantro), plus extra to garnish

1 Cook the potatoes in boiling salted water until tender but still firm. Remove from the heat and drain off the water. Set aside until needed.

2 In a deep frying pan, heat the oil over a medium-high heat, then reduce the heat to medium. Add the crushed chillies, cumin, fennel and coriander seeds and salt and fry, stirring, for 30–40 seconds.

3 Add the sliced onion and fry until softened and golden brown. Then add the potatoes, red chillies and chopped fresh coriander and stir well.

4 Reduce the heat to very low, then cover and cook for 5–7 minutes. Serve the potatoes hot, garnished with more fresh coriander.

Cook's Tips
• To prepare fresh chillies, trim the stalk end, slit down one side and scrape out the seeds, unless you want a really hot dish. Finely slice or chop the flesh.
• Wear rubber gloves if you have very sensitive skin and wash your hands thoroughly after handling chillies. Avoid touching your eyes if you have any trace of chilli on your fingers.

Aloo Saag Energy 201kcal/845kJ; Protein 6.2g; Carbohydrate 30.2g, of which sugars 4.7g; Fat 6.9g, of which saturates 0.9g; Cholesterol 0mg; Calcium 205mg; Fibre 4.3g; Sodium 668mg.
Cumin Potatoes Energy 260kcal/1091kJ; Protein 4.8g; Carbohydrate 35.2g, of which sugars 2.8g; Fat 12.1g, of which saturates 1.5g; Cholesterol 0mg; Calcium 39mg; Fibre 3.4g; Sodium 40mg.

Potatoes in Spicy Yogurt Sauce

Tiny potatoes cooked with their skins on are delicious in this fairly spicy yet tangy yogurt sauce. Serve with any vegetable dish or just with hot chapatis.

Serves 4

12 small new or salad
 potatoes, halved
275g/10oz/1¼ cups natural
 (plain) low-fat yogurt
300ml/½ pint/1¼ cups water

1.5ml/¼ tsp turmeric
5ml/1 tsp chilli powder
5ml/1 tsp ground coriander
2.5ml/½ tsp ground cumin
5ml/1 tsp salt
5ml/1 tsp soft brown sugar
30ml/2 tbsp vegetable oil
5ml/1 tsp white cumin seeds
15ml/1 tbsp chopped fresh
 coriander (cilantro)
2 fresh green chillies, sliced
1 coriander sprig, to
 garnish (optional)

1 Cook the potatoes in their skins in boiling salted water until just tender, then drain and set aside.

2 Mix together the yogurt, water, turmeric, chilli powder, ground coriander, ground cumin, salt and sugar in a bowl. Set aside.

3 Heat the oil in a medium pan over a medium-high heat and stir in the white cumin seeds.

4 Reduce the heat to medium, and stir in the prepared yogurt mixture. Cook the sauce, stirring continuously, for about 3 minutes.

5 Add the fresh coriander, green chillies and potatoes to the sauce. Mix well and cook for 5–7 minutes, stirring occasionally.

6 Transfer to a serving dish, garnish with the coriander sprig, if wished and serve hot.

Cook's Tip
If new or salad potatoes are unavailable, use 450g/1lb large potatoes instead, but choose a waxy not a floury variety. Peel them and cut into large chunks, then cook as described above.

Masala Mashed Potatoes

These well-spiced potatoes are delicious served alongside a vegetarian curry.

Serves 4

3 medium floury potatoes
15ml/1 tbsp mixed chopped fresh
 mint and coriander (cilantro)

5ml/1 tsp mango powder or
 mango chutney
5ml/1 tsp salt
5ml/1 tsp crushed black
 peppercorns
1 fresh red chilli, finely chopped
1 fresh green chilli, finely chopped
50g/2oz/4 tbsp butter, softened

1 Cook the potatoes in a large pan of lightly salted boiling water until tender. Drain thoroughly and mash them well with a potato masher.

2 Blend together the remaining ingredients in a small bowl. Reserve a little of the herb and chilli mixture for a garnish and stir the rest into the mashed potatoes, and mix together with a fork. Serve hot in a pile, with the remaining herb and chilli mixture on the top.

Garlic Mashed Potatoes

This wonderful creamy mash is ideal with fried fish.

Serves 6–8

3 whole garlic bulbs, separated
 into cloves, unpeeled

115g/4oz/8 tbsp butter
1.3kg/3llb floury potatoes, boiled
 until soft and drained
175ml/6fl oz/½ cup milk
salt and black pepper

1 Preheat the oven to 190°C/375°F/Gas 5. Blanch two-thirds of the garlic cloves in a pan of water for 2 minutes. Drain and then peel. Place the remaining cloves in a roasting pan and bake in the oven for 30–40 minutes. Gently fry the blanched garlic cloves in half the butter until golden and tender.

2 Warm the milk in a pan with the remaining butter. Put all the garlic into a food processor, purée, add the potatoes and milk and process until smooth. Reheat gently before serving.

Potatoes in Yogurt Sauce Energy 161kcal/677kJ; Protein 5.9g; Carbohydrate 24.7g, of which sugars 7g; Fat 5.1g, of which saturates 1g; Cholesterol 1mg; Calcium 154mg; Fibre 1.1g; Sodium 73mg.
Masala Potatoes Energy 219kcal/919kJ; Protein 3.1g; Carbohydrate 28.9g, of which sugars 3g; Fat 10.9g, of which saturates 6.7g; Cholesterol 27mg; Calcium 13mg; Fibre 1.8g; Sodium 600mg.
Garlic Potatoes Energy 261kcal/1093kJ; Protein 5g; Carbohydrate 33.3g, of which sugars 3.8g; Fat 12.8g, of which saturates 7.9g; Cholesterol 32mg; Calcium 43mg; Fibre 2.4g; Sodium 118mg.

Bombay Potatoes

This is a classic Indian vegetarian dish of potatoes slowly cooked in a richly flavoured curry sauce, with fresh chillies for an added kick. It is one of the most popular side dishes in Indian cuisine.

Serves 4–6

450g/1lb new or small salad potatoes
5ml/1 tsp turmeric
60ml/4 tbsp vegetable oil
2 dried red chillies
6–8 curry leaves
2 onions, finely chopped
2 fresh green chillies, finely chopped
50g/2oz coriander leaves, coarsely chopped
1.5ml/¼ tsp asafoetida
2.5ml/½ tsp each cumin, mustard, onion, fennel and nigella seeds
lemon juice
salt
fresh fried curry leaves, to garnish

1 Chop the potatoes into small chunks and cook in boiling lightly salted water with ½ tsp of the turmeric until tender. Drain, then coarsely mash. Set aside.

2 Heat the oil in a large heavy pan and fry the red chillies and curry leaves until the chillies are nearly burnt.

3 Add the onions, green chillies, coriander, remaining turmeric, asafoetida and spice seeds and cook until the onions are tender.

4 Fold in the potatoes and add a few drops of water. Cook on a low heat for about 10 minutes, mixing well to ensure the even distribution of the spices. Remove the dried chillies and curry leaves.

5 Serve the potatoes hot, with lemon juice squeezed or poured over, and garnish with the fresh fried curry leaves.

Cook's Tip
Asafoetida is the ground dried sap of a plant native to Iran. It is very pungent raw, but when cooked it becomes much milder and develops an onion-like aroma with a hint of truffle.

Sweet Potatoes with Ginger

Fried sweet potatoes acquire a candied coating when cooked with ginger, syrup and allspice. The addition of cayenne pepper, which is hot and rather pungent, cuts through the sweetness of the vegetable and prevents the dish from becoming cloying.

Serves 4

900g/2lb sweet potatoes
50g/2oz/¼ cup butter
45ml/3 tbsp vegetable oil
2 garlic cloves, crushed
2 pieces preserved stem ginger, drained and finely chopped
10ml/2 tsp ground allspice
15ml/1 tbsp syrup from the preserved ginger jar
salt and cayenne pepper
10ml/2 tsp chopped fresh thyme, plus a few thyme sprigs, to garnish

1 Peel the sweet potatoes and cut them into 1cm/½in cubes. Melt the butter with the oil in a large frying pan. Add the sweet potato cubes and fry, stirring frequently, for about 10 minutes, until they are just soft.

2 Stir in the garlic, chopped ginger and allspice. Cook, stirring constantly, for 5 minutes more. Stir in the ginger syrup. Season with salt and a generous pinch of cayenne pepper and add the chopped thyme. Stir for 1–2 minutes more, then serve, sprinkled with thyme sprigs.

Variation
For a less sweet, unglazed version of this dish, use a 2.5cm/1in piece of fresh ginger, finely chopped, instead of the preserved ginger and omit the syrup.

Cook's Tip
Some sweet potatoes have white flesh and some have yellow. Although they taste similar, the yellow-fleshed variety look particularly colourful and attractive.

Bombay Potatoes Energy 143kcal/595kJ; Protein 2.1g; Carbohydrate 17.4g, of which sugars 4.7g; Fat 7.7g, of which saturates 0.9g; Cholesterol 0mg; Calcium 21mg; Fibre 1.7g; Sodium 10mg.
Sweet Potatoes with Ginger Energy 375kcal/1576kJ; Protein 3.8g; Carbohydrate 50.1g, of which sugars 13.1g; Fat 19.3g, of which saturates 7.7g; Cholesterol 27mg; Calcium 59mg; Fibre 5.9g; Sodium 166mg.

Roasted Root Vegetables with Whole Spice Seeds

These spiced vegetables can be roasted alongside a vegetarian bake. They will virtually look after themselves and make a delicious side dish.

Serves 4
3 parsnips, peeled
3 potatoes, peeled
3 carrots, peeled

3 sweet potatoes, peeled
60ml/4 tbsp olive oil
8 shallots, peeled
2 garlic cloves, sliced
10ml/2 tsp white mustard seeds
10ml/2 tsp coriander seeds,
  lightly crushed
5ml/1 tsp cumin seeds
2 bay leaves
salt and ground black pepper

1 Preheat the oven to 190°C/375°F/Gas 5. Bring a saucepan of lightly salted water to the boil. Cut the parsnips, potatoes, carrots and sweet potatoes into chunks. Add them to the pan and bring the water back to the boil. Boil for 2 minutes, then drain the vegetables thoroughly.

2 Pour the olive oil into a large, heavy roasting pan and place over a moderate heat. When the oil is hot add the drained vegetables together with the whole shallots and garlic. Fry, tossing the vegetables over the heat, until they are pale golden at the edges.

3 Add the mustard, coriander and cumin seeds and the bay leaves. Cook for 1 minute, then season with salt and pepper.

4 Transfer the roasting pan to the oven and roast for about 45 minutes, turning the vegetables occasionally, until they are crisp and golden and cooked through.

> **Variation**
> Vary the selection of vegetables according to what is available. Try using swede (rutabaga) or pumpkin instead of, or as well as, the vegetables suggested.

Split Pea and Shallot Mash

This is a greatly underrated dish. Split peas are delicious when puréed with shallots and enlivened with cumin seeds and fresh herbs. The purée makes an excellent alternative to mashed potatoes, and is particularly good when served with winter pies and nut roasts. It can also be served with toast, naan bread or warmed pitta bread, accompanied by diced tomatoes and a splash of olive oil.

Serves 4–6
225g/8oz/1 cup yellow split peas
1 bay leaf
8 sage leaves, roughly chopped
15ml/1 tbsp olive oil
3 shallots, finely chopped
8ml/heaped 1 tsp cumin seeds
1 large garlic clove, chopped
50g/2oz/4 tbsp butter, softened
salt and ground black pepper

1 Put the split peas in a bowl and cover with cold water. Leave to soak overnight, then rinse and drain.

2 Transfer the peas to a pan, cover with fresh cold water and bring to the boil. Skim off any foam that rises to the surface, then reduce the heat. Add the bay leaf and sage, and simmer for 30–40 minutes until the peas are tender. Add more water during cooking, if necessary.

3 Meanwhile, heat the oil in a frying pan, and cook the shallots with the cumin seeds and garlic for 3 minutes or until the shallots soften, stirring occasionally. Add the mixture to the split peas while they are still cooking.

4 Drain the split peas, reserving the cooking water. Remove the bay leaf, then put the split peas in a food processor or blender with the butter and season well.

5 Add 105ml/7 tbsp of the reserved cooking water and blend until the mixture forms a coarse purée. Add more water if the purée seems to be too dry. Adjust the seasoning and serve warm with your choice of bread.

Roasted Vegetables Energy 290kcal/1213kJ; Protein 11.5g; Carbohydrate 32.5g, of which sugars 13.3g; Fat 13.6g, of which saturates 1.6g; Cholesterol 0mg; Calcium 175mg; Fibre 9.1g; Sodium 271mg.
Split Pea Mash Energy 156kcal/658kJ; Protein 9.1g; Carbohydrate 21.9g, of which sugars 1.5g; Fat 4.2g, of which saturates 0.6g; Cholesterol 0mg; Calcium 22mg; Fibre 2g; Sodium 14mg.

Sweet and Sour Rice

This popular Middle Eastern rice dish is flavoured with fruit and spices. Zereshk are small dried berries – use cranberries as a substitute.

Serves 4
50g/2oz/½ cup zereshk or
    fresh cranberries
45g/1½oz/3 tbsp butter
50g/2oz/⅓ cup raisins
50g/2oz/1¼ cup sugar
5ml/1 tsp ground cinnamon
5ml/1 tsp ground cumin
350g/12oz/1¾ cups basmati
    rice, soaked
2–3 saffron strands, soaked in
    15ml/1 tbsp boiling water
pinch of salt

1 Thoroughly wash the zereshk in cold water at least four or five times to rinse off any bits of grit. Drain well. Melt 15g/½oz/1 tbsp of the butter in a frying pan and fry the raisins for 1–2 minutes.

2 Add the zereshk, fry for a few seconds, and then add the sugar, with half of the cinnamon and cumin. Cook briefly and then set aside.

3 Drain the rice, then put it in a pan with plenty of boiling, lightly salted water. Bring back to the boil, reduce the heat and simmer for 4 minutes. Drain and rinse once again.

4 Melt half the remaining butter in the cleaned pan, add 15ml/1 tbsp water and stir in half the rice. Sprinkle with half the raisin and zereshk mixture and top with all but 45ml/3 tbsp of the rice. Sprinkle over the remaining raisin and zereshk mixture.

5 Mix the remaining cinnamon and cumin with the reserved rice, and sprinkle this mixture evenly over the layered mixture. Melt the remaining butter, drizzle it over the surface, then cover the pan with a clean dish towel. Cover with a tight-fitting lid, lifting the corners of the cloth back over the lid. Steam the rice over a very low heat for 20–30 minutes.

6 Just before serving, mix 45ml/3 tbsp of the rice with the saffron water. Spoon the sweet and sour rice on to a large, flat serving dish and sprinkle the saffron rice over the top, to garnish.

Garlic and Ginger Rice with Coriander

In Vietnam and Cambodia, when rice is served as a side dish it may be either plain or fragrant with the flavours of ginger and herbs. The combination of garlic and ginger is popular in both countries and complements almost any vegetable dish.

Serves 4–6
15ml/1 tbsp vegetable or
    groundnut (peanut) oil
2–3 garlic cloves, finely chopped
25g/1oz fresh root ginger,
    finely chopped
225g/8oz/generous 1 cup long
    grain rice, rinsed in several
    changes of water and drained
900ml/1½ pints/3¾ cups
    vegetable stock
bunch of fresh coriander
    (cilantro), stalks removed, leaves
    finely chopped
bunch of fresh basil and mint,
    stalks removed, leaves finely
    chopped (optional)

1 Heat the oil in a clay pot or heavy pan. Stir in the garlic and ginger and fry until golden. Stir in the rice and allow it to absorb the flavours for 1–2 minutes. Pour in the stock and stir to make sure the rice doesn't stick. Bring the stock to the boil, then reduce the heat.

2 Sprinkle the coriander, and other herbs if using, over the surface of the stock, cover the pan, and leave to cook gently for 20–25 minutes, until the rice has absorbed all the liquid. Turn off the heat and gently fluff up the rice to mix in the herbs. Cover and leave to infuse for 10 minutes before serving.

Variations
Rice cooked this way can be spiced up with many different combinations of flavourings. Take inspiration from the dish you are serving with the rice, and add warm Indian spices such as turmeric and cinnamon, or cardamom and cloves, or add Thai flavours with lemon grass and kaffir lime leaves. Simply adding a couple of cardamom pods will give rice a lovely mild fragrance, and stirring in fresh herbs adds colour and flavour.

Sweet and Sour Rice Energy 465kcal/1943kJ; Protein 7g; Carbohydrate 87g, of which sugars 17.2g; Fat 9.8g, of which saturates 5.9g; Cholesterol 24mg; Calcium 32mg; Fibre 0.6g; Sodium 77mg.
Garlic and Ginger Rice Energy 151Kcal/632kJ; Protein 3g; Carbohydrate 30g, of which sugars 0g; Fat 2g, of which saturates 0.3g; Cholesterol 0mg; Calcium 9mg; Fibre 0.1g; Sodium 124mg.

Persian Rice with Fried Onions

Persian cuisine is delicious, with intense flavours. This dish forms a lovely crust at the bottom of the pan.

Serves 6–8

450g/1lb/2⅓ cups basmati rice, soaked and drained
150ml/¼ pint/⅔ cup sunflower oil
2 garlic cloves, crushed
2 onions, 1 chopped, 1 sliced
150g/5oz/⅔ cup green lentils, soaked
600ml/1 pint/2½ cups stock
50g/2oz/⅓ cup raisins
10ml/2 tsp ground coriander
45ml/3 tbsp tomato purée (paste)
1 egg yolk, beaten
10ml/2 tsp natural (plain) yogurt
75g/3oz/6 tbsp melted butter
a few saffron strands, soaked in a little hot water
salt and ground black pepper

1 Cook the rice for 10–12 minutes. Drain. Heat 30ml/2 tbsp of the oil and fry the garlic and onion for 5 minutes. Stir in the lentils, stock, raisins, coriander and tomato purée. Bring to the boil, lower the heat, cover and simmer for 20 minutes.

2 Mix the egg yolk and yogurt in a bowl. Spoon in about 120ml/4 fl oz/½ cup of the cooked rice and mix. Season. Heat two-thirds of the remaining oil in a pan and sprinkle the egg mixture over the bottom.

3 Place a layer of rice in the pan, then a layer of lentils. Build up the layers in a pyramid shape away from the sides. Finish with a layer of plain rice. Make three holes down to the bottom of the pan; drizzle over the melted butter. Bring to a high heat, then wrap the pan lid in a wet dish towel and place on top. When the rice is steaming, lower the heat and cook for 30 minutes.

4 Fry the onion slices in the remaining oil until browned and crisp. Drain. Remove the rice pan from the heat, and dip the base into cold water to loosen the crust.

5 Strain the saffron water into a bowl and stir in a few spoons of cooked rice. Toss the rice and lentils together in the pan and spoon on to a serving dish. Sprinkle the saffron rice on top. Break up the crust and place around the mound. Top with the onions and serve.

Sour Cherry and Caraway Pilaff

Turkey is famous for its succulent cherries, and this is a popular summer pilaff, made with small, sour cherries rather than the plump, sweet ones. With its refreshing fruity bursts of intense cherry flavour, it is a good accompaniment to many vegetable dishes.

Serves 3–4

30ml/2 tbsp butter
225g/8oz fresh sour cherries, such as morello, pitted
5–10ml/1–2 tsp sugar
5ml/1 tsp caraway seeds
225g/8oz/generous 1 cup long grain rice, well rinsed and drained
salt and ground black pepper

1 Melt the butter in a heavy pan. Set a handful of the cherries aside to garnish the finished dish, and toss the rest in the butter with the sugar and caraway seeds. Cook for a few minutes.

2 Add the rice and 600ml/1 pint/2½ cups water and season with salt and pepper. Bring to the boil, lower the heat and partially cover the pan. Simmer for 10–12 minutes, until most of the water has been absorbed.

3 Turn off the heat, cover the pan with a clean dish towel and put the lid tightly on top. Leave for 20 minutes.

4 Fluff up the rice with a fork, tip on to a serving dish and garnish with the reserved cherries.

Variation
Use dried cranberries as a sweeter alternative to the sour cherries in this dish.

Cook's Tip
Due to their acidity, sour cherries are usually consumed cooked. They are delicious in savoury dishes like this one, but can also be poached with sugar and used in sorbets, jam, cakes or tangy compôtes to spoon over rice or yogurt.

Persian Rice Energy 398kcal/1658kJ; Protein 6.5g; Carbohydrate 69.9g, of which sugars 0.1g; Fat 9.7g, of which saturates 5.9g; Cholesterol 24mg; Calcium 19mg; Fibre 0g; Sodium 559mg.
Cherry Pilaff Energy 295kcal/1231kJ; Protein 4.7g; Carbohydrate 54g, of which sugars 9.1g; Fat 6.5g, of which saturates 3.9g; Cholesterol 16mg; Calcium 21mg; Fibre 0.5g; Sodium 46mg.

Brown Rice with Lime, Spices and Lemon Grass

It is unusual to find brown rice used in a Thai recipe, but the nutty flavour of the grains is enhanced by the fragrance of limes and lemon grass in this delicious dish.

Serves 4

2 limes
1 lemon grass stalk
225g/8oz/generous 1 cup brown long grain rice
15ml/1 tbsp olive oil
1 onion, chopped
2.5cm/1in piece fresh root ginger, peeled and finely chopped
7.5ml/1½ tsp coriander seeds
7.5ml/1½ tsp cumin seeds
750ml/1¼ pints/3 cups vegetable stock
60ml/4 tbsp chopped fresh coriander (cilantro)
spring onions (scallions) and toasted coconut strips, to garnish
lime wedges, to serve

1 Pare the limes, using a cannelle knife (zester) or fine grater, taking care to avoid cutting into the bitter white pith. Set the rind aside. Finely chop the lower portion of the lemon grass stalk and set it aside.

2 Rinse the rice in plenty of cold water until the water runs clear. Tip it into a sieve (strainer) and drain thoroughly.

3 Heat the oil in a large pan. Add the onion, ginger, coriander and cumin seeds, lemon grass and lime rind and cook over a low heat for 2–3 minutes.

4 Add the rice to the pan and cook, stirring constantly, for 1 minute, then pour in the stock and bring to the boil. Reduce the heat to very low and cover the pan. Cook gently for 30 minutes, then check the rice. If it is still crunchy, cover the pan and cook for 3–5 minutes more until the rice is tender. Remove from the heat.

5 Stir in the fresh coriander, fluff up the rice grains with a fork, cover the pan and leave to stand for 10 minutes. Transfer to a warmed dish, garnish with the green part of spring onions and toasted coconut strips, and serve with lime wedges.

Rice with Cinnamon and Star Anise

Originating from China, this thick rice porridge or "congee", known as *bubur* in Malaysia and Indonesia, has become popular all over South-east Asia. The basic recipe is nourishing but rather bland, and the joy of the dish is derived from the ingredients that are added.

Serves 4–6

25g/1oz fresh root ginger, peeled and sliced
1 cinnamon stick
2 star anise
2.5ml/½ tsp salt
115g/4oz/½ cup short grain rice, thoroughly washed and drained

1 Bring 1.2 litres/2 pints/5 cups water to the boil in a heavy pan. Stir in the spices, the salt and the rice.

2 Reduce the heat, cover the pan, and simmer gently for 1 hour, or longer if you prefer a thicker, smoother consistency. Serve piping hot.

Variations
The Teochew version of bubur is called muay. *With its addition of pickles, strips of omelette and braised dishes, it is popular for supper in Singapore. In Malaysia, bubur is enjoyed as a breakfast dish accompanied by pickles. Often flavoured with ginger, cinnamon and star anise, it is usually cooked until it is thick but the grains are still visible, whereas some of the Chinese versions are cooked for longer, so that the rice breaks down completely and the texture is quite smooth and slightly sticky. The consistency varies from family to family: some people like it soupy and eat it with a spoon.*

Cook's Tip
This dish is often eaten for breakfast, in Malaysia, and some domestic rice cookers have a "congee" setting, which allows the dish to be prepared the night before and slowly cooked overnight, in order to be ready in the morning.

Rice with Spices Energy 235kcal/996kJ; Protein 4.3g; Carbohydrate 47.3g, of which sugars 1.9g; Fat 4.5g, of which saturates 0.8g; Cholesterol 0mg; Calcium 35mg; Fibre 1.9g; Sodium 6mg.
Rice with Cinnamon Energy 69Kcal/288kJ; Protein 1.4g; Carbohydrate 15.3g, of which sugars 0g; Fat 0.1g, of which saturates 0g; Cholesterol 0mg; Calcium 4mg; Fibre 0g; Sodium 164mg.

Aromatic Indian Rice with Peas

This fragrant, versatile rice dish is often served as part of an elaborate meal at Indian festivals and celebratory feasts, which might include several vegetable curries, a yogurt dish, and chutneys. Ground turmeric or grated carrot is sometimes added for an extra splash of colour. Sprinkle the pilaff with chopped fresh mint and coriander (cilantro), if you like, or with roasted chilli and coconut.

Serves 4

350g/12oz/1¾ cups basmati rice
45ml/3 tbsp ghee or 30ml/2 tbsp
  vegetable oil and a small
  amount of butter
1 cinnamon stick
6–8 cardamom pods, crushed
4 cloves
1 onion, halved lengthways and
  sliced
25g/1oz fresh root ginger, peeled
  and grated
5ml/1 tsp sugar
130g/4½oz fresh peas, shelled, or
  frozen peas
5ml/1 tsp salt

1 Rinse the rice and put it in a bowl. Cover with plenty of water and leave to soak for 30 minutes. Drain thoroughly.

2 Heat the ghee, or oil and butter, in a heavy pan. Stir in the cinnamon stick, cardamom and cloves. Add the onion, ginger and sugar, and fry until golden. Add the peas, followed by the rice, and stir for 1 minute to coat the rice in ghee.

3 Pour in 600ml/1 pint/2½ cups water. Add the salt, stir once and bring the liquid to the boil. Reduce the heat and allow to simmer for 15–20 minutes, until the liquid has been absorbed.

4 Turn off the heat, cover the pan with a clean dish towel and the lid, and leave the rice to steam for a further 10 minutes. Spoon the rice on to a serving dish.

Variation
This Indian pilaff also works with diced carrot or beetroot (beet), or chickpeas. Instead of turmeric, you can add a little tomato paste to give the rice a red tinge.

Malay Yellow Rice

Coloured yellow by vibrant turmeric powder, this is a delicately flavoured rice often served at Malay festivals. It is also one of the popular dishes at the Malay *nasi campur* and Indonesian *nasi padang* stalls, where it is often served with other vegetable dishes. This simple rice dish is cooked in the same way as plain steamed rice, using the absorption method, to produce fluffy, tender grains.

Serves 4

30ml/2 tbsp vegetable or
  sesame oil
3 shallots, finely chopped
2 garlic cloves, peeled and
  finely chopped
450g/1lb/generous 2 cups long
  grain rice, thoroughly washed
  and drained
400ml/14fl oz/1⅔ cups
  coconut milk
10ml/2 tsp ground turmeric
4 fresh curry leaves
2.5ml/½ tsp salt
ground black pepper
2 red chillies, seeded and finely
  sliced, to garnish

1 Heat the oil in a heavy pan and stir in the shallots and garlic. Just as they begin to colour, stir in the rice until the grains are coated in the oil.

2 Add the coconut milk, 450ml/¾ pint/scant 2 cups water, turmeric, curry leaves, salt and pepper.

3 Bring to the boil, then turn down the heat and cover. Cook the rice and spice mixture gently for 15–20 minutes, until all the liquid has been absorbed.

4 Turn off the heat and leave the rice to steam in the pan for 10 minutes. Fluff up the rice with a fork and serve garnished with red chillies.

Cook's Tip
Regular long grain rice, or other types such as jasmine rice, short grain or sticky rice, would all work equally well in this simple but tasty recipe.

Yellow Rice Energy 481Kcal/2011kJ; Protein 8.8g; Carbohydrate 95.9g, of which sugars 5.8g; Fat 6.4g, of which saturates 0.9g; Cholesterol 0mg; Calcium 54mg; Fibre 0.2g; Sodium 356mg.
Indian Rice Energy 451Kcal/1880kJ; Protein 8.9g; Carbohydrate 75.7g, of which sugars 2.6g; Fat 12.2g, of which saturates 5.4g; Cholesterol 0mg; Calcium 28mg; Fibre 1.8g; Sodium 328mg.

Braised Baby Leeks in Red Wine

Coriander seeds and oregano lend a Greek flavour to this dish of braised leeks. Serve it as part of a mixed hors d'oeuvre or with other vegetable dishes for a buffet.

Serves 6
12 baby leeks or 6 thick leeks
15ml/1 tbsp coriander seeds, lightly crushed
5cm/2in cinnamon stick
120ml/4fl oz/½ cup olive oil
3 fresh bay leaves
2 strips pared orange rind
5–6 fresh or dried oregano sprigs
5ml/1 tsp sugar
150ml/¼ pint/⅔ cup fruity red wine
10ml/2 tsp balsamic or sherry vinegar
30ml/2 tbsp coarsely chopped fresh oregano or marjoram
salt and ground black pepper

1 Wash and trim the leeks. Leave baby leeks whole, but if you are using large, thicker ones cut them into 5–7.5cm/ 2–3in lengths.

2 Place the coriander seeds and cinnamon stick in a pan wide enough to take all the leeks in a single layer. Dry-fry the whole spices over a medium heat for 2–3 minutes, until they are fragrant, then stir in the oil, bay leaves, orange rind, oregano, sugar, wine and vinegar. Bring the mixture to the boil and simmer for 5 minutes.

3 Add the leeks. Bring back to the boil, reduce the heat and cover the pan. Cook gently for 5 minutes. Uncover and simmer gently for another 5–8 minutes, until the leeks are just tender when tested with the tip of a sharp knife.

4 Use a draining spoon to transfer the leeks to a serving dish. Boil the juices rapidly until reduced to about 75–90ml/5–6 tbsp. Add salt and pepper to taste and pour the liquid over the leeks. Leave to cool.

5 The leeks can be left to stand for several hours. If you chill them, bring them back to room temperature again before serving. Sprinkle chopped oregano or marjoram over the leeks just before serving them.

Spiced Pumpkin Wedges with Spinach

Warmly spiced roasted pumpkin, combined with creamy spinach and the fire of chilli, makes a lovely accompaniment for other vegetarian dishes.

Serves 4–6
10ml/2 tsp coriander seeds
5ml/1 tsp cumin seeds
5ml/1 tsp fennel seeds
5–10ml/1–2 tsp cinnamon
2 dried red chillies, chopped
coarse salt
2 garlic cloves
30ml/2 tbsp olive oil
1 medium pumpkin, halved, seeded, cut into 6–8 wedges

For the sautéed spinach
30–45ml/2–3 tbsp pine nuts
30–45ml/2–3 tbsp olive oil
1 red onion, halved and sliced
1–2 dried red chillies, finely sliced
1 apple, peeled, cored and sliced
2 garlic cloves, crushed
5–10ml/1–2 tsp ground roasted cumin
10ml/2 tsp clear honey
450g/1lb spinach, steamed and roughly chopped
60–75ml/4–5 tbsp double (heavy) cream
salt and ground black pepper
a handful of fresh coriander (cilantro) leaves, chopped, to garnish

1 Preheat the oven to 200°C/400°F/Gas 6. Grind the coriander, cumin and fennel seeds, cinnamon and chillies with a little coarse salt in a mortar with a pestle. Add the garlic and a little of the olive oil and pound the mixtue until it forms a paste. Rub the spice mixture over the pumpkin segments and place them, skin-side down, in an ovenproof dish or roasting pan. Bake the spiced pumpkin for 35–40 minutes, or until tender.

2 To make the sautéed spinach, roast the pine nuts in a dry frying pan until golden, then tip on to a plate. Add the olive oil to the pan. Sauté the onion with the chilli until soft, then add the apple and garlic. Once the apple begins to colour, stir in most of the pine nuts, most of the ground roasted cumin and the honey.

3 Toss in the spinach and, once it has heated through, stir in most of the cream. Season to taste and remove from the heat. Swirl the last of the cream on top, sprinkle with the reserved pine nuts and roasted cumin, and a little coriander. Serve.

Braised Leeks Energy 151kcal/621kJ; Protein 1.1g; Carbohydrate 1.7g, of which sugars 1.3g; Fat 13.7g, of which saturates 2g; Cholesterol 0mg; Calcium 29mg; Fibre 1.5g; Sodium 5mg.
Spiced Pumpkin Energy 456kcal/1897kJ; Protein 18.9g; Carbohydrate 22.1g, of which sugars 17.1g; Fat 31.9g, of which saturates 13.2g; Cholesterol 45mg; Calcium 635mg; Fibre 10g; Sodium 337mg.

Southern Thai Curried Vegetables

Rich curry flavours are found in the food of southern Thailand, where many dishes are made with coconut milk and spiced with turmeric.

Serves 4
90g/3¹/₂oz Chinese leaves (Chinese cabbage), shredded
90g/3¹/₂oz/generous 1 cup beansprouts
90g/3¹/₂oz/scant 1 cup green beans, trimmed
100g/3¹/₂oz broccoli florets
15ml/1 tbsp sesame seeds, toasted

For the sauce
60ml/4 tbsp coconut cream (see Cook's Tip)
5ml/1 tsp Thai red curry paste
90g/3¹/₂oz/1¹/₄ cups oyster mushrooms or field (portobello) mushrooms, sliced
60ml/4 tbsp coconut milk
5ml/1 tsp ground turmeric
5ml/1 tsp thick tamarind juice, made by mixing tamarind paste with a little warm water
juice of ¹/₂ lemon
60ml/4 tbsp light soy sauce
5ml/1 tsp palm sugar (jaggery) or light muscovado (brown) sugar

1 Blanch the shredded Chinese leaves, beansprouts, green beans and broccoli in boiling water for 1 minute per batch. Drain, place in a bowl and leave to cool.

2 To make the sauce, pour the coconut cream into a wok or frying pan and heat gently for 2–3 minutes, until it separates. Stir in the red curry paste. Cook over a low heat for 30 seconds. Increase the heat, add the mushrooms and cook for a further 2–3 minutes. Pour in the coconut milk and stir in the turmeric, tamarind juice, lemon juice, soy sauce and sugar.

3 Pour the mixture over the prepared vegetables and toss well to combine. Sprinkle with the toasted sesame seeds and serve.

Cook's Tips
To make coconut cream use a carton or can of coconut milk. Skim the cream off the top and cook 60ml/4 tbsp of it before adding the curry paste. Add the measured coconut milk later, as described in the recipe.

Malay Pak Choi in Coconut Milk

Among the rich and varied food traditions of Melaka, Penang and Singapore, the cooking that evolved among early immigrants from China is a unique blend of Chinese, Malay and Portuguese influences. The style is sweet and rich with the addition of sugar and myriad flavours, and Malaysia's abundant vegetables are often cooked in coconut milk. For this dish, you could use green beans, curly kale, or any type of cabbage, all of which are delicious served with steamed vegetables or other vegetable dishes.

Serves 4
4 shallots, chopped
2 garlic cloves, peeled and finely chopped
1 lemon grass stalk, trimmed and chopped
25g/1oz fresh root ginger, peeled and chopped
2 red chillies, seeded and chopped
5ml/1 tsp soy sauce
5ml/1 tsp ground turmeric
5ml/1 tsp palm sugar (jaggery)
15ml/1 tbsp sesame or groundnut (peanut) oil
400ml/14fl oz/1²/₃ cups coconut milk
450g/1lb pak choi (bok choy), separated into leaves
salt and ground black pepper

1 Using a mortar and pestle or food processor, grind the shallots, garlic, lemon grass, ginger and chillies to a paste. Add the soy sauce, turmeric and sugar.

2 Heat the oil in a wok or heavy pan, and stir in the spice paste mixture. Cook until it is fragrant and beginning to colour. Pour in the coconut milk, mix well, and increase the heat to bubble it up until it thickens. Drop in the cabbage leaves, coating them in the coconut milk, and cook for a minute or two until they are wilted. Season to taste and serve immediately.

Variation
Make the dish using Chinese leaves (Chinese cabbage) or kale, cut into thick ribbons, or a mixture of the two.

Thai Curried Vegetables Energy 162kcal/672kJ; Protein 5g; Carbohydrate 6.3g, of which sugars 5.4g; Fat 13.2g, of which saturates 9.4g; Cholesterol 0mg; Calcium 75mg; Fibre 2.5g; Sodium 1096mg.
Pak Choi in Coconut Milk Energy 112Kcal/469kJ; Protein 2.1g; Carbohydrate 13g, of which sugars 12.6g; Fat 6.1g, of which saturates 1g; Cholesterol 0mg; Calcium 89mg; Fibre 2.6g; Sodium 119mg.

Spicy Chickpeas with Spinach

This richly flavoured dish makes a great main meal for vegetarians, but it will be equally popular with meat-eaters. It is particularly good served drizzled with a little lightly beaten natural yogurt – the sharp, creamy flavour complements the complex spices perfectly.

Serves 4
200g/7oz dried chickpeas
30ml/2 tbsp sunflower oil
2 onions, halved and thinly sliced
  along the grain
10ml/2 tsp ground coriander
10ml/2 tsp ground cumin
5ml/1 tsp hot chilli powder
2.5ml/½ tsp turmeric
15ml/1 tbsp medium
  curry powder
400g/14oz can chopped
  tomatoes
5ml/1 tsp caster (superfine) sugar
30ml/2 tbsp chopped fresh
  mint leaves
115g/4oz baby leaf spinach
salt and ground black pepper
plain steamed rice or bread and
  natural (plain) yogurt, to serve

1 Soak the chickpeas in cold water overnight. Drain, rinse and place in a large pan. Cover with water and bring to the boil. Reduce the heat and simmer for 45 minutes, or until just tender. Drain and set aside.

2 Heat the oil in a wok or large frying pan, add the sliced onions and cook over a low heat for 15 minutes, stirring occasionally, until soft and lightly golden.

3 Add the ground coriander and cumin, chilli powder, turmeric and curry powder and stir-fry for 1–2 minutes.

4 Add the tomatoes, sugar and 105ml/7 tbsp water to the wok and bring to the boil. Cover, reduce the heat and simmer gently for 15 minutes.

5 Add the chickpeas to the wok, season well and cook gently for 8–10 minutes. Stir in the chopped mint.

6 Divide the spinach leaves between shallow bowls, top with the chickpea mixture and serve with some steamed rice or bread and natural yogurt.

Stir-fried Spinach with Garlic

There are endless versions of traditional spinach and yogurt *meze* dishes in Turkish cookery, ranging from plain steamed spinach served with yogurt, to this sweet and tangy creation, which is tempered with garlic-flavoured yogurt. Serve warm, with flatbread or chunks of a crusty loaf to accompany it.

Serves 3–4
350g/12oz fresh spinach leaves,
  thoroughly washed and drained
about 200g/7oz/scant 1 cup thick
  natural (plain) yogurt
2 garlic cloves, crushed
30–45ml/2–3 tbsp olive oil
1 red onion, cut in half
  lengthways, in half again
  crossways, and sliced along
  the grain
5ml/1 tsp sugar
15–30ml/1–2 tbsp currants,
  soaked in warm water for
  5–10 minutes and drained
30ml/2 tbsp pine nuts
5–10ml/1–2 tsp hot paprika, or
  1 fresh red chilli, seeded and
  finely chopped
juice of 1 lemon
salt and ground black pepper
a pinch of paprika, to garnish

1 Steam the spinach for 3–4 minutes, until wilted and soft. Drain off any excess water and chop the spinach.

2 In a bowl, beat the yogurt with the garlic. Season to taste and set aside.

3 Heat the oil in a heavy pan and fry the onion and sugar, stirring constantly to prevent the sugar burning, until the onion begins to colour. Add the currants, pine nuts and paprika or chilli and fry until the nuts begin to colour.

4 Add the spinach, tossing it around the pan until well mixed with the other ingredients, then pour in the lemon juice and season with salt and pepper.

5 Serve the spinach straight from the pan with the yogurt spooned on top, or tip into a serving dish and make a well in the middle, then spoon the yogurt into the well, drizzling some of it over the spinach. Serve hot, sprinkled with a little paprika.

Spicy Chickpeas Energy 267kcal/1122kJ; Protein 13.3g; Carbohydrate 35.5g, of which sugars 10.2g; Fat 9g, of which saturates 1.1g; Cholesterol 0mg; Calcium 170mg; Fibre 8.2g; Sodium 83mg.
Spinach with Garlic Energy 145kcal/603kJ; Protein 5.8g; Carbohydrate 10.2g, of which sugars 9.8g; Fat 9.3g, of which saturates 1.3g; Cholesterol 1mg; Calcium 252mg; Fibre 2.2g; Sodium 165mg.

Grilled Polenta with Chilli Salsa

This creamy polenta dish served with a tangy salsa is from Chile, where it is often served for Sunday brunch.

Serves 6–12
10ml/2 tsp dried chilli flakes
1.3 litres/2¼ pints/5⅔ cups water
250g/9oz/1¼ cups quick cook polenta
50g/2oz/¼ cup butter
75g/3oz Parmesan cheese, grated
30ml/2 tbsp chopped fresh dill
30ml/2 tbsp chopped fresh coriander (cilantro)
30ml/2 tbsp olive oil
salt

For the salsa
½ pink onion, finely chopped
4 drained bottled sweet cherry peppers, finely chopped
1 fresh medium hot red chilli, seeded and finely chopped
1 small red (bell) pepper, quartered
10ml/2 tsp raspberry vinegar
30ml/2 tbsp olive oil
4 tomatoes, halved, cored, seeded and roughly chopped
45ml/3 tbsp chopped fresh coriander (cilantro)

1 Put the dried chilli flakes in a pan with the water. Bring to the boil and add a pinch of salt. Pour the polenta into the water in a continuous stream, whisking. Reduce the heat and continue to whisk for a few minutes.

2 When the polenta is thick and bubbling like a volcano, whisk in the butter, Parmesan and herbs. Season with salt. Pour into a greased 33 × 23cm/13 × 9in baking tray and leave to cool. Chill overnight.

3 About an hour before you plan to serve the meal, make the salsa. Place the onion, sweet cherry peppers and chilli in a mortar. Slice the skin from the red pepper quarters. Dice the flesh finely and place in a food processor, with the raspberry vinegar and olive oil. Process until smooth, then tip into a serving dish. Stir in the tomatoes and coriander. Cover.

4 Cut the polenta into 12 even triangles and brush the top with oil. Heat a griddle and grill in batches, oiled-side down, for about 2 minutes, then turn through 180 degrees and cook for 1 minute more, to get a chequered effect. Serve with the salsa.

Root Vegetable Gratin with Indian Spices

Subtly spiced with curry powder, turmeric, coriander and mild chilli powder, this rich gratin is substantial enough to serve on its own for lunch or supper. It also makes a good accompaniment to a vegetable or bean curry.

Serves 4
2 large potatoes, total weight about 450g/1lb
2 sweet potatoes, total weight about 275g/10oz
175g/6oz celeriac
15ml/1 tbsp unsalted butter
5ml/1 tsp medium curry powder
5ml/1 tsp ground turmeric
2.5ml/½ tsp ground coriander
5ml/1 tsp mild chilli powder
3 shallots, chopped
salt and ground black pepper
150ml/¼ pint/⅔ cup single (light) cream
150ml/¼ pint/⅔ cup semi-skimmed (low-fat) milk
chopped fresh flat leaf parsley, to garnish

1 Thinly slice the potatoes, sweet potatoes and celeriac, using a sharp knife or the slicing attachment on a food processor. Immediately place the vegetables in a bowl of cold water to prevent them discolouring.

2 Preheat the oven to 180°C/350°F/Gas 4. Heat half the butter in a heavy pan and add the curry powder, turmeric and coriander and half the chilli powder. Cook for 2 minutes, then leave to cool slightly.

3 Drain the vegetables, then pat dry with kitchen paper. Place in a bowl, add the spice mixture and the shallots and mix well.

4 Arrange the vegetables in layers in a gratin dish, seasoning each layer. Mix together the cream and milk, pour over the vegetables, then sprinkle the remaining chilli powder on top.

5 Cover with greaseproof (waxed) paper and bake for about 45 minutes. Remove the greaseproof paper, dot with the remaining butter and bake for a further 50 minutes until the top is golden. Serve garnished with chopped fresh parsley.

Polenta with Salsa Energy 154kcal/639kJ; Protein 4.6g; Carbohydrate 15.4g, of which sugars 0.1g; Fat 8g, of which saturates 3.7g; Cholesterol 15mg; Calcium 85mg; Fibre 0.7g; Sodium 95mg.
Vegetable Gratin Energy 268kcal/1129kJ; Protein 5.8g; Carbohydrate 37.7g, of which sugars 9.8g; Fat 11.6g, of which saturates 7.1g; Cholesterol 31mg; Calcium 127mg; Fibre 3.6g; Sodium 117mg.

Fiery Dhal with Spicy Topping

Boost your pulse rate with this delectable dish of red lentils with a spicy topping.

Serves 4
50g/2oz/¼ cup butter
10ml/2 tsp black mustard seeds
1 onion, finely chopped
2 garlic cloves, finely chopped
5ml/1 tsp ground turmeric
5ml/1 tsp ground cumin
2 fresh green chillies, seeded and
 finely chopped

225g/8oz/1 cup red lentils
300ml/½ pint/1¼ cups canned
 coconut milk
crisply fried sliced onion and
 sprigs of fresh coriander
 (cilantro), to garnish
warm naan, to serve

For the spicy topping
30ml/2 tbsp ghee
10ml/2 tsp black mustard seeds
2.5ml/½ tsp asafoetida
8 dried curry leaves

1 Melt the butter in a large heavy pan. Add the mustard seeds. When they start to pop, add the onion and garlic and cook for 5–10 minutes until soft.

2 Stir in the turmeric, cumin and chillies and cook for about 2 minutes. Stir in the lentils, 1 litre/1¾ pints/4 cups water and coconut milk. Bring to the boil, then cover and simmer for 40 minutes, adding water if needed. The lentils should be soft and should have absorbed most of the liquid.

3 To prepare the topping, melt the ghee in a frying pan. When it is hot add the black mustard seeds and cover the pan until they start to pop. Remove from the heat and add the asafoetida and curry leaves. Stir into the hot ghee, then pour immediately over the dhal.

4 Garnish the dish with onion rings, fried until deep brown and crisp, and coriander leaves and serve at once, with warm naan to mop up the sauce.

> **Variation**
> *This dish is excellent made with moong dhal, the yellow split mung bean that is widely used in Indian cookery.*

Garlic-flavoured Lentils with Coriander and Sage

Adapted from a traditional Ottoman Turkish dish, which is flavoured with mint and dill, this simple recipe uses sage instead. Dried sage leaves have an intense, herby aroma, and are ideal for this dish, though you could also make it using fresh sage. Serve these lentils with grilled, broiled or barbecued meats, or on their own with a dollop of yogurt seasoned with garlic, salt and pepper.

Serves 4–6
175g/6oz/¾ cup green lentils
45–60ml/3–4 tbsp fruity olive oil
1 onion, sliced
3–4 plump garlic cloves, roughly
 chopped and bruised
5ml/1 tsp coriander seeds
a handful of dried sage leaves
5–10ml/1–2 tsp sugar
4 carrots, sliced
15–30ml/1–2 tbsp tomato
 purée (paste)
salt and ground black pepper
1 bunch of fresh sage or flat leaf
 parsley, to garnish

1 Pick over the lentils, rinse them in cold water and drain. Bring a pan of water to the boil and tip in the lentils. Lower the heat, partially cover the pan and simmer for 10 minutes. Drain and rinse well under cold running water.

2 Heat the oil in a heavy pan, stir in the onion, garlic, coriander, sage and sugar, and cook until the onion begins to colour. Toss in the carrots and cook for 2–3 minutes.

3 Add the drained lentils to the carrots in the pan and pour in 250ml/8fl oz/1 cup water, making sure the lentils and carrots are covered.

4 Stir in the tomato purée and cover the pan, then cook the lentils and carrots gently for about 20 minutes, until most of the liquid has been absorbed. The lentils and carrots should both be tender, but still have some bite.

5 Season the dish with salt and pepper to taste. Transfer to a serving dish and garnish with the fresh sage or flat leaf parsley. Serve hot or at room temperature.

Dhal with Spicy Topping Energy 381kcal/1599kJ; Protein 14.9g; Carbohydrate 39.1g, of which sugars 6g; Fat 19.7g, of which saturates 10.4g; Cholesterol 27mg; Calcium 69mg; Fibre 3g; Sodium 182mg.
Garlic Lentils Energy 166kcal/696kJ; Protein 7.6g; Carbohydrate 21.1g, of which sugars 6.7g; Fat 6.2g, of which saturates 0.9g; Cholesterol 0mg; Calcium 38mg; Fibre 4g; Sodium 22mg.

Falafel

The secret to making good falafel is to use well-soaked, but not cooked, chickpeas. Do not try to use canned chickpeas for this recipe, as the texture will be mushy and the finished falafel will fall apart.

Serves 6
250g/9oz/generous 1⅓ cups dried chickpeas
1 litre/1¾ pints/4 cups water
45–60ml/3–4 tbsp bulgur wheat
1 large onion, finely chopped
5 garlic cloves, crushed
75ml/5 tbsp chopped fresh parsley
75ml/5 tbsp chopped fresh coriander (cilantro) leaves
45ml/3 tbsp ground cumin
15ml/1 tbsp ground coriander
5ml/1 tsp baking powder
5m/1 tsp salt
small pinch to 1.5ml/¼ tsp ground black pepper
small pinch to 1.5ml/¼ tsp cayenne pepper
5ml/1 tsp curry powder with a pinch of cardamom seeds
45–60ml/3–4 tbsp gram flour
extra flour, if necessary
vegetable oil, for deep-frying
6 pitta breads, hummus, tahini, chilli sauce, pickles, olives and salads, to serve

1 Place the chickpeas in a large bowl and pour over the water. Leave to soak for 4 hours, drain and grind in a food processor.

2 Put the ground chickpeas in a bowl and stir in the bulgur wheat, onion, garlic, parsley, fresh coriander, ground cumin and coriander, baking powder, salt, black pepper and cayenne pepper, and curry powder, if using. Stir in 45ml/3 tbsp water and leave to stand for about 45 minutes.

3 Stir the gram flour into the falafel batter, adding a little water if it is too thick or a little flour if it is too thin. Using a wet tablespoon and wet hands, shape the mixture into 12–18 balls.

4 In a deep pan or wok, heat the oil for deep-frying to 180°C/350°F. Add the falafel in batches and cook for 3–4 minutes until golden brown.

5 Serve tucked into warmed pitta bread with a spoonful of hummus and a drizzle of tahini. Accompany with chilli sauce, pickles, olives and some salads.

Spiced Chickpea Rissoles

Sesame seeds are used to give a crunchy coating to these spicy patties. Serve with the tahini yogurt dip and warm pitta bread as a light lunch or supper dish.

Serves 4
250g/9oz/1⅓ cups dried chickpeas
2 garlic cloves, crushed
1 red chilli, seeded and sliced
5ml/1 tsp ground coriander
5ml/1 tsp ground cumin
15ml/1 tbsp chopped fresh mint
15ml/1 tbsp chopped fresh parsley
2 spring onions (scallions), finely chopped
1 large egg, beaten
sesame seeds, for coating
sunflower oil, for frying
salt and ground black pepper

For the tahini yogurt dip
30ml/2 tbsp light tahini
200g/7oz/scant 1 cup natural (plain) yogurt
5ml/1 tsp cayenne pepper, plus extra for sprinkling
15ml/1 tbsp chopped fresh mint
1 spring onion (scallion), finely sliced

1 Place the chickpeas in a bowl, cover with cold water and leave to soak overnight. Drain and rinse the chickpeas, then place in a pan and cover with cold water. Bring to the boil and boil rapidly for 10 minutes, then reduce the heat and simmer for 1½–2 hours until tender.

2 Meanwhile, make the tahini yogurt dip. Mix together the tahini, yogurt, cayenne pepper and chopped mint in a small bowl. Sprinkle with the spring onion, extra cayenne pepper and mint and chill.

3 Combine the chickpeas with the garlic, chilli, ground spices, herbs, spring onions and seasoning, then mix in the egg. Place in a blender or food processor and blend until the mixture forms a coarse paste. If the paste seems too soft, chill it for 30 minutes.

4 Form the chilled chickpea paste into 12 patties with your hands, then roll each one in the sesame seeds to coat. Heat enough oil to cover the base of a large frying pan. Fry the rissoles, in batches if necessary, for 6 minutes, turning once.

Falafel Energy 303kcal/1282kJ; Protein 18.5g; Carbohydrate 44.7g, of which sugars 5.2g; Fat 6.9g, of which saturates 1.2g; Cholesterol 0mg; Calcium 88mg; Fibre 7.2g; Sodium 16mg.
Chickpea Rissoles Energy 552kcal/2312kJ; Protein 21.3g; Carbohydrate 63.7g, of which sugars 8.2g; Fat 25.3g, of which saturates 3.6g; Cholesterol 48mg; Calcium 234mg; Fibre 10.8g; Sodium 95mg.

Greek-style Aromatic Mushrooms

There are many variations of this classic dish of mushrooms stewed in olive oil, but they all contain coriander seeds.

Serves 4
60ml/4 tbsp olive oil
2 carrots, peeled and diced
375g/12oz baby onions
120ml/4fl oz/½ cup dry
  white wine
5ml/1 tsp coriander seeds,
  lightly crushed
2 bay leaves
pinch of cayenne pepper
1 garlic clove, crushed
375g/12oz button mushrooms
3 tomatoes, peeled, seeded and
  quartered
salt and ground black pepper
45ml/3 tbsp chopped fresh
  parsley, to garnish
crusty bread, to serve

1 Heat 45ml/3 tbsp of the olive oil in a deep frying pan. Add the carrots and onions and cook, stirring occasionally, for about 20 minutes until the vegetables have browned lightly and are beginning to soften.

2 Add the white wine, coriander seeds, bay leaves, cayenne, garlic, button mushrooms and tomatoes, with salt and pepper to taste. Cook gently, uncovered, for 20–30 minutes until the vegetables are soft and the sauce has thickened.

3 Transfer to a serving dish and leave to cool. Cover and chill until needed. Before serving, pour over the remaining olive oil and sprinkle with the parsley. Serve with crusty bread.

Variation
This treatment is ideal for other vegetables. Try leeks, fennel or artichokes, with or without baby onions.

Cook's Tip
Don't trim too much from either the top or root end of the onions: if you do, the centres will pop out during cooking.

Japanese Fried Chilli Aubergine

In this tasty traditional recipe, stir-fried aubergine is coated in a rich miso sauce. Make sure the oil is very hot when adding the aubergine, so that it does not absorb too much oil.

Serves 4
2 large aubergines (eggplants)
1–2 dried red chillies
45ml/3 tbsp sake
45ml/3 tbsp mirin
45ml/3 tbsp caster
  (superfine) sugar
30ml/2 tbsp shoyu
45ml/3 tbsp red miso (use either
  dark red aka miso or even
  darker hatcho miso)
90ml/6 tbsp sesame oil
salt

1 Cut the aubergines into bitesize pieces and place in a large colander, sprinkle with some salt and leave for 30 minutes to remove the bitter juices. Squeeze the aubergine pieces with your hands to extract the moisture. Remove the seeds from the chillies and chop the chillies into thin rings.

2 Mix the sake, mirin, sugar and shoyu in a cup. In a separate bowl, mix the red miso with 45ml/3 tbsp water to make a loose paste.

3 Heat the oil in a large pan and add the chilli. When you see pale smoke rising from the oil, add the aubergine, and stir-fry for about 8 minutes, or until browned and tender. Lower the heat to medium.

4 Add the sake mixture to the pan, and stir for 2–3 minutes. If the sauce starts to burn, lower the heat. Add the miso paste to the pan and cook, stirring, for another 2 minutes. Serve hot.

Variation
Sweet (bell) peppers could be used for this dish instead of aubergine. Take 1 red, 1 yellow and 2 green peppers. Remove the seeds and chop them into 1cm/½in strips, then follow the rest of the recipe.

Greek Mushrooms Energy 122kcal/502kJ; Protein 2.7g; Carbohydrate 1.5g, of which sugars 0.5g; Fat 11.7g, of which saturates 1.7g; Cholesterol 0mg; Calcium 23mg; Fibre 1.9g; Sodium 9mg.
Chilli Aubergine Energy 198kcal/819kJ; Protein 1.5g; Carbohydrate 3.7g, of which sugars 3.4g; Fat 17g, of which saturates 2.5g; Cholesterol 0mg; Calcium 17mg; Fibre 2.5g; Sodium 716mg.

Carrots with Mango and Ginger

Ripe mango adds its unique fruity sweetness to carrots and ginger in this spicy vegetable dish from Morocco. Cooked in this way, humble carrots are turned into an excellent and exciting dish. It can be served as an accompaniment for grilled meat or couscous, but the dish is also very good on its own with yogurt and a salad. The mango must be ripe, otherwise you will need to add a little honey to balance the flavours.

Serves 4–6
15–30ml/1–2 tbsp olive oil
1 onion, chopped
25g/1oz fresh root ginger, peeled and chopped
2–3 garlic cloves, chopped
5–6 carrots, sliced
30–45ml/2–3 tbsp shelled pistachio nuts, roasted
5ml/1 tsp ground cinnamon
5–10ml/1–2 tsp mixed spice
1 small firm but ripe mango, peeled and coarsely diced
small bunch of fresh coriander (cilantro), finely chopped
juice of ½ lemon
salt

1 Heat the olive oil in a large, heavy frying pan or wok. Stir in the onion, ginger and garlic and fry for 1 minute.

2 Add the carrots, tossing them in the pan to make sure that they are thoroughly mixed with the flavouring ingredients, and cook until they begin to brown.

3 Add the pistachio nuts, cinnamon and *ras el hanout*, then mix in the pieces of mango, stirring gently to avoid breaking them up. Sprinkle with coriander, season with salt and pour over the lemon juice. Serve immediately.

Cook's Tip
To prepare a mango, use a sharp knife to cut down either side of the large stone. Score a lattice into the flesh of each half without cutting the skin, then run the knife between the flesh and the skin to release the cubes of mango. If you prefer slices of mango, peel the fruit, cut either side of the stone and thinly slice the flesh just before serving.

Warm Carrot Salad

Packed with exotic spices, this colourful Middle-Eastern salad is sure to go down well. It is delicious served with a topping of tangy, garlicky yogurt.

Serves 4
450g/1lb carrots, cut into sticks
30–45ml/2–3 tbsp olive oil
juice of 1 lemon
2–3 garlic cloves, crushed
10ml/2 tsp sugar
5–10ml/1–2 tsp cumin seeds, roasted
5ml/1 tsp ground cinnamon
5ml/1 tsp paprika
1 small bunch fresh coriander (cilantro), finely chopped
1 small bunch fresh mint, finely chopped
salt and ground black pepper

1 Steam the carrots over boiling water for about 15 minutes, or until tender.

2 While they are still warm, toss the carrots in a serving bowl with the olive oil, lemon juice, garlic and sugar.

3 Season to taste, then add the cumin seeds, cinnamon and paprika. Finally, toss in the fresh coriander and mint, and serve warm or at room temperature.

Cook's Tip
To roast the cumin seeds, stir them in a heavy pan over a low heat until they change colour slightly and emit a warm, nutty aroma. Be careful not to burn them.

Variation
For a spiced carrot dip, put 3 grated carrots, 1 chopped onion and the grated rind and juice of 2 oranges in a pan with 15ml/1 tbsp hot curry paste. Bring to the boil, then simmer for 10 minutes until tender. Process until smooth, allow to cool. Stir in 150ml/¼ pint/⅔ cup natural (plain) yogurt. Add a handful basil, then season with lemon juice and salt and pepper. Serve.

Carrots with Mango Energy 89kcal/371kJ; Protein 1.7g; Carbohydrate 8.2g, of which sugars 7.5g; Fat 5.7g, of which saturates 0.8g; Cholesterol 0mg; Calcium 23mg; Fibre 2.2g; Sodium 47mg.
Carrot salad Energy 114kcal/473kJ; Protein 1.6g; Carbohydrate 13.2g, of which sugars 11.2g; Fat 6.5g, of which saturates 1g; Cholesterol 0mg; Calcium 61mg; Fibre 3.3g; Sodium 34mg

Herbed Potato Salad

Mixing the potatoes with the dressing when hot means they absorb it better.

Serves 4–6

675g/1½lb new potatoes
4 spring onions (scallions)
45ml/3 tbsp white wine vinegar
45ml/3 tbsp olive oil
175ml/6fl oz/¾ cup mayonnaise
a handful of fresh chives, snipped
salt and ground black pepper

1 Boil the potatoes in their skins until tender. Slice the spring onions into thin rounds. Whisk the vinegar and oil together. Drain the potatoes and immediately toss in the oil and vinegar.

2 Stir the mayonnaise and chives together, season, then mix in with the dressed potatoes. Leave to cool a little, then serve.

Hot Cajun Potato Salad

In Cajun country in Louisiana, where Tabasco sauce originates, hot means really hot, so you can go to town with this salad if you think you can take it.

Serves 6–8

8 waxy potatoes
1 green (bell) pepper, diced
1 large gherkin, chopped
4 spring onions (scallions), shredded
3 hard-boiled eggs, shelled and chopped
250ml/8fl oz/1 cup mayonnaise
15ml/1 tbsp Dijon mustard
salt and ground black pepper
Tabasco sauce, to taste
pinch or two of cayenne
sliced gherkin, to garnish
mayonnaise, to serve

1 Cook the potatoes in their skins in boiling salted water until tender. Drain and leave to cool.

2 When the potatoes are cool enough to handle, but while they are still warm, peel them and cut into coarse chunks. Place them in a large bowl.

3 Add the green pepper, gherkin, spring onions and hard-boiled eggs to the potatoes and toss gently to combine.

4 In a separate bowl, mix the mayonnaise with the mustard and season with salt, black pepper and Tabasco sauce to taste.

5 Pour the dressing over the potato mixture and toss gently so that the potatoes are well coated. Sprinkle with a pinch or two of cayenne and garnish with a few slices of gherkin. Serve with extra mayonnaise.

Cook's Tips
• The salad is good to eat immediately, when the potatoes are just cool. If you make it in advance and chill it, let it come back to room temperature before serving.
• Tabasco is one of thousands of commercial hot pepper sauces on the market, of varying intensity: use your favourite brand to make this salad.

Potato Salad with Mango Dressing

This sweet and spicy salad is a wonderful accompaniment to a vegetarian meal.

Serves 4–6

15ml/1 tbsp olive oil
1 onion, sliced into rings
1 garlic clove, crushed
5ml/1 tsp ground cumin
5ml/1 tsp ground coriander
1 mango, diced
30ml/2 tbsp demerara (raw) sugar
30ml/2 tbsp lime juice
900g/2lb new potatoes, cut in half and boiled
15ml/1 tbsp sesame seeds
salt and ground black pepper
deep-fried coriander (cilantro) leaves, to garnish

1 Heat the oil in a frying pan and fry the onion and garlic over a low heat for 10 minutes until they start to brown. Stir in the cumin and coriander and fry for a few seconds. Stir in the mango and sugar and fry for 5 minutes, until soft. Remove the pan from the heat and squeeze in the lime juice. Season.

2 Place the potatoes in a large bowl and spoon the mango dressing over. Sprinkle with sesame seeds and garnish with the coriander leaves. Serve while the dressing is still warm.

Cajun Potato Salad Energy 289kcal/1197kJ; Protein 4g; Carbohydrate 10.3g, of which sugars 2.7g; Fat 26.1g, of which saturates 4.2g; Cholesterol 95mg; Calcium 21mg; Fibre 0.9g; Sodium 229mg.
Herbed Potato Salad Energy 218kcal/913kJ; Protein 3g; Carbohydrate 27g, of which sugars 2.3g; Fat 11.6g, of which saturates 1.7g; Cholesterol 0mg; Calcium 23mg; Fibre 2g; Sodium 21mg.
Potato Salad with Mango Energy 174kcal/737kJ; Protein 3.3g; Carbohydrate 33.7g, of which sugars 11.2g; Fat 3.8g, of which saturates 0.7g; Cholesterol 0mg; Calcium 34mg; Fibre 2.5g; Sodium 18mg.

Lentil Salad with Red Onion and Garlic

This delicious, garlicky Moroccan lentil salad is frequently served as an accompaniment to kebabs, as part of a *meze* or by itself as an appetizer. It is equally good eaten warm or cooled. Try it together with a generous spoonful of natural yogurt.

Serves 4

45ml/3 tbsp olive oil
2 red onions, chopped
2 tomatoes, peeled, seeded and chopped
10ml/2 tsp ground turmeric
10ml/2 tsp ground cumin
175g/6oz/¾ cup brown or green lentils, picked over, rinsed and drained
900ml/1½ pints/3¾ cups vegetable stock or water
4 garlic cloves, crushed
small bunch of fresh coriander (cilantro), finely chopped
salt and ground black pepper
1 lemon, cut into wedges, to serve

1 Heat 30ml/2 tbsp of the oil in a large pan or flameproof casserole and fry the onions until soft. Add the tomatoes, turmeric and cumin, then stir in the lentils.

2 Pour in the stock or water and bring to the boil, then reduce the heat and simmer until the lentils are tender and almost all the liquid has been absorbed.

3 In a separate pan, fry the garlic in the remaining oil until brown and frizzled. Toss the garlic into the lentils with the fresh coriander and season to taste.

4 Serve warm or at room temperature, with wedges of lemon for squeezing over.

> **Cook's Tips**
> • If you prefer, you can replace the lentils with mung beans – they work just as well.
> • When including this dish in a meze, serve it with a creamy dip and a fruity salad to balance the different textures.

Herb Salad with Chilli and Preserved Lemon

Firm-leafed fresh herbs, such as flat leaf parsley, mint and coriander (cilantro), can be used as tasty ingredients in their own right rather than just as flavourings. Tossed in a little olive oil and seasoned with salt, they make a fabulous salad to serve as part of a *meze* spread, and they also go wonderfully with spicy kebabs or tagines. Lightly sautéed with garlic and served warm with yogurt, this dish is delightful even on its own.

Serves 4

large bunch of flat leaf parsley
large bunch of mint
large bunch of fresh coriander (cilantro)
bunch of rocket (arugula)
large bunch of spinach leaves (about 115g/4oz)
60–75ml/4–5 tbsp olive oil
2 garlic cloves, finely chopped
1 green or red chilli, seeded and finely chopped
½ preserved lemon, finely chopped
salt and ground black pepper
45–60ml/3–4 tbsp strained natural (plain) yogurt, to serve

1 Roughly chop the parsley, mint, coriander, rocket and spinach leaves.

2 Heat the olive oil in a wide, heavy pan. Stir in the garlic and chilli, and fry until they begin to colour.

3 Toss in the chopped herbs, rocket and spinach and cook over a low heat, stirring gently, until they begin to soften and wilt. Add the preserved lemon and season to taste.

4 Turn the salad into a serving dish and serve while still warm with a dollop of yogurt.

> **Variation**
> Garlic-flavoured yogurt makes a good accompaniment: crush a clove of garlic and stir it into the yogurt with salt and ground pepper to taste.

Lentil Salad Energy 244kcal/1025kJ; Protein 12.3g; Carbohydrate 29.2g, of which sugars 6.6g; Fat 9.5g, of which saturates 1.3g; Cholesterol 0mg; Calcium 78mg; Fibre 6.1g; Sodium 16mg.
Herb Salad with Chilli Energy 142kcal/585kJ; Protein 3.6g; Carbohydrate 3.1g, of which sugars 2.7g; Fat 12.9g, of which saturates 2.1g; Cholesterol 2mg; Calcium 216mg; Fibre 4.4g; Sodium 82mg.

Winter Melon Relish

Cooks in southern India make a variety of side dishes like this one, Known as *pachadi* or raita, they are all designed to cool the palate and aid digestion when eating the hot, spicy food for which the region is renowned. The dishes are yogurt-based and are made with a variety of cooling vegetables and herbs, such as winter melon, okra, courgette, spinach, pumpkin and cucumber with mint. They also often include small amounts of spicier ingredients such as chilli.

Serves 4

225g/8oz winter melon, peeled, seeded and diced
5ml/1 tsp ground turmeric
5ml/1 tsp red chilli powder
300ml/½ pint/1¼ cups strained natural (plain) yogurt
2.5ml/½ tsp salt
2.5ml/½ tsp sugar
15g/½oz fresh root ginger, peeled and grated
1 green chilli, seeded and finely chopped
15ml/1 tbsp vegetable oil
1.5ml/¼ tsp ground asafoetida
5ml/1 tsp brown mustard seeds
8–10 dried curry leaves
1 dried red chilli, seeded and roughly chopped

1 Put the winter melon in a heavy pan with the turmeric and chilli powder and pour in enough water to just cover. Bring to the boil and cook gently, uncovered, until the winter melon is tender and all the water has evaporated.

2 In a bowl, beat the yogurt with the salt and sugar until smooth and creamy. Add the ginger and green chilli, and fold in the warm winter melon.

3 Heat the oil in small pan. Stir in the asafoetida and mustard seeds. As soon as the seeds begin to pop, stir in the curry leaves and dried chilli. When the chilli darkens, add the spices to the yogurt and mix thoroughly. Serve at room temperature.

> **Cook's Tip**
> *This dish can made a day or two in advance, so that the flavours have time to mingle and blend.*

Spiced Tomato Salsa

This is the traditional tomato-based salsa that most people associate with Mexican food. There are innumerable recipes for it, but the basics of onion, tomato, chilli and coriander are common to all. Serve as a condiment with a wide variety of dishes.

Serves 6 as an accompaniment

3–6 fresh serrano chillies
1 large white onion
grated rind and juice of 2 limes, plus strips of rind, to garnish
8 ripe, firm tomatoes
bunch of fresh coriander (cilantro)
1.5ml/¼ tsp sugar
salt

1 Use three chillies for a salsa of medium heat; up to six if you like it hot. Spear the chillies on a metal skewer and roast them over a gas flame until the skins blister. Do not let the flesh burn. Alternatively, dry-fry them in a griddle. Place them in a strong plastic bag and tie the top. Set aside for 20 minutes.

2 Meanwhile, chop the onion finely and put it in a bowl with the lime rind and juice. The lime juice will soften the onion.

3 Remove the chillies from the bag and peel off the skins. Cut off the stalks, then slit the chillies and scrape out the seeds with a sharp knife. Chop the flesh roughly and set aside.

4 Cut a small cross in the base of each tomato. Place them in a heatproof bowl and pour over boiling water to cover.

5 Leave the tomatoes in the water for 3 minutes, then lift out and plunge into a bowl of cold water. Drain. The skins will be peeling back from the crosses. Remove the skins completely.

6 Dice the peeled tomatoes and put them in a bowl. Add the chopped onion and lime mixture; the onion should have softened. Chop the fresh coriander finely.

7 Add the coriander, with the chillies and the sugar. Mix gently until the sugar has dissolved and all the ingredients are coated in lime juice. Cover and chill for 2–3 hours. The salsa will keep for 3–4 days in the refrigerator. Garnish with lime rind before serving.

Melon Relish Energy 127Kcal/527kJ; Protein 5.1g; Carbohydrate 5.3g, of which sugars 5.3g; Fat 10.5g, of which saturates 4.2g; Cholesterol 0mg; Calcium 120mg; Fibre 0.2g; Sodium 316mg.
Tomato Salsa Energy 42kcal/176kJ; Protein 2g; Carbohydrate 8g, of which sugars 7g; Fat 1g, of which saturates 0g; Cholesterol 0mg; Calcium 31mg; Fibre 1.7g; Sodium 100mg.

Coriander and Coconut Chutney

Cooling fragrant chutneys are very popular with the Jewish community in India, and this delicious blend of coriander, mint and coconut, with a hint of chilli, a tang of tamarind and the sweet flavour of dates, is a traditional condiment.

Makes about 450g/1lb/ 2 cups

30ml/2 tbsp tamarind paste
30ml/2 tbsp boiling water
1 large bunch fresh coriander (cilantro), roughly chopped
1 bunch fresh mint, roughly chopped
8–10 pitted dates, roughly chopped
75g/3oz dried coconut or 50g/2oz creamed coconut, coarsely grated
2.5cm/1in piece fresh root ginger, chopped
3–5 garlic cloves, chopped
2–3 fresh chillies, chopped
juice of 2 limes or lemons
about 5ml/1 tsp sugar
salt
30–45ml/2–3 tbsp natural (plain) yogurt to serve

1 Place the tamarind paste in a bowl and pour over the boiling water. Stir thoroughly until the paste is completely dissolved and set aside.

2 Place the fresh coriander, mint leaves and pitted dates in a food processor and process briefly until finely chopped. Alternatively, chop the ingredients finely by hand using a sharp knife. Place in a bowl.

3 Add the coconut, ginger, garlic and chillies to the chopped herbs and dates and stir in the tamarind. Season with citrus juice, sugar and salt. Spoon into sterilized jars, seal and chill. To serve, thin the chutney with the yogurt.

Cook's Tips
• This chutney can be stored in the refrigerator for up to 2 weeks, adding the yogurt just before serving.
• Adjust the amount of ginger, garlic and chillies to taste.

Cucumber and Shallot Salad

In Malaysia and Singapore, this light, refreshing salad is served with Indian food almost as often as the cooling and familiar mint-flavoured cucumber raita. The Malays enjoy this salad with many of their spicy dishes. It can be made ahead of time and kept in the refrigerator. Serve it as a salad, or a relish.

Serves 4

5–10ml/1–2 tsp whole cumin seeds
1 cucumber, peeled, halved lengthways and seeded
4 shallots, halved lengthways and sliced finely along the grain
1–2 green chillies, seeded and sliced finely lengthways
60ml/4 tbsp coconut milk
salt
1 lime, quartered, to serve

1 Dry-roast the cumin seeds in a heavy frying pan until they emit their aroma. Put them in a mortar and grind to a fine power using a pestle, or grind them in a spice mill. Set aside.

2 Slice the cucumber halves finely. Put them on a plate and sprinkle with salt. Set aside for about 15 minutes then rinse well and leave in a colander to drain off any excess water.

3 Put the cucumber in a bowl with the sliced shallots and chillies. Pour in the coconut milk and toss well. Sprinkle most of the roasted cumin over the top.

4 Just before serving, toss the salad again, season with salt, and sprinkle the rest of the roasted cumin over the top. Serve with lime wedges to squeeze over the salad.

Cook's Tip
Cumin seeds are a key flavouring in Indian food, and therefore often appear in Malay dishes with Indian influences, but they are equally popular in Central America, the Middle East and the Mediterranean. Cumin has a distinctive taste; it is a warm spice but slightly bitter. Its aromatic, nutty-flavoured seeds, enhanced by roasting, bring out the natural sweetness of other ingredients.

Coriander Chutney Energy 536kcal/2232kJ; Protein 10.1g; Carbohydrate 47g, of which sugars 39.5g; Fat 35.5g, of which saturates 29.8g; Cholesterol 0mg; Calcium 144mg; Fibre 6.6g; Sodium 39mg.
Cucumber Salad Energy 17Kcal/68kJ; Protein 0.7g; Carbohydrate 3.3g, of which sugars 2.7g; Fat 0.1g, of which saturates 0g; Cholesterol 0mg; Calcium 19mg; Fibre 0.7g; Sodium 15mg.

Fragrant Persian Halek

Charoset, the sweet mixture of apples, nuts, honey and cinnamon, is made by Jews at Passover in remembrance of the mortar used by the Israelites to bond bricks while in slavery in Egypt. Persian Jews make this more elaborate version, which is fragrant with rose water and the sweet flavours of many different dried fruits and nuts, which are so important a part of the Persian culinary tradition.

Serves 10

60ml/4 tbsp blanched almonds
60ml/4 tbsp unsalted pistachio nuts
60ml/4 tbsp walnuts
15–30ml/1–2 tbsp skinned hazelnuts
30ml/2 tbsp unsalted shelled pumpkin seeds
90ml/6 tbsp raisins, chopped
90ml/6 tbsp pitted prunes, diced
90ml/6 tbsp dried apricots, diced
60ml/4 tbsp dried cherries
sugar or honey, to taste
juice of ½ lemon
30ml/2 tbsp rose water
seeds from 4–5 cardamom pods
pinch of ground cloves
pinch of freshly grated nutmeg
1.5ml/¼ tsp ground cinnamon
fruit juice of choice, if necessary

1 Roughly chop the almonds, pistachio nuts, walnuts, hazelnuts and pumpkin seeds and put in a bowl. Add the chopped raisins, prunes, apricots and cherries to the nuts and seeds and toss to combine. Stir in sugar or honey to taste and mix well until thoroughly combined.

2 Add the lemon juice, rose water, cardamom seeds, cloves, nutmeg and cinnamon to the fruit and nut mixture and mix until thoroughly combined.

3 If the halek is too thick, add a little fruit juice to thin the mixture. Pour into a serving bowl, cover and chill in the refrigerator until ready to serve.

> **Cook's Tip**
> Some cooks observe a tradition of using 40 ingredients to make halek, echoing 40 years of wandering in the desert.

Pineapple Pickle

This spicy sweet and sour pickle is ideal to serve with hot grilled foods or as an accompaniment to curries or vegetable dishes.

Serves 6–8

15ml/1 tbsp brown mustard seeds
2 dried chillies, soaked in water until soft, seeded, and squeezed dry
15g/½oz fresh root ginger, peeled and chopped
1 garlic clove, chopped
5ml/1 tsp ground turmeric
200ml/7fl oz/scant 1 cup white wine vinegar or rice vinegar
15ml/1 tbsp palm sugar (jaggery)
1 ripe pineapple, peeled, cored and diced
salt

1 Put the mustard seeds a small, heavy pan over a medium heat. Cover the pan and dry-roast the seeds until they pop. Remove from the heat.

2 Using a mortar and pestle or food processor, grind the chillies, ginger and garlic to a paste. Stir in the mustard seeds and ground turmeric. Add the vinegar and sugar, stirring until the sugar has completely dissolved.

3 Put the pineapple pieces in a bowl and pour over the pickling sauce. Add salt to taste.

> **Variation**
> Try adding spices such as cloves, cinnamon and allspice to the spice paste for a sweeter flavour.

> **Cook's Tips**
> • Malays and Indians often serve a selection of condiments with every meal. Sambals, pickles and chutneys can all be interchanged with the spicy food of these cultures.
> • This pickle will keep for 2–3 days in the refrigerator, and in fact is better made in advance as it will improve as the flavours mingle.

Persian Halek Energy 207kcal/863kJ; Protein 5.1g; Carbohydrate 14.9g, of which sugars 14.5g; Fat 14.6g, of which saturates 1.4g; Cholesterol 0mg; Calcium 66mg; Fibre 2.8g; Sodium 42mg.
Pineapple Pickle Energy 56Kcal/238kJ; Protein 0.7g; Carbohydrate 12.5g, of which sugars 12.2g; Fat 0.2g, of which saturates 0g; Cholesterol 0mg; Calcium 20mg; Fibre 1.3g; Sodium 4mg.

Onion, Garlic and Lemon Relish

This powerful relish is flavoured with North African spices and punchy preserved lemons, which are available from delicatessens and larger supermarkets or from specialist Middle Eastern food stores.

Serves 6

45ml/3 tbsp olive oil
3 large red onions, sliced
2 heads of garlic, separated into
  cloves and peeled
10ml/2 tsp coriander seeds,
  crushed but not finely ground
10ml/2 tsp light muscovado
  (brown) sugar, plus a little extra
pinch of saffron strands
5cm/2in piece cinnamon stick
2–3 small whole dried red
  chillies (optional)
2 fresh bay leaves
30–45ml/2–3 tbsp sherry vinegar
juice of ½ small orange
30ml/2 tbsp chopped
  preserved lemon
salt and ground black pepper

1 Heat the oil in a heavy pan. Add the onions and stir, then cover with a tightly fitting lid and reduce the heat to the lowest setting. Cook for 10–15 minutes, stirring occasionally, until the onions are soft.

2 Add the garlic cloves and coriander seeds. Cover and cook for 5–8 minutes until they are soft. Add a pinch of salt, several grindings of pepper and the sugar, and cook, uncovered, for 5 minutes.

3 Soak the saffron in about 45ml/3 tbsp warm water for 5 minutes, then add to the onions, with the soaking water. Add the cinnamon stick, dried chillies, if using, and bay leaves. Stir in 30ml/2 tbsp of the sherry vinegar and the orange juice.

4 Cook over a low heat, uncovered, until the onions are very soft and most of the liquid has evaporated. Stir in the preserved lemon and cook gently for a further 5 minutes, then taste and adjust the seasoning, adding more salt, sugar and/or vinegar to taste.

5 Serve warm or cold, but not hot or chilled. The relish tastes best if it is allowed to stand for 24 hours before serving for the flavours to blend and mellow.

Lime Pickle

This classic Indian pickle is popular everywhere, and various commercial brands are widely available in supermarkets and Asian stores, but the homemade version is far finer, and you can adjust the heat to suit your family's preferences. In India the pickle is eaten mainly as an accompaniment to fiery curries.

Serves 8–10

8–10 limes
30ml/2 tbsp salt
150ml/5fl oz/⅔ cup sesame or
  groundnut (peanut) oil
10–15ml/2–3 tsp brown
  mustard seeds
3–4 garlic cloves, cut into
  thin sticks
25g/1oz fresh root ginger, peeled
  and cut into thin sticks
5ml/1 tsp coriander seeds
5ml/1 tsp cumin seeds
5ml/1 tsp fennel seeds
10ml/2 tsp ground turmeric
10ml/2 tsp hot chilli powder
  or paste
handful of fresh or dried
  curry leaves

1 Put the whole limes in a bowl. Cover them with boiling water and leave to stand for 30 minutes. Drain the limes and cut each into quarters. Rub the lime pieces with salt and put them into a sealed sterilized jar. Leave the limes to cure in the salt for 1 week.

2 Heat the oil in a wok and stir in the mustard seeds. When they begin to pop, stir in the garlic, ginger, spices and curry leaves. Cook gently for a few minutes to flavour the oil, then stir in the lime pieces and the juices from the jar. Reduce the heat and simmer for about 45 minutes, stirring from time to time.

3 Store the pickle in sterilized jars and keep in a cool place for 1–2 months.

> **Cook's Tips**
> • Lime pickle is delicious served with roasted vegetables, and spicy stir-fried noodles.
> • You can make the pickle as fiery as you like by adding more chilli powder.

Onion Relish Energy 79kcal/326kJ; Protein 1.3g; Carbohydrate 10.4g, of which sugars 8.1g; Fat 3.9g, of which saturates 0.5g; Cholesterol 0mg; Calcium 27mg; Fibre 1.4g; Sodium 4mg.
Lime Pickle Energy 96Kcal/395kJ; Protein 0.3g; Carbohydrate 0.9g, of which sugars 0.6g; Fat 10.1g, of which saturates 1.5g; Cholesterol 0mg; Calcium 25mg; Fibre 0.2g; Sodium 1185mg.

Harissa

This hot sauce features strongly in North African cooking. It can be used as a condiment, served with food according to individual tastes; it can be added to dishes to give them a fiery kick; or it can be served as a dip for warm bread, either on its own or blended with a little yogurt. Traditionally, the ingredients are pounded to a paste using a pestle and mortar, but whizzing them in a blender is far simpler and quicker. This recipe makes a small amount for a dip, or enough for several dishes.

Makes 1 small jar
6–8 dried red chillies (preferably New Mexico variety), seeded
2 garlic cloves, crushed
2.5ml/½ tsp sea salt
5ml/1 tsp ground cumin
2.5ml/½ tsp ground coriander
120ml/4fl oz/1½ cup olive oil

1 Soak the chillies in warm water for about 40 minutes, until soft. Drain and squeeze out the excess water. Place them in a blender with the other ingredients and process the mixture to form a paste.

2 Spoon the harissa into a small jar, cover with a thin layer of olive oil and seal tightly. Store in the refrigerator for up to 1 month.

Cook's Tip
Though harissa is perhaps the most famous of the spice mixes of the Middle East and North Africa, the most complex and refined is probably ras el hanout, which originates in Morocco. Its name means "top of the shop" in Arabic – referring to the fact that it is made from the shopkeeper's best spices – and its composition reflects the centuries of trade, war and cross-cultural exchange of Morocco's history. It includes cardamoms, nutmeg, mace, galangal, cinnamon, ginger and curcuma from India and the Far East and guinea pepper, cloves and cyparacee from Africa, plus orris root, ash berries, monk's pepper, belladonna berries, fennel flowers, lavender, black pepper and rose buds.

Tahini Sauce

Made of ground sesame seeds and spiced with garlic and lemon juice, this is a versatile and popular Middle Eastern sauce. It makes a delicious dip, served with pitta bread, and can also be thinned with water to a pouring consistency.

Serves 4–6
150–175g/5–6oz/⅔–¾ cup tahini
3 garlic cloves, finely chopped
juice of 1 lemon
1.5ml/¼ tsp ground cumin
small pinch of ground coriander
small pinch of curry powder
50–120ml/2–4fl oz/¼–½ cup water
cayenne pepper
salt

For the garnish
15–30ml/1–2 tbsp extra virgin olive oil
chopped fresh coriander (cilantro) leaves or parsley
handful of olives and/or pickled vegetables
a few chillies or a hot pepper sauce

1 Put the tahini and garlic in a food processor or bowl and mix together well. Stir in the lemon juice, cumin, ground coriander and curry powder.

2 Slowly add the water to the tahini, beating all the time. The mixture will thicken, then become thin. Season with cayenne pepper and salt.

3 To serve, spread the mixture on to a serving plate, individual plates or into a shallow bowl. Drizzle over the oil and sprinkle with the other garnishes.

Cook's Tip
Tahini sauce forms the basis of many salads and dips made throughout the Middle East. It is most often poured over falafel, the spicy fried balls made from chickpeas, typically eaten in a pitta as street food. But tahini sauce can also be used as a sauce for grilled vegetables such as potatoes or cauliflower. By adding a little more olive oil it can be turned into a tasty salad dressing.

Tahini Sauce Energy 175kcal/725kJ; Protein 5.2g; Carbohydrate 1.2g, of which sugars 0.3g; Fat 16.7g, of which saturates 2.4g; Cholesterol 0mg; Calcium 184mg; Fibre 2.5g; Sodium 7mg.
Harissa Energy 306kcal/1280kJ; Protein 15.6g; Carbohydrate 37.2g, of which sugars 0.6g; Fat 13.7g, of which saturates 2g; Cholesterol 0mg; Calcium 191mg; Fibre 0g; Sodium 36mg.

Spiced Apple Pie

If you use eating apples bursting with flavour, and make your own shortcrust pastry with butter and sugar, you will achieve a delicious result. Cooking the apples in butter and sugar adds a lovely caramel flavour, and together with the mixed spice, gives a rich flavour to the juices in the pie.

Serves 6
900g/2lb eating apples
75g/3oz/6 tbsp unsalted
   (sweet) butter
45–60ml/3–4 tbsp demerara
   (raw) sugar

3 cloves
2.5ml/½ tsp mixed (apple
   pie) spice

For the pastry
250g/9oz/2¼ cups plain
   (all-purpose) flour
pinch of salt
50g/2oz/¼ cup white vegetable
   fat, chilled and diced
75g/3oz/6 tbsp unsalted (sweet)
   butter, chilled and diced
30–45ml/2–3 tbsp chilled water
a little milk, for brushing
caster (superfine) sugar,
   for dredging
clotted cream, ice cream or
   double (heavy) cream, to serve

1 Preheat the oven to 200°C/400°F/Gas 6. Sift the flour and salt into a bowl. Rub in the lard or fat and butter until the mixture resembles fine breadcrumbs. Stir in enough chilled water to bring the pastry together. Knead lightly then wrap in cling film (plastic wrap) and chill for 30 minutes.

2 To make the filling, peel, core and thickly slice the apples. Melt the butter in a frying pan, add the sugar and cook for 3–4 minutes allowing it to melt and caramelize. Add the apples and stir around to coat. Cook over a brisk heat until the apples take on a little colour, add the spices and tip out into a bowl.

3 Divide the pastry in two and, on a lightly floured surface, roll out into two rounds to fit a deep 23cm/9in pie plate. Line the plate with one round. Spoon in the cooled apple. Cover with the remaining pastry, sealing and crimping the edges. Make a 5cm/2in long slit through the top of the pastry to allow the steam to escape. Brush the pie with milk and dredge with caster sugar. Place the pie on a baking sheet and bake in the oven for 25–35 minutes until golden and firm. Serve warm.

Almond-stuffed Baked Apples

The first spoonful of this baked apple dessert is always a delightful surprise. The pastry wrapping the apple acts as an oven, which bakes the apple and keeps in its flavour, and this mingles perfectly with the almonds.

Serves 8
8 eating apples
1 egg yolk
30ml/2 tbsp water
double (heavy) cream, whipped
   with 5ml/1 tsp vanilla sugar,
   to serve

For the pastry
575g/1¼lb/5 cups plain (all-
   purpose) flour
225g/8oz/1 cup unsalted
   (sweet) butter
100g/4oz/½ cup caster
   (superfine) sugar
1 egg, beaten

For the almond stuffing
25g/1oz/2 tbsp unsalted
   (sweet) butter
100g/4oz/1 cup ground almonds
50g/2oz/4 tbsp caster
   (superfine) sugar
10ml/2 tsp ground cinnamon

1 To make the pastry, put the flour in a food processor. Cut the butter into small pieces, add to the flour and then, using a pulsating action, mix together until the mixture resembles fine breadcrumbs. Add the sugar and egg and mix to form a dough. Wrap in greaseproof (waxed) paper and place in the refrigerator for 1 hour.

2 Preheat the oven to 200°C/400°F/Gas 6. To make the almond stuffing, melt the butter and leave to cool but not set. Put the ground almonds, caster sugar and cinnamon in a bowl. Add the melted butter and mix together. Remove the cores from the apples and then use the stuffing to fill their centres.

3 Divide the pastry into eight pieces. On a floured surface, roll each piece out to a thickness of about 5mm/¼in and, using a 20–23cm/8–9in plate, cut into a round. Put a round over the top of each apple and wrap the pastry around, pinching it in at the bottom. Place on a baking sheet.

4 Beat the egg yolk and water together and brush over the pastry to glaze. Bake in the oven for about 30 minutes until golden brown. Serve hot, with the vanilla-flavoured cream.

Spiced Apple Pie Energy 610kcal/2566kJ; Protein 8.1g; Carbohydrate 86.1g, of which sugars 40.2g; Fat 28.5g, of which saturates 8.8g; Cholesterol 14mg; Calcium 168mg; Fibre 8.1g; Sodium 413mg.
Almond-stuffed Apples Energy 735kcal/3080kJ; Protein 11.2g; Carbohydrate 87.7g, of which sugars 32.6g; Fat 40.2g, of which saturates 20.6g; Cholesterol 129mg; Calcium 159mg; Fibre 5.2g; Sodium 245mg.

Cardamom-spiced Pear Tarte Tatin

Cardamom is a spice that is equally at home in sweet and savoury dishes and is delicious with pears. It has an exquisite but evanescent fragrance, so it is best to buy whole pods and extract the seeds as you need them.

Serves 2–4
50g/2oz/¼ cup butter, softened
50g/2oz/¼ cup caster
  (superfine) sugar
10 cardamom pods
225g/8oz puff pastry, thawed
  if frozen
3 ripe pears

1 Preheat the oven to 220°C/425°F/Gas 7. Spread the butter over the base of a 18cm/7in heavy cake tin or an omelette pan with an ovenproof handle. Spread the sugar evenly over the bottom of the tin or pan. Extract the seeds from the cardamom pods and sprinkle them evenly over the butter and sugar.

2 On a floured surface, roll out the pastry to a circle slightly larger than the cake tin or omelette pan. Prick the pastry lightly, support it on a baking sheet and chill.

3 Peel the pears, cut out the cores and slice them lengthways into halves. Arrange the pear halves, rounded-side down, on top of the butter and sugar. Set the cake tin or omelette pan over a medium heat until the sugar melts and begins to bubble with the butter and juice from the pears. If any areas appear to be browning more than others, move the pan around, but do not stir the contents.

4 As soon as the sugar has caramelized, remove the pan carefully from the heat. Place the circle of pastry on top of the pears, tucking the edges down the side of the pan. Transfer to the oven and bake for 25 minutes until the pastry is well risen and golden.

5 Leave the tart in the tin or pan for 2–3 minutes until the juices have stopped bubbling. Invert the tin over a plate and shake to release the tart. It may be necessary to slide a spatula underneath the pears to loosen them. Serve the tart warm with cream.

Sweet and Spicy Rice Fritters

These delicious little golden balls of rice are scented with sweet, warm spices and will fill the kitchen with wonderful aromas while cooking. To enjoy them at their best, serve them piping hot. They are great at any time of day – as a mid-morning or late afternoon snack, a simple dessert, or even as a late night treat.

Serves 4
175g/6oz cooked basmati rice
2 eggs, lightly beaten
60ml/4 tbsp caster
  (superfine) sugar
a pinch of nutmeg
2.5ml/½ tsp ground cinnamon
a pinch of ground cloves
10ml/2 tsp vanilla extract
50g/2oz/½ cup plain
  (all-purpose) flour
10ml/2 tsp baking powder
a pinch of salt
25g/1oz desiccated
  (dry unsweetened
  shredded) coconut
sunflower oil, for frying
icing (confectioners') sugar,
  to dust

1 Place the cooked rice, eggs, sugar, nutmeg, cinnamon, cloves and vanilla extract in a large bowl and whisk to combine. Sift in the flour, baking powder and salt and add the coconut. Mix well.

2 Fill a wok or deep pan one-third full of oil and heat to 180°C/350°F (or until a cube of bread, dropped into the oil, browns in 30 seconds).

3 Very gently, drop tablespoonfuls of the mixture into the oil, one at a time, and fry for 2–3 minutes, or until golden. Carefully remove the fritters from the wok using a slotted spoon and drain well on kitchen paper.

4 Divide the fritters into four portions, or simply pile them up on a single large platter. Dust them with icing sugar and serve immediately.

> **Cook's Tip**
> *Unlike many cookies, these little fritters are gluten-free, so make a perfect snack for anyone with a gluten intolerance.*

Pear Tarte Tatin Energy 265kcal/1107kJ; Protein 2.5g; Carbohydrate 30.2g, of which sugars 16.8g; Fat 16.1g, of which saturates 4.4g; Cholesterol 18mg; Calcium 36mg; Fibre 1.7g; Sodium 170mg.
Spicy Rice Fritters Energy 316kcal/1321kJ; Protein 6.6g; Carbohydrate 45.7g, of which sugars 16.3g; Fat 12.4g, of which saturates 4.8g; Cholesterol 95mg; Calcium 46mg; Fibre 1.3g; Sodium 38mg.

Rich Cinnamon-spiced Pumpkin

Rich, sticky and sweet, this Mexican way of cooking pumpkin in brown sugar creates a warming and indulgent dessert that looks very attractive and is not at all difficult to prepare. The mildly flavoured flesh of the pumpkin, equally suited to sweet and savoury dishes, responds particularly well to cooking with sweet spices.

Serves 6
1 small pumpkin, about 800g/1¾lb
350g/12oz/1½ cups soft dark brown sugar
120ml/4fl oz/½ cup water
5ml/1 tsp ground cloves
12 cinnamon sticks, each about 10cm/4in long
fresh mint sprigs, to decorate
thick yogurt or crème fraîche, to serve

1 Halve the pumpkin, remove the seeds and fibres and cut into wedges. Arrange in a single layer in a shallow, flameproof casserole or heavy pan. Fill the hollows with the sugar.

2 Pour the water carefully into the pan, taking care not to wash all the sugar to the bottom. Make sure that some of the water trickles down to the bottom to prevent the pumpkin from burning. Sprinkle on the ground cloves and add two of the cinnamon sticks.

3 Cover the pan tightly and cook over a low heat for about 30 minutes, or until the pumpkin is tender and the sugar and water have formed a syrup. Check the casserole or pan occasionally to make sure that the pumpkin does not dry out or catch on the bottom.

4 Transfer the pumpkin to a platter and pour the hot syrup over. Decorate each portion with mint and cinnamon sticks and serve with thick yogurt or crème fraîche.

> **Cook's Tip**
> Pumpkin cooked in this way makes an ideal filling for sweet empanadas, so it's worth cooking the whole pumpkin and using the leftovers in this way for another meal.

Spiced Spanish Leche Frita

The name of this dessert means "fried milk". It has a melting, creamy centre and crunchy, golden coating.

Serves 6–8
550ml/18fl oz/2½ cups milk
3 finely pared strips of lemon rind
½ cinnamon stick
90g/3½oz/½ cup caster (superfine) sugar
60ml/4 tbsp cornflour (cornstarch)
30ml/2 tbsp plain (all-purpose) flour
3 egg yolks and 2 whole eggs
90–120ml/6–8 tbsp breadcrumbs
sunflower oil, for frying
ground cinnamon, for dusting

For the sauce
450g/1lb blackberries or blackcurrants
90g/3½oz/½ cup caster (superfine) sugar

1 Put the milk, lemon rind, cinnamon stick and sugar in a pan and bring to the boil. Cover and leave to infuse for 20 minutes. Mix the cornflour and flour in a bowl and beat in the egg yolks. Add a little of the milk and beat to make a smooth batter.

2 Strain the remaining hot milk into the batter, then pour back into the pan. Cook over a low heat, stirring constantly until it thickens. Beat the mixture hard for a smooth consistency. Pour into an 18–20cm/7–8in, 1cm/½in deep rectangular dish, and smooth the top. Cool, then chill until firm.

3 To make the sauce, cook the fruit with the sugar and a little water for about 10 minutes until soft. Reserving 30–45ml/ 2–3 tbsp whole fruit, put the rest in a processor and blend to make a smooth purée. Return to the pan and keep warm.

4 Cut the chilled custard into eight or twelve squares. Beat the eggs in a shallow dish and spread the breadcrumbs on a plate. Coat each square in egg, then in crumbs.

5 Heat about 1cm/½in oil in a frying pan until very hot. Fry the squares in batches for a couple of minutes, shaking or spooning the oil over the top, until golden. Drain on kitchen paper while frying the other batches. Arrange on plates and sprinkle with sugar and cinnamon. Pour a circle of warm sauce round the squares, distributing the whole berries evenly.

Spiced Pumpkin Energy 247kcal/1054kJ; Protein 1.2g; Carbohydrate 63.9g, of which sugars 63.2g; Fat 0.3g, of which saturates 0.1g; Cholesterol 0mg; Calcium 70mg; Fibre 1.3g; Sodium 4mg.
Spiced Leche Frita Energy 257kcal/1089kJ; Protein 6.9g; Carbohydrate 45.9g, of which sugars 30.6g; Fat 6.4g, of which saturates 2.7g; Cholesterol 133mg; Calcium 159mg; Fibre 2.3g; Sodium 143mg.

Pears with Vanilla and Honey

These sweet juicy pears, poached in a honey syrup fragrant with vanilla, saffron and lime, make a truly elegant dessert. They are lovely eaten just as they are, but for a really luxurious, indulgent treat, serve them with thin pouring cream or ice cream.

Serves 4
150g/5oz/³⁄₄ cup caster (superfine) sugar
105ml/7 tbsp clear honey
5ml/1 tsp finely grated lime rind
a large pinch of saffron
2 vanilla pods (beans)
4 large, firm ripe dessert pears
single (light) cream or ice cream, to serve

1 Place the caster sugar and honey in a medium, non-stick wok or large pan, then add the lime rind and the saffron strands. Using a small, sharp knife, split the vanilla pods in half and scrape the seeds into the wok, then add the pods as well.

2 Pour 500ml/17fl oz/scant 2¼ cups water into the wok and bring the mixture to the boil. Reduce the heat to low and simmer, stirring occasionally, while you prepare the pears.

3 Peel the pears, then add to the wok and gently turn in the syrup to coat evenly. Cover the wok and simmer gently for 12–15 minutes, turning the pears halfway through cooking, until they are just tender.

4 Lift the pears from the syrup using a slotted spoon and transfer to four serving bowls. Set aside.

5 Bring the syrup back to the boil and cook gently for about 10 minutes, or until thickened. Spoon the syrup over the pears and serve warm or chilled with single cream or ice cream.

Variations
Try using different flavourings in the syrup: add 10ml/2 tsp chopped fresh root ginger and 1–2 star anise, or 1 cinnamon stick and 3 cloves. The honey can be replaced with the same quantity of maple syrup.

Spiced Carrot and Raisin Halwa

Halwa is a traditional Indian sweet, and there are many variations on the basic recipe. In this version, which comes from the Udupi cuisine of south-west India, grated carrots are cooked in milk with ghee, sugar, spices and raisins until meltingly tender and sweet. You will only need a small bowl of this delicious dessert because it is very rich.

Serves 4
90g/3½oz ghee
300g/11oz carrots, coarsely grated
250ml/8fl oz/1 cup milk
150g/5oz/³⁄₄ cup golden caster (superfine) sugar
5–6 lightly crushed cardamom pods
1 clove
1 cinnamon stick
50g/2oz/scant ½ cup raisins

1 Place a wok or a large deep frying pan over a low heat and add half the ghee. When the ghee has melted, add the grated carrot and stir-fry for 6–8 minutes.

2 Pour the milk into the wok, stir into the carrots and raise the heat to bring the mixture to the boil. Once it is bubbling reduce the heat to low again and leave to simmer gently for 10–12 minutes, stirring occasionally.

3 Stir the remaining ghee into the carrot mixture, then add the caster sugar, crushed cardamom pods, clove, cinnamon stick and raisins.

4 Gently simmer the carrot mixture for 6–7 minutes, stirring occasionally, until it is thickened and glossy. Using a spoon, remove and discard the whole spices if you wish, and serve scoops of the halwa immediately in small serving bowls.

Cook's Tip
Ghee is clarified butter, widely used in Indian cooking. It is an essential ingredient in halwa and is available in cans from Asian stores and many supermarkets.

Pears with Vanilla Energy 283kcal/1207kJ; Protein 0.8g; Carbohydrate 74.3g, of which sugars 74.3g; Fat 0.2g, of which saturates 0g; Cholesterol 0mg; Calcium 38mg; Fibre 3.3g; Sodium 10mg.
Carrot Halwa Energy 439kcal/1838kJ; Protein 3g; Carbohydrate 56.7g, of which sugars 56.3g; Fat 23.8g, of which saturates 15.6g; Cholesterol 67mg; Calcium 119mg; Fibre 2.1g; Sodium 56mg.

Baklava

This famous Turkish confection is one of the greatest creations of the Ottoman pastry chefs. It is traditionally made with eight layers of pastry and seven layers of chopped walnuts, but fillings vary from a mixture of chopped nuts to a moist, creamy almond paste or a delicately flavoured pumpkin purée.

Serves 12

175g/6oz/³/₄ cup butter
100ml/3¹/₂fl oz/scant ¹/₂ cup
   sunflower oil
450g/1lb filo pastry
450g/1lb walnuts, or a mixture of
   walnuts and almonds, chopped
5ml/1 tsp ground cinnamon

For the syrup
450g/1lb sugar
30ml/2 tbsp rose water

1 Preheat the oven to 160°C/325°F/Gas 3. Melt the butter and oil in a small pan, then brush a little over the bottom and sides of a 30cm/12in round or square cake tin (pan).

2 Place a sheet of filo in the bottom of the tin and brush it with melted butter and oil. Continue until you have used half the filo sheets, brushing each one with butter and oil. Ease the sheets into the corners and trim the edges if they flop over the rim.

3 Spread the nuts over the last buttered sheet and sprinkle with the cinnamon, then continue as before with the remaining filo sheets. Brush the top one as well, then, using a sharp knife, cut diagonal parallel lines right through all the layers to the bottom to form small diamond shapes.

4 Bake for about 1 hour, until the top is golden. Meanwhile make the syrup. Put the sugar into a heavy pan, pour in 250ml/8fl oz/1 cup water and bring to the boil, stirring all the time. When the sugar has dissolved, lower the heat and stir in the rose water, then simmer for about 15 minutes, until the syrup thickens. Leave to cool in the pan.

5 When the baklava is ready, remove it from the oven and slowly pour the cooled syrup over the hot pastry. Return to the oven for 2–3 minutes to soak up the syrup, then take it out and leave to cool before lifting the pieces out of the tin.

Nutmeg Custard Tarts

These luxurious little tarts are a real treat to eat with afternoon tea or as a classic dessert at a supper party.

Serves 8
600ml/1 pint/2¹/₂ cups full-cream
   (whole) milk
6 egg yolks
75g/3oz/6 tbsp caster
   (superfine) sugar
a whole nutmeg

For the rich butter pastry
175g/6oz/1¹/₂ cups plain (all-
   purpose) flour
a good pinch of salt
75g/3oz/6 tbsp unsalted
   (sweet) butter, at room
   temperature
75g/3oz/6 tbsp caster
   (superfine) sugar
3 egg yolks, at room temperature
2.5ml/¹/₂ tsp vanilla extract

1 Make the pastry first. Sift the flour and salt on to a sheet of baking parchment. Put the butter, sugar, egg yolks and vanilla extract in a food processor and process until the mixture resembles scrambled eggs. Tip in the flour and combine. Transfer the dough to a floured surface and knead gently until smooth. Form into a ball, flatten and wrap in cling film (plastic wrap). Chill for at least 30 minutes.

2 Roll out the pastry thinly and use to line eight individual 10cm/4in loose-based tart pans. (You can use smaller, deeper pans, but remember they will need slightly longer cooking.) Place the pans on a baking sheet and chill for 30 minutes.

3 Preheat the oven to 200°C/400°F/Gas 6. To make the filling, heat the milk in a pan until just warmed but not boiling. Beat the egg yolks and sugar together in a bowl until pale and creamy. Pour the milk on to the yolks and stir well to mix. Do not whisk as this will produce too many bubbles. Strain the milk mixture into a jug (pitcher) and pour into the tart cases.

4 Liberally grate fresh nutmeg over the surface of the tartlets. Bake for about 10 minutes, then lower the heat to 180°C/350°F/Gas 4 and bake for another 10 minutes, or until the filling has set and is just turning golden. Don't overbake as the filling should be a bit wobbly when the tartlets come out of the oven. Remove from the pans to cool slightly but serve warm.

Baklava Energy 973kcal/4059kJ; Protein 12.2g; Carbohydrate 89.9g, of which sugars 60.9g; Fat 65.2g, of which saturates 15.6g; Cholesterol 47mg; Calcium 139mg; Fibre 3.1g; Sodium 141mg.
Custard Tarts Energy 336kcal/1409kJ; Protein 7.9g; Carbohydrate 40g, of which sugars 23.4g; Fat 17.1g, of which saturates 8.6g; Cholesterol 257mg; Calcium 157mg; Fibre 0.7g; Sodium 101mg.

Moroccan Cinnamon Swirl

This pastry, whose Arabic name means "the snake", is the most famous, traditional sweet dish in Morocco. The coiled pastry looks impressive and tastes divine when freshly made.

Serves 8–10
115g/4oz/1 cup blanched almonds
300g/11oz/2¾ cups ground almonds
50g/2oz/½ cup icing (confectioners') sugar
115g/4oz/⅔ cup caster (superfine) sugar
115g/4oz/½ cup butter, softened, plus 20g/¾oz for cooking nuts
5–10ml/1–2 tsp ground cinnamon
15ml/1 tbsp orange flower water
3–4 sheets filo pastry
1 egg yolk
icing (confectioners') sugar and ground cinnamon, to dust

1 Fry the blanched almonds in a little butter until golden brown, then pound them using a pestle and mortar. Place the nuts in a bowl and add the ground almonds, icing sugar, caster sugar, butter, cinnamon and orange flower water. Form the mixture into a smooth paste. Cover and chill.

2 Preheat the oven to 180°C/350°F/Gas 4. Open out the sheets of filo pastry, keeping them in a pile so they do not dry out, and brush the top one with a little melted butter. Take lumps of the almond paste and roll them into fingers. Place them end to end along the long edge of the top sheet of filo, then roll the filo up into a roll the thickness of your thumb, tucking in the ends to stop the filling oozing out. Repeat with the other sheets of filo, until all the filling is used up.

3 Grease a large baking sheet. Lift one of the filo rolls in both hands and gently push it together from both ends, like an accordion, to relax the pastry before coiling it in the centre of the pan or baking sheet. Do the same with the other rolls, placing them end to end to form a tight coil like a snake.

4 Mix the egg yolk with a little water and brush the pastry, then bake for 30–35 minutes, until crisp. Top the freshly cooked pastry with a liberal sprinkling of icing sugar, and add lines of cinnamon. Serve at room temperature.

Aromatic Stuffed Pastries

These aromatic sweet pastry crescents from Greece are packed with candied citrus peel and walnuts, which have been soaked in a coffee syrup.

Makes 16
60ml/4 tbsp clear honey
60ml/4 tbsp strong brewed coffee
75g/3oz/½ cup mixed candied citrus peel, finely chopped
175g/6oz/1½ cups walnuts, chopped
1.5ml/¼ tsp freshly grated nutmeg
milk, to glaze
caster (superfine) sugar, for sprinkling

For the pastry
450g/1lb/4 cups plain (all-purpose) flour
2.5ml/½ tsp ground cinnamon
2.5ml/½ tsp baking powder
pinch of salt
150g/5oz/10 tbsp butter
30ml/2 tbsp caster (superfine) sugar
1 egg
120ml/4fl oz/½ cup milk, chilled

1 Preheat the oven to 180°C/350°F/Gas 4. To make the pastry, sift the flour, cinnamon, baking powder and salt into a bowl. Rub or cut in the butter until the mixture resembles breadcrumbs. Stir in the sugar and make a well in the mixture.

2 Beat the egg and milk together and pour into the well in the dry ingredients. Mix to a soft dough. Divide the dough into two and chill for 30 minutes. Meanwhile, mix the honey and coffee in a mixing bowl. Add the candied peel, walnuts and nutmeg. Stir well, cover and leave for 20 minutes.

3 Roll out one portion of the dough on a lightly floured surface to a thickness of 3mm/⅛in. Stamp out rounds, using a 10cm/4in plain pastry cutter. Place a heaped teaspoonful of filling on one side of each round. Brush the edges with a little milk, then fold over and press together to seal. Repeat with the second piece of pastry until all the filling has been used.

4 Place the pastries on lightly greased baking sheets, brush lightly with a little milk, and then sprinkle with a little caster sugar. Make a steam hole in the centre of each. Bake for 35 minutes, until golden. Cool on a wire rack before serving.

Cinnamon Swirl Energy 261kcal/1091kJ; Protein 3.8g; Carbohydrate 25.9g, of which sugars 17.9g; Fat 16.6g, of which saturates 6.7g; Cholesterol 45mg; Calcium 55mg; Fibre 1.2g; Sodium 74mg.
Stuffed Pastries Energy 278kcal/1162kJ; Protein 5g; Carbohydrate 30.2g, of which sugars 8.7g; Fat 16.1g, of which saturates 5.7g; Cholesterol 32mg; Calcium 69mg; Fibre 1.5g; Sodium 80mg.

Spicy Pumpkin and Orange Bombe

Pumpkin has a subtle flavour that is truly transformed with the addition of citrus fruits and spices.

Serves 8
For the sponge
115g/4oz/½ cup unsalted butter
115g/4oz/½ cup caster (superfine) sugar
115g/4oz/1 cup self-raising (self-rising) flour
2.5ml/½ tsp baking powder
2 eggs

For the ice cream
Juice and pared rind of 1 orange
300g/11oz/scant 1½ cups golden granulated sugar
300ml/½ pint/1¼ cups water
2 cinnamon sticks, halved
10ml/2 tsp whole cloves
30ml/2 tbsp orange flower water
400g/14oz can unsweetened pumpkin purée
300ml/½ pint/1¼ cups extra thick double cream
2 pieces stem ginger, grated
icing (confectioners') sugar, to dust

1 Preheat the oven to 180°C/350°F/Gas 4. Grease and line a 450g/1lb loaf tin (pan). Beat the butter, caster sugar, flour, baking powder and eggs until creamy. Turn into the tin, level the surface and bake for 30 minutes, until firm in the centre. Leave to cool.

2 Make the ice cream. Cut the pared orange rind into very fine shreds. Heat the sugar and water in a heavy pan until the sugar dissolves, then boil rapidly for 3 minutes. Stir in the orange shreds, juice, cinnamon and cloves and heat gently for 5 minutes. Strain, reserving the rind and spices. Measure 300ml/ ½ pint/1¼ cups of the syrup and reserve. Return the spices to the remaining syrup with the orange flower water.

3 Beat the pumpkin purée with 175ml/6fl oz/¾ cup of the measured syrup, the cream and ginger. Pour the mixture into a shallow container and freeze until firm.

4 Line a 1.5 litre/2½ pint/6¼ cup basin with clear film (plastic wrap). Cut the cake into 1cm/½in slices. Dip them briefly in the remaining strained syrup and use to line the basin, trimming the pieces to fit. Chill, then fill with the ice cream, level the surface and freeze until firm, preferably overnight. To serve, invert the ice cream on to a serving plate and peel away the film. Dust with icing sugar and serve in wedges with the spiced syrup.

Crème Caramel with Butter Cookies

This Moroccan version of a simple but much-loved dessert adds the subtle colour and flavour of saffron and the fragrance of delicate cardamom. Crisp orange-flower-scented cookies are a lovely accompaniment.

Serves 4–6
600ml/1 pint/2½ cups milk
115g/4oz/⅔ cup sugar, plus 60ml/4 tbsp for caramel
pinch of saffron threads
2.5ml/½ tsp cardamom seeds
15–30ml/1–2 tbsp rose water
4 eggs, lightly beaten
60ml/4 tbsp boiling water

For the cookies
200g/7oz/scant 1 cup butter
130g/4½oz/generous 1 cup icing (confectioners') sugar, sifted
5–10ml/1–2 tsp orange flower water
250g/9oz/2¼ cups plain (all-purpose) flour, sifted
handful of blanched almonds

1 Preheat the oven to 180°C/350°F/Gas 4. Heat the milk, sugar, saffron and cardamom in a pan until the milk is just about to boil. Set aside to cool. Add the rose water, then gradually pour the mixture into the eggs, beating all the time. Set aside.

2 To make the caramel, heat the 60ml/4 tbsp sugar in a small heavy pan until melted and dark brown. Stir in the boiling water and let it bubble before tipping it into individual dishes. Swirl the dishes to coat evenly. Leave to cool.

3 Pour the custard into the dishes and stand them in a roasting pan. Add water to two-thirds of the way up the dishes. Bake for about 1 hour, until set. Cool, then chill for several hours or overnight.

4 To make the cookies, melt the butter in a pan and leave to cool. Stir in the icing sugar and orange flower water, then gradually beat in the flour to form a smooth, stiff dough. Chill.

5 Preheat the oven to 180°C/350°F/Gas 4. Grease a baking sheet. Break off walnut-size pieces of dough and roll into balls. Place on the baking sheet and flatten slightly. Press a nut into the centre of each. Bake for 20 minutes, or until golden. Invert the crème caramel on to plates. Serve with the butter cookies.

Pumpkin Bombe Energy 571kcal/2387kJ; Protein 4.2g; Carbohydrate 67g, of which sugars 56.1g; Fat 33.6g, of which saturates 20.5g; Cholesterol 130mg; Calcium 122mg; Fibre 1g; Sodium 168mg.
Crème Caramel Energy 969kcal/4065kJ; Protein 17.8g; Carbohydrate 120g, of which sugars 72.3g; Fat 50g, of which saturates 29.3g; Cholesterol 306mg; Calcium 338mg; Fibre 1.9g; Sodium 443mg.

Date and Walnut Spice Cake

This deliciously moist and richly spiced cake is topped with a sticky honey and orange glaze. Serve it as a dessert with a generous spoonful of crème fraîche.

Serves 8
115g/4oz/½ cup unsalted butter, plus extra for greasing
175g/6oz/¾ cup soft dark brown sugar
2 eggs
175g/6oz/1½ cups unbleached self-raising (self-rising) flour
5ml/1 tsp bicarbonate of soda (baking soda)
2.5ml/½ tsp grated nutmeg
5ml/1 tsp mixed (apple pie) spice
pinch of salt
175ml/6fl oz/¾ cup buttermilk
50g/2oz/⅓ cup ready-to-eat stoned dates, chopped
25g/1oz/¼ cup walnuts, chopped

For the topping
60ml/4 tbsp clear honey
45ml/3 tbsp fresh orange juice
15ml/1 tbsp grated orange rind, plus extra to decorate

1 Grease and lightly flour a 23cm/9in spring-form cake tin (pan). Preheat the oven to 180°C/350°F/Gas 4. Cream together the butter and sugar until fluffy and creamy. Add the eggs, one at a time, and beat well to combine. Sift together the flour, bicarbonate of soda, spices and salt. Gradually add this to the creamed mixture, alternating with the buttermilk. Stir in the dates and walnuts.

2 Spoon the mixture into the prepared tin and level the top. Bake for 50 minutes or until a skewer inserted into the centre of the cake comes out clean. Leave to cool for 5 minutes, then turn out on to a wire rack to cool completely.

3 To make the topping, heat the honey, orange juice and rind in a small pan. Boil rapidly for 3 minutes, without stirring, until syrupy. Make holes in the cake with a skewer, and pour over the syrup. Decorate with orange rind.

> **Cook's Tip**
> To make your own buttermilk substitute, mix 15ml/1 tbsp lemon juice with 250ml/8fl oz/1 cup semi-skimmed milk.

Spicy Overnight Cake

Many old recipes for cakes contained lists of ingredients with weights and proportions that were easy to remember – ideal for passing down from generation to generation. This one has no added sugar; all its sweetness comes from the dried fruit it contains. It is at its most delicious if eaten when just cooled, on the day it is baked. Its crust is crisp and flaky while the inside is soft and moist.

Makes a thin 23cm/9in round cake
225g/8oz/2 cups plain (all-purpose) flour
5ml/1 tsp ground cinnamon
5ml/1 tsp ground ginger
115g/4oz/½ cup butter, cut into cubes
115g/4oz/⅔ cup mixed dried fruit
2.5ml/½ tsp bicarbonate of soda (baking soda)
15ml/1 tbsp vinegar
300ml/½ pint/1¼ cups full-cream (whole) milk

1 Sift the flour and spices. Add the butter and rub in until the mixture resembles fine breadcrumbs. Stir in the dried fruit and enough milk to make a soft mix.

2 Mix the bicarbonate of soda with the vinegar and, as the combination begins to froth, quickly stir it into the cake mixture. Cover the bowl and leave at room temperature for about 8 hours, or overnight.

3 Preheat the oven to 180°C/360°F/Gas 4. Grease a shallow 23cm/9in round cake tin (pan) and line its base with baking parchment.

4 Spoon the cake mixture into the prepared tin and level the top. Put into the hot oven and cook for about 1 hour or until the cake is firm to the touch and cooked through – a skewer inserted in the centre should come out free of sticky mixture. If the top starts to get too brown during cooking, cover it with baking parchment.

5 Leave the cake in the tin to cool for 15–20 minutes, then turn out and cool completely on a wire rack.

Date Spice Cake Energy 2666kcal/11243kJ; Protein 61.2g; Carbohydrate 429.6g, of which sugars 243.9g; Fat 90.2g, of which saturates 12.3g; Cholesterol 18mg; Calcium 650mg; Fibre 34.8g; Sodium 163mg.
Overnight Cake Energy 2069kcal/8681kJ; Protein 34.7g; Carbohydrate 267.9g, of which sugars 96.5g; Fat 103g, of which saturates 63.6g; Cholesterol 263mg; Calcium 780mg; Fibre 9.5g; Sodium 888mg.

Spicy Apple Cake

Hundreds of German cakes and desserts include apples. This moist and spicy *apfelkuchen* is perfect with a cup of coffee or tea.

Serves 12
115g/4oz/1 cup plain (all-purpose) flour
115g/4oz/1 cup wholemeal (whole-wheat) flour
10ml/2 tsp baking powder
5ml/1 tsp cinnamon
2.5ml/1/2 tsp mixed spice (apple pie spice)
225g/8oz cooking apple, cored, peeled and chopped

75g/3oz/6 tbsp butter
175g/6oz/generous 3/4 cup soft light brown sugar
finely grated rind of 1 small orange
2 eggs, beaten
30ml/2 tbsp milk
whipped cream dusted with cinnamon, to serve

For the topping
4 eating apples, cored and thinly sliced
juice of 1/2 orange
10ml/2 tsp caster (superfine) sugar
45ml/3 tbsp apricot jam, warmed and sieved (strained)

1 Preheat the oven to 180°C/350°F/Gas 4. Grease and line a 23cm/9in round loose-bottomed cake tin (pan). Sift the flours, baking powder and spices together into a bowl. Toss the chopped cooking apple in 30ml/2 tbsp of the flour mixture.

2 Cream the butter, brown sugar and orange rind together until light and fluffy. Gradually beat in the eggs, then fold in the flour mixture, the chopped apple and the milk. Spoon the mixture into the cake tin and level the surface.

3 For the topping, toss the apple slices in the orange juice and set them in overlapping circles on top of the cake mixture, pressing down lightly.

4 Sprinkle the caster sugar over the top of the cake and bake for 1–1 1/4 hours, or until risen and firm. Cover with foil if the apples start to brown too much.

5 Cool in the tin for 10 minutes, then remove to a wire rack. Glaze the apples with the sieved jam. Cut into wedges and serve with whipped cream, sprinkled with cinnamon.

Spiced Walnut Cake

This luscious cake is the finest Greek dessert of all. Its soft texture, with the sweetness of the walnuts, makes it irresistible. The cake tastes even better the day after it is made.

2.5ml/1/2 tsp ground cinnamon
300g/11oz/2 3/4 cups shelled walnuts, coarsely chopped
150g/5oz/1 1/4 cups self-raising (self-rising) flour
5ml/1 tsp baking powder
salt

Serves 10–12
150g/5oz/2/3 cup butter
115g/4oz/1/2 cup caster (superfine) sugar
4 eggs, separated
60ml/4 tbsp brandy

For the syrup
250g/9oz/generous 1 cup caster (superfine) sugar
30ml/2 tbsp brandy
2–3 strips of pared orange rind
2 cinnamon sticks

1 Preheat the oven to 190°C/375°F/Gas 5. Grease a 35 × 23cm/14 × 9in baking dish that is at least 5cm/2in deep. Cream the butter in a large mixing bowl until soft, then add the sugar and beat well until the mixture is light and fluffy.

2 Add the egg yolks one by one, beating after each addition. Stir in the brandy and cinnamon. Mix the chopped walnuts in to the mixture. Sift the flour with the baking powder and set aside.

3 Whisk the egg whites with a pinch of salt until they are stiff. Fold them into the creamed mixture, alternating with tablespoons of flour until both have all been incorporated. Spread the mixture evenly in the prepared pan or dish. It should be about 4cm/1 1/2in deep. Bake for about 40 minutes, until the top is golden and a skewer inserted in the cake comes out clean. Take the cake out of the oven and let it rest in the pan or dish while you make the syrup.

4 Mix the sugar and 300ml/1/2 pint/1 1/4 cups water in a small pan. Heat gently, stirring, until the sugar dissolves. Bring to the boil, lower the heat, add the brandy, orange rind and cinnamon sticks. Simmer for 10 minutes. Slice the cake into diamond shapes and strain the syrup slowly over it. Let it stand for 10–20 minutes until the syrup is absorbed.

Spicy Apple Cake Energy 587kcal/2471kJ; Protein 5.5g; Carbohydrate 92g, of which sugars 69.7g; Fat 24.5g, of which saturates 10.6g; Cholesterol 40mg; Calcium 95mg; Fibre 2.5g; Sodium 129mg.
Walnut Cake Energy 563kcal/2349kJ; Protein 8.5g; Carbohydrate 50.6g, of which sugars 39.2g; Fat 35.3g, of which saturates 10.1g; Cholesterol 108mg; Calcium 114mg; Fibre 1.5g; Sodium 177mg.

Swedish Spice Bread

Cardamom and caraway seeds are widely used in Scandinavian cooking. Serve this interesting bread sliced with butter.

Makes a 23cm/9in round loaf
25g/1oz/2 tbsp butter
45ml/3 tbsp clear honey
225g/8oz/2 cups strong white bread flour
225g/8oz/2 cups rye flour
2.5ml/½ tsp salt
7g/¼oz sachet easy-blend (rapid-rise) dried yeast
5ml/1 tsp ground cardamom
5ml/1 tsp ground caraway seeds
2.5ml/½ tsp ground star anise
30ml/2 tbsp caster (superfine) sugar
grated rind and juice of 1 orange
175ml/6fl oz/¾ cup lager
1 egg, beaten

For the glaze
4 tbsp boiling water
1 tbsp clear honey

1 Melt the butter with the honey in a small pan, then leave to cool. Sift the flours and salt into a bowl and stir in the yeast, cardamom, caraway, star anise, caster sugar and orange rind.

2 Mix the lager with the boiling water. Stir the orange juice and beaten egg into the melted butter and honey, then stir this mixture into the flour. Add enough of the warm lager and water to make a soft and slightly sticky, but manageable dough. Place the dough on a lightly floured surface and knead for 5 minutes until smooth and elastic. Place in an oiled bowl, cover and leave to rise until doubled in bulk. Knead briefly, then divide the dough in two. Roll out each piece into a long snake.

3 Grease a 23cm/9in round cake tin (pan). Starting at the edge of the tin, coil the dough round and round to the centre, joining the second piece to the first with a little water. Cover with oiled clear film (plastic wrap) and leave until doubled in size. Preheat the oven to 190°C/375°F/Gas 5. Bake the bread for 10 minutes, then turn the oven down to 160°C/325°F/Gas 3 and bake for 40–50 minutes more, until the bread is lightly browned and sounds hollow when rapped underneath.

4 To make the glaze, mix the honey with 15ml/1 tbsp hot water, then brush it over the loaf. Leave on a wire rack to cool.

Orange and Coriander Brioches

The warm spicy flavour of coriander seeds combines really well with orange.

Makes 12
225g/8oz/2 cups strong white bread flour
10ml/2 tsp easy-blend (rapid rise) dried yeast
2.5ml/½ tsp salt
15ml/1 tbsp caster (superfine) sugar
10ml/2 tsp coriander seeds, coarsely ground
grated rind of 1 orange
2 eggs, beaten
50g/2oz/¼ cup butter, melted
1 small egg, beaten, to glaze

1 Grease 12 individual brioche tins (pans). Sift the flour into a bowl and stir in the yeast, salt, sugar, coriander seeds and orange rind. Make a well in the centre, pour in 30ml/2 tbsp hand-hot water, the eggs and the melted butter and beat to make a soft dough. Turn on to a lightly floured surface and knead for 5 minutes until smooth and elastic. Return to the clean, lightly oiled bowl, cover with clear film (plastic wrap) and leave in a warm place for 1 hour until doubled in bulk.

2 Turn on to a floured surface, knead again briefly and roll into a sausage. Cut into 12 pieces. Break off a quarter of each piece and set aside. Shape the larger pieces of dough into balls and place in the prepared tins.

3 With a floured wooden spoon, press a hole in each dough ball. Shape each small piece of dough into a little plug and press into the holes. Place the brioche tins on a baking sheet. Cover with lightly oiled clear film and leave in a warm place until the dough rises almost to the top of the tins.

4 Preheat the oven to 220°C/425°F/Gas 7. Brush the brioches with beaten egg and bake for 15 minutes until golden brown. Sprinkle over shreds of orange rind, and serve warm with butter.

Cook's Tip
These brioches look particularly attractive if they are made in special brioche tins, but they can also be made in muffin tins.

Spice Bread Energy 2195kcal/9299kJ; Protein 52.8g; Carbohydrate 425.4g, of which sugars 69.3g; Fat 38.7g, of which saturates 16.5g; Cholesterol 244mg; Calcium 519mg; Fibre 33.3g; Sodium 263mg.
Orange Brioches Energy 112kcal/471kJ; Protein 2.8g; Carbohydrate 15.9g, of which sugars 1.6g; Fat 4.6g, of which saturates 2.5g; Cholesterol 41mg; Calcium 32mg; Fibre 0.6g; Sodium 119mg.

Cinnamon Doughnuts

These doughnuts are made to an Eastern European recipe and are, of course, best eaten on the day they are made. They are dusted with sugar and cinnamon, and are also an ideal showcase for your finest homemade jam: in the Balkans they are usually filled with a thick fruity jam such as cherry, plum or apricot.

Makes 10–12

225g/8oz/2 cups strong flour
2.5ml/½ tsp salt
7g/¼oz sachet easy-blend (rapid-rise) dried yeast
1 egg, beaten
60–90ml/4–6 tbsp milk
15ml/1 tbsp sugar
about 60ml/4 tbsp cherry jam
oil, for deep-fat frying
50g/2oz/¼ cup caster (superfine) sugar
2.5ml/½ tsp cinnamon

1 Sift the flour into a bowl with the salt. Stir in the yeast. Make a well in the dry ingredients and add the egg, milk and sugar.

2 Mix together thoroughly, adding a little more milk if necessary, to make a smooth, but not sticky, dough. Beat well, then cover with clear film (plastic wrap) and leave for 1–1½ hours in a warm place until the dough has doubled in size.

3 Grease a baking sheet. Knead the dough on a lightly floured surface and divide it into 10–12 pieces. Shape each into a round and put 5ml/1 tsp of jam in the centre.

4 Dampen the edges of the dough with water, then draw up to form a ball, closing firmly so the jam will not escape during cooking. Place on the baking sheet and leave for 15 minutes.

5 Heat the oil in a large saucepan or deep fryer to 180°C/350°F, or until a 2.5cm/1in cube of bread dropped into the oil turns golden in about 60 seconds. Fry the doughnuts fairly gently for 5–10 minutes, until golden brown. Drain well on kitchen paper.

6 Mix the caster sugar and ground cinnamon together on a plate or in a large plastic bag and use to liberally coat the doughnuts while still warm.

Cornish Saffron Bread

This loaf is traditionally made at Easter, and is served sliced and buttered. Saffron, the precious spice from western Asia, may have been introduced to Cornwall by Phoenician traders 3,000 years ago.

Makes 1 loaf
good pinch of saffron threads
450g/1lb/4 cups plain (all-purpose) flour

2.5ml/½ tsp salt
50g/2oz/4 tbsp butter, diced
50g/2oz/4 tbsp lard, diced
10ml/2 tsp fast-action yeast granules
50g/2oz caster (superfine) sugar
115g/4oz/½ cup currants, raisins or sultanas (golden raisins), or a mixture
50g/2oz chopped mixed candied peel
150ml/¼ pint/⅔ cup milk
beaten egg, to glaze

1 Put the saffron in a bowl and add 150ml/¼ pint/⅔ cup boiling water. Cover and leave for several hours to allow the colour and flavour to develop.

2 Sift the flour and salt into a large bowl. Add the butter and lard and rub them into the flour until the mixture resembles fine breadcrumbs. Stir in the yeast granules, sugar, dried fruit and chopped mixed peel. Make a well in the centre.

3 Add the milk to the saffron water and warm to body heat. Tip the liquid into the flour and stir until it can be gathered into a ball. Cover with oiled clear film (plastic wrap) and leave in a warm place for about 1 hour, until doubled in size.

4 Grease and line a 900g/2lb loaf tin (pan) with baking parchment. Turn the dough on to a lightly floured surface and knead gently and briefly. Put the dough in the prepared tin, cover and leave in a warm place for 30 minutes until nearly doubled in size.

5 Preheat the oven to 200°C/400°F/Gas 6. Brush the top of the loaf with beaten egg and cook for 40 minutes or until risen and cooked through; cover with foil if it starts to brown too much. Leave in the tin for about 15 minutes before turning out on to a wire rack to cool.

Cinnamon Doughnuts Energy 192kcal/803kJ; Protein 2.5g; Carbohydrate 22.6g, of which sugars 8.3g; Fat 10.8g, of which saturates 1.4g; Cholesterol 16mg; Calcium 37mg; Fibre 0.6g; Sodium 11mg.
Saffron Bread Energy 3041kcal/12821kJ; Protein 50.7g; Carbohydrate 516.8g, of which sugars 173.9g; Fat 99.9g, of which saturates 48.7g; Cholesterol 162mg; Calcium 1018mg; Fibre 18.5g; Sodium 541mg.

Cinnamon and Vanilla Biscuits

These melt-in-the-mouth cinnamon and vanilla biscuits are traditionally served at Mexican weddings. They are perfect for serving with coffee.

Makes about 40
225g/8oz/1 cup butter, softened
50g/2oz/¼ cup caster (superfine) sugar

225g/8oz/2 cups plain (all-purpose) flour
115g/4oz/1 cup cornflour (cornstarch)
5ml/1 tsp vanilla extract

For dusting
50g/2oz/½ cup icing (confectioners') sugar
5ml/1 tsp ground cinnamon

1 Preheat the oven to 160°C/325°F/Gas 3. Lightly grease two or three baking sheets.

2 In a bowl, cream the butter with the caster sugar until light and fluffy. Sift the flour and cornflour together and gradually work into the creamed butter and sugar mixture with the vanilla extract.

3 Roll heaped teaspoons of the mixture into balls and place on the prepared baking sheets. Bake for 30 minutes or until the biscuits (cookies) are pale golden.

4 Sift the icing sugar and ground cinnamon together into a bowl. While the biscuits are still warm, toss them in the icing sugar mixture. Leave on a wire rack to cool, then store in an airtight tin for up to 2 weeks.

Cook's Tips
• The biscuit mixture can be prepared in a food processor.
• Vanilla is one of the most complex of spices, and is available in various forms. Pure vanilla extract is made by soaking chopped vanilla pods (beans) in alcohol and water. The best quality extracts are expensive, but keep indefinitely. Don't be tempted to buy cheaper products that use imitation vanilla flavouring, as the taste is synthetic and inferior.

Dutch Marzipan Cookies

These Dutch cookies, made from a spicy dough wrapped around a rich marzipan filling, are eaten on the feast of St Nicholas, 6 December.

Makes about 35
175g/6oz/1½ cups ground hazelnuts
175g/6oz/1½ cups ground almonds
175g/6oz/scant 1 cup caster (superfine) sugar
175g/6oz/1½ cups icing (confectioners') sugar

1 egg, beaten
10–15ml/2–3 tsp lemon juice
250g/9oz/2¼ cups self-raising (self-rising) flour
5ml/1 tsp mixed (apple pie) spice
75g/3oz/⅓ cup light muscovado (brown) sugar
115g/4oz/½ cup unsalted (sweet) butter, diced
2 eggs
15ml/1 tbsp milk
15ml/1 tbsp caster (superfine) sugar
about 35 blanched almond halves

1 To make the filling, put the ground hazelnuts, almonds, caster sugar, icing sugar, beaten egg and 10ml/2 tsp lemon juice in a bowl and mix to a firm paste, adding more lemon juice if needed. Divide the mixture in half and roll each piece into a sausage shape about 25cm/10in long. Wrap in foil and chill.

2 To make the dough, sift the flour and mixed spice into a large mixing bowl then stir in the muscovado sugar. Add the butter and rub in well with your fingertips. Beat one of the eggs, add to the mixture and mix together to form a dough. Knead lightly, then wrap in clear film (plastic wrap) and chill for 15 minutes. Preheat the oven to 180°C/350°F/Gas 4 and line a baking sheet with baking parchment.

3 Roll out the pastry on a lightly floured surface to a 30cm/12in square and cut in half to make two rectangles. Beat the remaining egg and brush some all over the pastry rectangles.

4 Place a roll of filling on each piece of pastry and roll to enclose the filling. Place, join-side down, on the baking sheet. Beat the remains of the egg with the milk and sugar and brush over the rolls. Press almond halves along the top, bake for 35 minutes, and leave to cool before cutting diagonally into slices.

Cinnamon Biscuits Energy 65kcal/273kJ; Protein 0.9g; Carbohydrate 7.8g, of which sugars 3.1g; Fat 3.6g, of which saturates 2.2g; Cholesterol 14mg; Calcium 15mg; Fibre 0.2g; Sodium 28mg.
Marzipan Cookies Energy 181kcal/757kJ; Protein 3.5g; Carbohydrate 19.5g, of which sugars 13.8g; Fat 10.4g, of which saturates 2.4g; Cholesterol 23mg; Calcium 44mg; Fibre 1.1g; Sodium 28mg.

Chilli Cornbread

This golden yellow cornbread spiked with chilli makes an excellent accompaniment to soups and salads.

Makes 9 slices
2 eggs
450ml/³/₄ pint/1⁷/₈
   cups buttermilk
50g/2oz/¹/₄ cup butter, melted

65g/2¹/₂oz/¹/₂ cup plain (all-
   purpose) flour
2.5ml/¹/₂ tsp ground mace
5ml/1 tsp bicarbonate of soda
   (baking soda)
10ml/2 tsp salt
250g/9oz/2¹/₄ cups fine cornmeal
2 fresh red chillies, seeded and
   finely chopped
shredded red chillies and sea salt,
   to serve

1 Preheat the oven to 200°C/400°F/Gas 6. Grease and line a 23 × 7.5 cm/9 × 3 in loaf tin (pan). In a large bowl, whisk the eggs until frothy, then whisk in the buttermilk and melted butter.

2 Sift the flour, mace, bicarbonate of soda and salt together and gradually stir into the egg mixture. Fold in the cornmeal a little at a time, then stir in the fresh chillies.

3 Pour the mixture into the prepared tin and bake for 25–30 minutes until the top is firm to the touch.

4 Leave the loaf to cool in the tin for a few minutes before turning out. Scatter over the red chillies and sea salt, then cut into slices and serve warm.

Variation
For a loaf with a more rustic appearance, use medium or coarse cornmeal.

Cook's Tip
This cornbread is flavoured with ground mace, a spice that comes from the same plant as nutmeg. It has a similar but more delicate flavour and also adds a bright orange colour.

Chilli Cheese Muffins

These muffins are flavoured with chilli purée, which is widely available in tubes or jars and is a really instant way to add spicy heat to recipes of all kinds.

Makes 12
115 g/4 oz/1 cup self-raising
   (self-rising) flour

15ml/1 tbsp baking powder
5ml/1 tsp salt
225g/8oz/2 cups fine cornmeal
150g/5oz/1¹/₄ cups grated
   mature Cheddar cheese
50g/2oz/4 tbsp butter, melted
2 eggs, beaten
5ml/1 tsp chilli purée
1 garlic clove, crushed
300ml/¹/₂ pint/1¹/₄ cups milk

1 Preheat the oven to 200°C/400°F/Gas 6. Thoroughly grease 12 deep muffin tins (pans) or line the tins with paper muffin cases.

2 Sift the flour, baking powder and salt into a bowl, then stir in the cornmeal and 115g/4oz/1 cup of the grated cheese.

3 Pour the melted butter into a bowl and stir in the eggs, chilli purée, crushed garlic and milk. Pour on to the dry ingredients and mix quickly until just combined.

4 Spoon the batter into the prepared muffin tins, sprinkle the remaining cheese on top and bake for 20 minutes until risen and golden brown.

5 Leave to cool for a few minutes before turning the muffins out on to a wire rack to cool completely.

Cook's Tips
• Take care not to over-mix the mixture or the finished muffins will be heavy. Stir the mixture just enough to combine the ingredients roughly.
• The muffins are best eaten on the same day they are made, preferably while still slightly warm.
• Other strongly flavoured cheeses, such as Parmesan or Gruyère, can also be used.

Chilli Cornbread Energy 229kcal/959kJ; Protein 6.9g; Carbohydrate 32.8g, of which sugars 4.9g; Fat 8.2g, of which saturates 1.4g; Cholesterol 48mg; Calcium 98mg; Fibre 1g; Sodium 514mg.
Chilli Muffins Energy 166kcal/698kJ; Protein 5.1g; Carbohydrate 19.3g, of which sugars 4.4g; Fat 8.1g, of which saturates 4.6g; Cholesterol 60mg; Calcium 93mg; Fibre 0.6g; Sodium 96mg.

Spiced Cocktail Biscuits

These savoury biscuits are ideal for serving with pre-dinner drinks. Each of the spice seeds in the mixture contributes its own distinct character to the flavour. For bitesize cocktail snacks use a tiny round cookie cutter, or you could cut out fancy shapes such as stars and crescents.

Makes 20–30
150g/5oz/1¼ cups plain
   (all-purpose) flour
10ml/2 tsp curry powder
115g/4oz/½ cup butter
75g/3oz/¾ cup grated mature
   Cheddar cheese
10ml/2 tsp poppy seeds
5ml/1 tsp black onion seeds
1 egg yolk
cumin seeds, to decorate

1 Grease two baking sheets or line them with sheets of baking parchment. Sift the flour and curry powder into a bowl.

2 Rub in the butter until the mixture resembles breadcrumbs, then stir in the grated cheese, poppy seeds and black onion seeds.

3 Stir in the egg yolk and mix to a firm dough. Wrap the dough in clear film (plastic wrap) and chill for 30 minutes.

4 Roll out the dough on a floured surface to a thickness of about 3mm/⅛in. Cut into shapes with a cookie cutter. Arrange on the prepared baking sheets and sprinkle with the cumin seeds. Chill for 15 minutes.

5 Preheat the oven to 190°C/375°F/Gas 5. Bake the biscuits (cookies) for about 20 minutes until crisp and golden. Transfer to a wire rack to cool, and serve soon after baking.

Cook's Tip
These biscuits are at their best when they are freshly baked. The dough can be made in advance and chilled until required, so that all you need to do is cut out the shapes and put the biscuits in the oven.

Fennel and Chilli Ring Cookies

Based on an Italian recipe, these cookies are made with yeast and are appetizingly savoury and crumbly. Try them as nibbles with drinks, to go with dips or with antipasti. Fennel seeds have an anise-like taste similar to that of the herb, and they add a rounded flavour that goes well with the heat added by the chillis.

Makes about 30
500g/1lb 2oz/4½ cups type
   00 flour
115g/4oz/½ cup white
   vegetable fat
5ml/1 tsp easy-blend (rapid-rise)
   dried yeast
15ml/1 tbsp fennel seeds
10ml/2 tsp crushed chilli flakes
15ml/1 tbsp olive oil
400–550ml/14–18fl oz/1⅔–2½
   cups lukewarm water
olive oil, for brushing

1 Put the flour in a bowl and rub in the fat until the mixture resembles fine breadcrumbs. Add the yeast, fennel and chilli and mix well. Add the oil and enough water to make a soft but not sticky dough. Turn out on to a floured surface and knead lightly.

2 Take small pieces of dough and shape into sausages about 15cm/6in long. Shape into rings and pinch the ends together.

3 Place the rings on a non-stick baking sheet and brush lightly with olive oil. Cover with a dish towel and set aside at room temperature for 1 hour to rise slightly.

4 Meanwhile, preheat the oven to 150°C/300°F/Gas 2. Bake the cookies for 1 hour until they are dry and very slightly browned. Leave on the baking sheet to cool completely.

Cook's Tip
Type 00 is an Italian grade of flour, principally used for pasta. It is milled from the centre part of the endosperm so that the resulting flour is much whiter than plain (all-purpose) flour. It contains 70 per cent of the wheat grain. It is available from Italian delicatessens and some large supermarkets. If you cannot find it, try using strong white bread flour instead.

Cocktail Biscuits Energy 67kcal/278kJ; Protein 1.5g; Carbohydrate 4g, of which sugars 0.1g; Fat 5g, of which saturates 2.7g; Cholesterol 17mg; Calcium 38mg; Fibre 0.3g; Sodium 44mg.
Fennel Cookies Energy 94kcal/396kJ; Protein 1.8g; Carbohydrate 13g, of which sugars 0.3g; Fat 4.3g, of which saturates 1.5g; Cholesterol 1mg; Calcium 30mg; Fibre 0.6g; Sodium 31mg.

Index